W9-CBZ-874

To Ivory,
I hope you enjoy this
chapter on little known African
American history, not taught
in schools.

BLACK, BUCKSKIN, AND BLUE

Peace &
Blessings!

African American Scouts and Soldiers on the Western Frontier

Art T. Burton

by *11-29-'99*

Art T. Burton

"Black To The West"

EAKIN PRESS ✦ Austin, Texas

This book is dedicated to my parents,
Mr. and Mrs. Arthur Burton, Sr.,
who taught me the importance of reading;
to my father-in-law, James P. Davis, and my uncles,
Roland Traylor, Lester Traylor, and Henry Parks,
all U.S. Army veterans of World War II.

FIRST EDITION

Copyright © 1999
By Art T. Burton

Published in the United States of America
By Eakin Press
A Division of Sunbelt Media, Inc.
P.O. Box 90159
Austin, TX 78709
email: eakinpub@sig.net
www.eakinpress.com

ALL RIGHTS RESERVED.

2 3 4 5 6 7 8 9

1-57168-295-3

Contents

Acknowledgments . . . v
Introduction . . . vii

Section I: Scouts 1
   1. Edward Rose . . . 5
   2. Jim Beckwourth . . . 15
   3. Britton Johnson . . . 21
   4. Henry Wilson . . . 25
   5. Jim Ned . . . 27
   6. Alfred Wood . . . 30
   7. Tom Tobin . . . 35
   8. Isaiah Dorman . . . 41
   9. Frank Grouard . . . 45
  10. Charles "Smokey" Wilson . . . 71
  11. Sam Bowman . . . 79
  12. Wash Robinson . . . 81
  13. Seminole Negro Indian Scouts . . . 87

Section II: Civil War in the West 103

   14. 1st Kansas Colored Volunteer Infantry Regiment . . . 105
   15. Remember Poison Springs . . . 118
   16. 2nd Kansas Colored Volunteer Infantry . . . 121
   17. 1st Iowa Regiment of African Descent . . . 126
   18. Other Units in the West . . . 129

Section III: Buffalo Soldiers 133

   19. Inception . . . 135
   20. The Black Infantry . . . 139
   21. The Wham Payroll Robbery . . . 143
   22. 9th U.S. Cavalry . . . 147
   23. 10th U.S. Cavalry . . . 177
   24. Buffalo Soldiers to the Rescue . . . 209
   25. Buffalo Soldiers Fighting Outlaws . . . 226
   26. A Soldier's Soldier . . . 239
   Buffalo Soldier Narratives . . . 248

Appendices:

Military Engagements of the Buffalo Soldiers
   and Seminole Negro Indian Scouts in the Indian Wars . . . 259

Muster Rolls of the Seminole Negro Indian Scouts . . . 265

Battles Fought on the Western Frontier
   by Black Civil War Soldiers . . . 267

   Bibliography . . . 269
   Index . . . 275

Acknowledgments

Many people gave encouragement and assistance in the preparation of this book. My biggest booster, after my wife and family, was Bennie J. McRae, Jr., a wonderful historian in his own right. Bennie has put together one of the finest African American history internet websites in the country entitled, "Lest We Forget."

Bill Gwaltney of the National Park Service provided materials and inspiration. Buffalo Soldier historian Anthony Powell provided insight into black military history. Also providing military history was the nationally renowned sculptor, Eddie Dixon, who designed the Buffalo Soldier monument in Leavenworth, Kansas. As a soldier, Eddie did two tours of duty during the Vietnam War.

Fort Sill U.S. Army base historian Towana Spivey was kind enough to give me a day long tour of the old historic Fort Sill in Lawton, Oklahoma. This was very enlightening in reference to the Buffalo Soldier history on the post and region. I highly recommend anyone interested in Buffalo Soldier history to visit Fort Sill.

Angela Walton-Raji and Diron Ahlquist were a big help in assisting with archival files on the United States military. Angela assisted with statistical information on USCT soldiers on the western frontier during the Civil War and is one of the top researchers on African Indian relations in the country. Diron has done thorough research on the history of law enforcement at frontier Fort Sill and its vicinity. Diron and I are also members of Oklahombres, the Association for the Preservation of Lawman and Outlaw History of the Indian Territory.

Kareem Abdul Jabbar supplied information on army scouts that was very helpful during my research on the manuscript. Kareem is an astute historian on Buffalo Soldier history and has written a great book on African American history.

I also have to thank the many readers who enjoyed my first book and told me to keep writing. This is not an easy task when you have a full time job, a family, and other duties to attend to. Kudos to Ed Eakin of Eakin Press for keeping the faith.

Bernard Williams was very gracious in allowing me to use his magnificent painting *Sergeant Buffalo* for the cover of the book. Bernard is at the forefront of artists who are interpreting the American frontier on canvas.

Last but not least, I would not be able to do any of this without the assistance of my wife Patrice. She is my proofreader, typist, and number one motivator and motivation. Above all, I thank the Creator for giving me the vision and the opportunity.

Introduction

As a young child I was intrigued by the frontier soldier, partly because my grandfather, Frank B. Traylor, of Arcadia, Oklahoma, told me stories of seeing black cavalry troopers riding on horseback through Arcadia. He saw them on the military road later to be known as Route 66, on their way to Fort Reno or Fort Sill.

This was the first time I ever heard anyone mention African American horse soldiers. My father, Arthur T. Burton, Sr., later told me his older sister had been married to a man named Stanley who said he chased Pancho Villa in Mexico while serving in the United States Army Cavalry. Amazed at the stories when I first heard them, I later learned they were true and that much more needed to be known about this forgotten history.

This book will examine the contributions of African Americans who were scouts and soldiers on the United States western frontier during the nineteenth and early twentieth centuries. I believe this is the first book to take an in-depth look at

African American scouts. There hasn't been much written on the topic in recent years, except a mention in a few books and articles.

This book is not intended to be a totally comprehensive or all inclusive study. It explores individuals, incidents, and occurrences in which black men were involved during the westward movement as scouts and soldiers.

Besides some of the information on scouts which may be new for readers, the work takes a look at African American soldiers involved in the Civil War west of the Mississippi River. During the war this area was referred to as the Trans-Mississippi campaign. Again, this is an area that has only been covered by a few books and then only peripherally.

Regarding the African American soldiers after the Civil War who are known today as Buffalo Soldiers, I will not examine the many racial hostilities and conflicts they endured in western frontier towns. This has already been well covered in *The Buffalo Soldiers*, by Leckie; *New Mexico's Buffalo Soldiers, 1866–1900*, by Billington; *Black Valor*, by Schubert; *In Search of the Racial Frontier*, by Taylor; and *Freedom on the Border* by Mulroy.

This manuscript examines military incidents that may not be well known to readers of western frontier history, such as Buffalo Soldiers versus the desperadoes and outlaws, or certain critical military engagements in which black soldiers made an important contribution.

Hollywood movies and television have mainly overlooked both the African American soldier and scout in their portrayal of the settling of the West. There is only one movie that I can highly recommend that portrays Buffalo Soldiers and that is John Ford's *Sergeant Rutledge* which starred one of the best black cowboy actors, Woody Strode. It was released in 1960. Ironically, even this movie was not told from an African American perspective, but from the white officer who served with the black troopers.

Symbolic of the paradox concerning the black soldier on the western frontier was that the black trooper was helping to subjugate another group of people of color while he was also discriminated against by the dominant society. Many black men joined the army trying to escape the political oppression and lack of job and educational opportunities that were not available in their local communities in the South and the North. The army offered a steady wage, adventure, prestige, and three square meals a day. Given the odds and obstacles placed in their path, I believe that the African American soldiers of the western frontier came through with flying colors. Then as now, the army wasn't a panacea, but it was an option.

In discussing the cavalry in the text, I describe the units in the regiments as troops. The cavalry was officially designated as having "companies" until January 1, 1881, when the Army officially designated these units as "troops." They kept the same size and command structure. The infantry kept the term "company" for units of approximately 100 men.

Some of the most important army scouts in the "Wild West" were black men. They performed various tasks from interpreting Indian languages and signing, locating trails, locating horse and human tracks, and leading military units to "hostile" Indian and outlaw bands.

Many of the black scouts had once served in the regular U.S. Army. Some of them married Indian or Mexican women on the frontier. And many of the black scouts and soldiers themselves were of mixed Indian blood.

The most important black scout in the book is Frank Grouard, a true hero of the "Wild West." He was undoubtedly the most important scout for military campaigns on the western frontier, bar none. I am sure you will find Grouard's life interesting. There are many other individuals in the scouts section that also merit recognition.

This book is a continuation of the study I started with my first book, *Black, Red, and Deadly: Black and Indian Gunfighters of the Indian Territory, 1870–1907*, on the African American's contribution to the settling of the western United States frontier.

I hope that in the near future, we will celebrate this history in homes, classrooms, and libraries throughout this great country. I hope you enjoy this trip to yesteryear down the dangerous and dusky trails of the Buffalo Soldiers and the scouts of bronze. I take all responsibility if there are any errors in the book, and I am honored to have you along for the ride.

Adiós . . .Vaya con Diós
Art T. Burton

9th Cavalry at dress parade, Fort Davis, Texas, 1875.

(Courtesy Fort Davis National Historic Site)

Section I:
Scouts

John T. Glass, Chief of Scouts (far right), with Bonito (left), and Sergeant Jim (center), Apache Scouts
(Courtesy Arizona Historical Society)

D uring the early days of exploration in North America, it was not uncommon for European explorers to be accompanied by African slaves. Estevanico, "little Steven," was a black slave from North Africa. He was one of the four survivors of the expedition led by the Spaniard Panfilo de Narvaez, which was shipwrecked in 1529 on the Texas coast. Many years afterwards, Estevanico lived among the Indians of the American southwest. He became noted for his abilities as a medicine man and linguist among the Native Americans. When Estevanico and his party finally reached the colonial settlements of northern Mexico, the viceroy sent Estevanico as leader of the advance party of an expedition northward. In 1539 the people of the Zuni pueblo of Cibola in New Mexico murdered him. To this day, his murder remains a mystery as to motive. Estevanico's travels inspired Coronado to search for the legendary Seven Cities of Cibola.

Africans were also found with the French explorers of the eighteenth century and the British explorers of the nineteenth century. One of the most famous slaves was York, who accompanied the Lewis and Clark expedition as Capt. William Clark's body servant. York became popular on the expedition as an entertainer, expert hunter, skillful swimmer, and peace maker with the many Indians they met on the trip. The Indians were awed by York's black skin. The explorers used this to their advantage.

In 1821 there was an African slave named Paul who accompanied his owner, Maj. Jacob Fowler, on an expedition. This group set out from Fort Smith, Arkansas Territory, and traveled through parts of present day Oklahoma, Kansas, and New Mexico into the settlement which is now Pueblo, Colorado. Fowler kept a diary that gave evidence Paul had his own gun, money, horse, and his opinions were valued as much as anyone's on the trip.

A free African accompanied John Charles Fremont on his second and third expeditions during the years 1843-1846. His name was Jacob Dodson; he served as Fremont's body servant, hunter, boatman, Indian fighter, rider, and roper.

In the fur trade, there were men such as Francois Duchoquette and Jean Baptiste Point du Sable. The latter, a

3

Haitian mulatto, married in 1778 a Potawatomi woman and later established a trading post on a site later to be known as the city of Chicago. Another important black family in the fur trade industry was the Bongas, descendants of a couple who during the 1780s were slaves of the British commandant at Fort Michilimackinac in the Minnesota area. The Bongas intermarried with the Chippewas and served in all areas of the fur trade as guides, interpreters, and independent traders.

CHAPTER ONE

Edward Rose

One of the first black men to earn a large reputation on the Western frontier as a scout, hunter, and guide was Edward Rose.

Rose was born in Kentucky in the vicinity of Louisville. His father was a mixed blood Cherokee trader and his mother was of African and Cherokee heritage. At seventeen Rose left home and traveled to New Orleans as a new crew member on a keelboat. It is said that while in New Orleans, Rose participated in more than a few waterfront fights and gained an unsavory reputation. Historians have stated that Rose became notorious as a Mississippi River pirate; Washington Irving wrote of Rose as "powerful in frame and fearless in spirit."

Irving also stated that Rose belonged "to one of the gangs of pirates who infested the islands of the Mississippi, plundering boats as they went up and down the river, and who sometimes shifted the scene of their robberies to the shore, waylaying travelers as they returned by land from New Orleans with the products of their downward voyage, plundering them of their money and effects, and often perpetuating the most atrocious murders."

The New Orleans police department broke the gang up and ran Ed Rose out of town. He next showed up in St. Louis in the spring of 1806. The St. Louis newspapers described Rose as big, strong, and hot-tempered with a swarthy, fierce looking face. Very noticeable on his forehead was a mark which some said was an improperly applied criminal brand. Rose said he got the mark from the teeth of a Frenchman in a fight in New Orleans. But that was not the most notable feature of Rose's face. The tip of his nose had been either cut off or bitten off in a fight. For many years, the Indians referred to Rose as "Cut Nose."

While in St. Louis in 1806, Rose traveled up the Osage River with a group of hunters. On his return to St. Louis, the teenage black man got permission to join the Manuel Lisa expedition that was traveling up the Missouri River. Rose and forty-one men set out for the Yellowstone country in the spring of 1807.

This particular trip initiated by Lisa was the first attempt to engage in the fur trade in an organized fashion at the headwaters of the Missouri. The trappers built Fort Lisa, also called Fort Manuel, on the Yellowstone River at the mouth of the Bighorn River. The Native Americans living in the area called themselves Absarokes, and the land they inhabited was called Absaroka. Translated into French Absaroke meant "Sparrow Hawk." The French translation was transformed into English as Crow. Since that time they have been known as the Crow tribe of the Northern Plains.

Rose had great admiration for the Crow tribe. They were among the finest horsemen in the Missouri Valley. Rose began living among the Crow where he learned their language, culture, and customs. The Crows admired Rose for his courage, marksmanship, horsemanship, hunting skills, and his ability to fight. Rose, besides learning the Crow language, learned how to sign, the universal language used by all the Plains Indians. As time went on, his influence grew with the Crows; Rose was always finding some supplies from the trapper's camp to give to the Indians who placed a high priority on gift giving.

While living with the Crows, Rose was given a new name; the details, of which, follow.

A small war party of Minnatarees and a boy were camped on a ridge overlooking a valley. They spied a Crow warrior and his wife approaching and quickly organized an ambush with bow and arrow. They were able to kill the Crow warrior, but his wife escaped. After relaying her horror to the Crow village, Rose and about fifty warriors mounted and took to the trail after the Minnatarees.

Rose was in the lead, and the chase went on for about three hours. The pursuit was perilous over rocky ravines, wind swept slopes, and heavy timber. They finally overtook the Minnatarees whose horses had given out. The object of their chase took refuge in a well-protected position on a forested mountain shelf.

The Crows were very hesitant to attack such a heavily forti-fied position. Ed Rose thought little of it; he seized two shields and placed them together. With his battle axe and knife, Rose attacked the Minnatarees position by himself. Although three arrows struck his shields, Rose gained entry to the position. The Crows were inspired by this act of bravery and attacked en masse. Rose proceeded to kill five warriors singlehandedly. He shot one and clubbed four others to death before taking their scalps. Thereafter, Rose became known by the Crow as "Five Scalps."

This incident only added to the prestige Rose already had among the Crows. He was made war chief of the tribe.

Rose thoroughly enjoyed living among the Crow and would give them gifts at every chance he received. Sometimes he would raid the trappers' camps and take items to the Crow villages. These acts enhanced his stature in the villages.

Rose became involved in a business enterprise with a French mountain man named Charbonneau. His full name was Touissant Charbonneau, and he had accompanied Lewis and Clark to the Pacific as interpreter. Charbonneau's wife was Sacajawea, who had saved the Lewis and Clark expedition on more than one occasion.

The enterprise that Rose and Charbonneau were involved in was escorting Arapaho women, who had been captured in warfare by the Snake, to the European trappers on the Missouri River. Trappers were without women and paid good money for these Indian maidens whom they took for their wives. On one trip from the Snake domain, Edward Rose traded his rifle for a quiver of arrows and a bow. Although his rifle was a superior weapon, Rose was an expert with bow and arrow. Nevertheless, Charbonneau criticized Rose for his trade of the weapons. As Rose and Charbonneau, with six females, continued their journey, they came across a small hunting party of Snakes. Rose proceeded to give his bow and arrows to this group of Indians with nothing in exchange. Charbonneau was now beside himself with anger. He thought Rose must be crazy or losing his mind. Rose must have thought his friend's tirade was hilarious, for he proceeded to give the same Indian whom he gave his bow and arrows, his only hunting knife.

Charbonneau had never witnessed anything like Rose's behavior on the frontier before. They only had provisions for one day. Rose replied by saying, "The man who can't live in a country of game like this, without arms deserves to die." Evidently, Charbonneau's rifle was defective, through some mishap, for he discarded it. The only weapon he had was his hunting knife. For three days Edward Rose and his party had no food to eat. The women were now complaining constantly, and Charbonneau's anger knew no bounds. Rose proceeded to ask for his business partner's knife. When Charbonneau relented, Rose took the knife and broke the blade from the handle. The only thing Charbonneau could do was groan; he was speechless and in a silent rage. Rose went into a clump of trees and came back with a sturdy, small branch. He took the knife and branch and made a credible spear with the items. As the day went on, Rose spotted a buffalo in the afternoon. With his ready-made spear Rose stalked the buffalo and killed it as proficiently as any hunter on the plains. The meat lasted for many days on the trip, and Rose was able to keep the small party in ample food for the remainder of the journey.

In the first decades of the 1800s Rose participated in just about every expedition into the Yellowstone area and surrounding country. In the spring of 1809 he led the first all-land expedition into the Rocky Mountains. The purpose of the trip was to escort Chief Big White back to his Mandan tribe on the Missouri River. The chief, his wife, and child had accompanied Lewis and

Clark to the national capitol in Washington D.C. The politicians had given Big White, whose Indian name was Shehake, a medal of honor for assisting Lewis and Clark on their trip to the Pacific. In 1809 the government paid the Missouri Fur Company a tidy sum of $7,000 for the safe return of Big White. The expedition left St. Charles, Missouri Territory, on June 15. This group of twenty men followed the Missouri River west to the Kansas River. During the trip, the party came upon many Indian villages at which Ed Rose's communication skills proved to be indispensable. After three months journey the party reached the Mandan villages. Chief Big White was finally home, safe and sound.

On the return trip back to St. Louis, Rose decided to stay with the Crow Indians on the Northern Plains. Two years later in the summer of 1811, Rose met the largest expedition to travel the western rivers up until that time. There were sixty-four people in the group. The purpose of this group was to establish a trading post on the Pacific Ocean in the Oregon Country. It was financed by John Jacob Astor, one of the most noted and wealthiest fur merchants in the country. The expedition was led by Wilson Price Hunt and also included the aforementioned Manuel Lisa. Rose met the group on the plains near the Arikara villages on the Missouri bottoms. None of the scouts were familiar with the territory. Rose led them as far as Crow country. Hunt didn't completely trust Rose so he contracted for Rose to only lead them as far as Absaroka, the land of the Crows. After leaving Rose, Hunt thought he could follow instructions to go through the mountains, but became lost when he couldn't find the pass. Again Rose came to the rescue along with some Crow comrades. He proceeded to show Hunt's party the trail they couldn't find in the Rocky Mountains. Hunt didn't offer Rose employment to lead them further. He should have. Hunt made some critical mistakes on the trip which became a failure. Some of the party did reach the west coast, but overall they did not accomplish what they set out to do.

Besides living with Crows it is also believed that Ed Rose lived three years with the Arikara. Manuel Lisa found Rose with the Arikaras in 1812 and hired him as a scout. In March 1813 Rose was on his way back to New Orleans with Lisa. In route he became enamored with a lady of the Omaha tribe. He never made it to New Orleans and stayed with the Omahas for a spell. Eventually, the Omahas became disgruntled with Rose; they had him arrested and taken to St. Louis. It is reported that Rose left two children with his Omaha wife. After agreeing to stay out of Indian country, for being drunk and fighting, Supt. of Indian Affairs William Clark, in the spring of 1813, let Rose go free.

Rose did stay out of Indian country for some time. It is said that during this period Rose may have spent time in the Gulf of Mexico as a pirate. He was familiar with this line of work.

The next time Ed Rose is mentioned, it is as an interpreter and scout in 1823. Gen. William H. Ashley and Andrew Henry co-owned the Rocky Mountain Fur Company. On March 10 Ashley left St. Louis with two keelboats and a hundred men. Ed Rose rode into Ashley's camp while they were camped south of the Arikara villages. Ashley offered Rose employment as a guide and scout, and Rose accepted. Ashley also was in need of horses as they were leaving the river. He thought he could trade for horses with the nearby Arikaras, and their chief did give Ashley an invitation to talk. Rose told Ashley he didn't think it was a good idea to barter with the Arikaras. He felt they had some ulterior motives planned. Ashley did not want to completely trust Rose, the same as Hunt before him. Rose advised him to moor his boats on the opposite side of the river bank—not on the bank near the Arikara villages. Although Ashley hired Rose, he didn't utilize his knowledge of Indian style and character. It must be assumed they were primarily interested in his skills as a guide and interpreter. They weren't ready to take advice from a black man, even one with Ed Rose's expertise.

The following morning after purchasing horses, Ashley's men were attacked by the Arikaras. They implored Rose to go, but he refused to leave the white men. They had to beat a hasty retreat up the river. If he had listened to Rose, this loss of men and supplies could have been avoided. With thirty men, Ashley set up camp on an island in the Missouri River. Rose was one of those men. The rest of the men went for help or were too scared to stay. Ashley called for military intervention, and on June 22, Col. Henry Leavenworth from Fort Atkinson left to aid Ashley. He came prepared with 200 men, two six-pound cannons, a couple of small cannons, and three keelboats. Along with Leavenworth's troops, the fur traders and mountain men were organized into "The Missouri Legion," a frontier militia. The forces were organized under the command of Colonel Leavenworth; he appointed Rose as an ensign. This particular honor was only to be recognized for this one engagement, by this particular militia. But it still gives some insight into the respect bestowed upon Rose by his fellow frontiersmen. The Legion was also assisted militarily by Lakota and Yankton warriors who were at odds with the Arikaras.

The Missouri Legion attacked the Arikara village on August 8, 1823. After one of the Arikara chiefs, Grey Eyes, was killed, the Indians asked for a truce from Leavenworth. Ed Rose was sent into the Arikara village to negotiate a peace settlement. Through several meetings, Rose was able to work out agreeable terms between the two adversarial parties. Although they were humbled on this occasion, Arikaras continued later to harass trappers traveling up the Missouri River.

Leavenworth, who later had a fort named after him, had this to say about Ed Rose in his official report to General Atkinson dated October 20, 1823:

> I had not found anyone willing to go into those villages, except a man by the name of Rose, who had the nominal rank of ensign in General Ashley's volunteers. He appeared to be a brave and enterprising man, and was well acquainted with those Indians. He had resided for about three years with them; understood their language, and they were much attached to him. He was with General Ashley when he was attacked. The Indians at that time called to him to take care of himself, before they fire upon General Ashley's party. This was all I knew of the man. I have since heard that he was not of good character. Everything he told us, however, was fully corroborated. He was perfectly willing to go into their villages, and did go in several times.

General Ashley resumed sending expeditions into the northern trapping grounds. One of these groups was led by the legendary mountain man Jedediah Smith. Rose was hired to go along with Smith as guide and interpreter because he was familiar with the Indians and the terrain. Rose saved Smith's expedition from several catastrophes. Ashley's men received Rose's assistance for a couple of years.

In 1825 Gen. Henry Atkinson and Maj. Benjamin O'Fallon hired Rose to lead their expedition into the Yellowstone country. Rose led a forty man contingent under the command of Lieutenant Armstrong on land via horseback. A larger contingent of 430 men in nine boats departed Fort Atkinson on May 16, 1825. On one occasion during the expedition, Rose disguised himself with twigs and parts of bushes and crawled into a group of eleven bison. He proceeded to kill six of the buffalo before the others ran off. Rose accomplished this feat without a repeating rifle, which didn't exist at the time. The meat from this hunt weighed in at 3,300 pounds, enough rations for everyone for a week.

The Atkinson-O'Fallon expedition was successful in signing peace treaties with most of the native tribes in the region. The place of negotiations became known as Council Bluffs. Among the tribes in agreement were the Oglalas, Cheyennes, and Siones. In signing a treaty with the Crow, the best documented story of Ed Rose's courage can be related.

In an argument with a Crow chief, over a minor disturbance, Major O'Fallon struck the Indian with his pistol. This action infuriated 600 Crow warriors. Just as the Indians were preparing to grab O'Fallon, Rose stepped forward, grabbed a rifle lying in front of the chiefs, and began to swing it in a circular motion protecting O'Fallon. At the same time, Rose placed one foot on a pile of muskets on the ground. He proceeded to injure a couple of Indians who came too close. The Crows knew Rose was deadly serious and didn't know how many would die trying to subdue him. In the midst of 600 warriors, Rose was able to control a situation which, minutes earlier, seemed hopeless. Cooler heads prevailed. Additionally, and not to be forgotten, is the fact that the Crows felt Rose was one of them. In his autobiography, James (Jim) Beckwourth said, "When this occurrence reached the ears of the Indian warriors, they became perfectly infuriated, and prepared for instant attack. General Atkinson pacified them through Rose, who was one of the best interpreters ever known in the whole Indian country."

After 1826 Rose's influence among the Crows and other Indian tribes was shared with Beckwourth, another famous African American frontiersman. But Rose was the first trailblazer, and his efforts in assisting the military, trappers, and mountainmen should and must be recognized.

It is said that sometime around 1834, Edward Rose was killed along with his friend Hugh Glass by a group of Arikara Indians that were hostile to the Crows. They caught the men traveling on foot down the frozen Yellowstone River and proceeded to murder and scalp them. Perhaps the Arikaras felt Rose, who had also lived with them, was for all practical purposes, a Crow Indian. He was buried on the banks of the Missouri River opposite the mouth of the Milk River in the land he loved. Edward Rose, the African Indian, was an important pioneer figure in the early days of the frontier. No one did a better job of scouting, hunting, trailblazing, interpreting, and fighting than the one and only Edward Rose, also known as Cut Nose and Five Scalps and a legendary hero of the Old West.

Jim Beckwourth, greatest trailblazer and scout of the Rocky Mountains.
(Courtesy Nevada Historical Society)

CHAPTER TWO

Jim Beckwourth

The most famous African American scout, trapper, guide, interpreter, and mountain man was Jim Beckwourth. His full name was James Pierson Beckwourth; he was born on April 26, 1798, in Frederick County, Virginia. Beckwourth's father's name was Jennings Beckwith; he was a descendant of Irish aristocrats and a prominent Virginia slaveholding family. Jim's mother was an African slave on the Beckwith plantation; she was said to have been a mulatto. Beckwith moved his family west to the Louisiana Territory in 1810, and eventually they settled in St. Louis. Jim attended school in St. Louis at the age of 10; he was able to become literate with good communication skills. He also spent a lot of time hunting and fishing with his father in the Missouri wilderness.

By adulthood, Beckwourth had become a complete out-doorsman, skilled in every area of survival on the frontier. In 1822 Beckwourth made a trip to New Orleans, no doubt looking for adventure. At manhood his father had declared him a free man, therefore he could come and go as he pleased. By 1824 Jim had decided he was ready for the western frontier. He joined General Ashley's famous expedition to the Rocky Mountains. On this trip Beckwourth met other famous mountain men such as Edward Rose, Jedediah Smith, Jim Bridger, and Hugh Glass. He became good friends with Smith and wintered with him in Cache Valley in 1825–26 where they were trapping for furs.

In 1828 Beckwourth was made a member of the Crow tribe in the far northern Rocky Mountain area. He went on to live with the Crow for six years and married a number of Crow, Snake, and Blackfoot maidens. As a Crow, Beckwourth was involved in many battles and raids and gained a great reputation as a warrior. During his stay with the Crows, Beckwourth was also working for the American Fur Company. His skills and knowledge were of great benefit to the fur company in that area of the Rockies. Beckwourth evidently longed for new adventure and after his stay with the Crow Indians traveled back to St. Louis.

While in the Gateway city he signed up as a scout with a Missouri volunteer company that was headed to Florida to fight the Seminoles. The Seminole Indian War was the most costly Indian war for the U.S. government; $30 million was spent, and over 1,500 U.S. soldiers died in combat. The Seminole Nation was a confederation of former African slaves, runaways or maroons, dissatisfied Creeks, Shawnees, and Choctaws. The Seminole did not agree with removal to the Indian Territory and fought to stay in the Southeast. Beckwourth was employed as a mule-skinner, messenger, and scout. He fought at the battle of Okeechobee against the African-Seminole Chief Osceola in central Florida. Beckwourth didn't find the land or weather to his liking. He also complained the Seminole had no horses worth stealing. In early 1838, Beckwourth left Florida and the Seminole War and headed for the west again.

There was a need for Beckwourth's skills on the Santa Fe Trail. Andrew Sublette and Louis Vasquez were trying to establish the fur trading industry with a small company in the Southwest. They needed Beckwourth to set up a dialogue with the Cheyenne to deal in buffalo robes. Vasquez had already established a small fort on the Platte River in north central Colorado, called Fort Vasquez. Beckwourth led the trading party south down the Santa Fe Trail serving as scout and guide. Sublette and Vasquez were successful in their trading ventures, and Beckwourth was very successful in his dealings with the Cheyenne. Also during this period Beckwourth worked for William Bent as a wagon leader at Bent's Fort. Jim took his money and set up a general store in Taos, New Mexico. He married a lady there named Luisa Sandoval; the relationship was very brief. But she did accompany him in October of 1842 to a location on the Arkansas River where Beckwourth set up a trading post. He was joined by other trappers and their families. This settlement went on to become the wild and wooly town of Pueblo, Colorado.

Beckwourth next found adventure in California, after leaving his wife and small daughter. He wanted to set up a trading post in Los Angeles. But on arrival Beckwourth and about fifteen men from Pueblo found themselves in the midst of the Bear Flag Rebellion. This was basically a war between Americans and the Mexican government that controlled California. Beckwourth said his greatest contribution was the 2,000 horses he stole along with five other Americans from a few Mexican haciendas near Los Angeles. The Americans took the horses back to Bent's Fort and Pueblo, where they sold them for a nice profit. Beckwourth took his share of the money and purchased a saloon and hotel in Santa Fe, New Mexico. The saloon was said to be the best furnished in Santa Fe at that time.

The Mexican-American War began in 1846, and Beckwourth rendered his services to the American army. He served as a messenger, carrying communiques between Santa Fe and Leavenworth, Kansas, a distance of over 700 miles. Beckwourth on horseback could make the trip in about three weeks. He also carried messages between other Army outposts. With the onset of the California gold rush in 1848, Beckwourth again traveled to the Golden State, where he moved around the Sierra mining camps. Initially Beckwourth gained employment as a dispatch rider, but after a few months he resigned from this job. He then traveled over the length and breadth of the state, showing up in Stockton, Sonora, San Francisco, and other towns. It is said that during this period Beckwourth dealt in horse rustling, prospecting, guiding prospectors to strike areas, and dealing and playing cards (Spanish Monte) wherever he could find games.

John Letts, a storeowner on the American River near Sacramento, remembered Beckwourth riding in one morning mounted on a grey horse, a poncho thrown over his shoulder, over which he slung a huge rifle, wearing deerskin leggings, Mexican spurs and boots, and a large sombrero on his head. Jim announced he was dead broke and needed a meal. Letts treated him to breakfast, whereupon after the meal, Beckwourth proceeded to talk about the various adventures in his life on the frontier. Letts had never heard such stories before. Beckwourth told of his life among the Crows and his many battles with them and then proceeded to teach him how to sign in Indian language. Letts recorded that Beckwourth was a mixture of Negro, Indian, and Anglo-Saxon blood. After a couple of days Beckwourth rode on, and Letts thought he would never be seen in those parts again. But Beckwourth never forgot a favor, and three weeks later he rode in again on the same grey horse. Jim came up to Letts' store at a gallop; after dismounting and entering the store he threw a handkerchief filled with gold and silver on the counter. He had been successful gambling upriver and wanted to repay his hospitality. Letts went on to report that Jim was able to win $18,000 on the gaming tables a few nights later. Beckwourth was always able to win money and shared it freely with anyone he could. Being a real mountain man, he didn't have any need for a lot of money weighing him and his horse down.

After being locked up for brawling in the saloons around Sacramento, Beckwourth headed for the mountains. He set up camp in the Sierra Nevada Range in the winter of 1850. This would lead to one of his greatest accomplishments on the frontier.

Beckwourth found a pass through the mountains that would allow wagons and horses accessibility. This was a major breakthrough that would save many months going around the mountains by wagon train. This passage became known as the Beckwourth Pass on the Beckwourth Trail through the Sierra Nevada Mountains. Many years later the pass would be utilized by a transcontinental railroad. Beckwourth built a trading post, ranch, and hotel on the trail in the valley where Grizzly Creek meets the middle fork of the Feather River. In 1855, 10,000 westward emigrant wagons passed through Beckwourth Pass. Jim was not able to retain his trading post and ranch because he was too generous with indigent families stopping by his home. But it wasn't in Beckwourth's nature to stay put too long even if he was getting up in age.

There was one incident that did happen to Beckwourth on his ranch that gave him national recognition. In the winter of 1854, Beckwourth dictated his life story to a writer named Thomas D. Bonner from Massachusetts, then living in California. Bonner felt the Beckwourth story was too good to pass up. The biography of Beckwourth was published by Harper Brothers in 1856.

In 1858 Beckwourth abandoned his ranch and traveled to cities such as St. Louis, Denver, and Kansas City. With the discovery of gold in the Pikes Peak region of Colorado, Beckwourth headed west to the Rockies once more. He worked for a while for his old friend Louis Vasquez, as a supplier and storekeeper. By 1862 Beckwourth had a Crow wife named Sue and worked as an army guide for E. G. Berthoud, of the Colorado Second Infantry. It was during this period that Beckwourth shot and killed a black blacksmith known as "Nigger Bill" in Denver. A jury eventually acquitted him of murder charges.

In 1864, Beckwourth was pressed into service to assist the Colorado Volunteer Cavalry. He was hired by Col. George L. Shoup. The army wanted to annihilate the Arapaho and Cheyenne in Colorado. Chief Black Kettle of the Cheyenne was encamped at Sand Creek near Fort Lyon. The chief believed that he and his people were under the protection of the army. In late November 1864 one of Col. John Chivington's patrols roused Beckwourth from his bed and took him to Chivington's headquarters. Beckwourth was then made to assist in helping the cavalry locate the Cheyenne and Arapaho camps at Sand Creek. The attack on the Indian camp took place on November 29, 1864, led by Colonel Chivington. The 600 volunteer cavalrymen went on to massacre men, women, and children in the Indian camp. Beckwourth was appalled by the killings of the people he once knew as his friends. Beckwourth later testified at hearings concerning the battle and said he served at the threat of death to his life.

Beckwourth tried his hand at trapping in 1865, but found many of the Indians didn't trust him any longer. He then went back into the employ of the army at Fort Laramie where he served as a dispatch rider and scout. Many times he would serve as a guide in tracking marauders or hostile Indian bands. Beckwourth left Fort Laramie on U.S. Army business with his business partner, Jim Bridger. This venture led him back to the Bighorn River that was part of his old stomping ground among the Crow. While visiting his old friends, in October 1866, Jim Beckwourth took sick and died among the people who loved him the most.

Jim Beckwourth was as good as any mountain man who was ever produced on the American western frontier. His name will echo in the Rockies and Sierras for seasons to come and, with a little luck, it will be heard from time to time.

CHAPTER THREE

Britton Johnson

In a conversation with the notable Texas historian Bill O'Neal, he informed me that portions of John Ford's movie *The Searchers* (starring John Wayne) were based on the legacy of Britton Johnson. Originally a slave on the West Texas frontier, Johnson was right at home on the wide open plains. He was said to have been a jet black African with a splendid physique. During his slave days, Britton belonged to Moses Johnson of Young County, Texas, near Wichita Falls.

Prior to the Civil War he had served as a scout and orderly for military officers at Fort Belknap. Britton gained a reputation from hunting forays and target shooting, as one of the best riflemen on the Texas frontier. He was also known for his physical strength.

In the fall of 1864, Little Buffalo, Comanche war chief, visited the Kiowa village at Rainy Mountain in the vicinity of the Wichita Mountains. Little Buffalo convinced the Kiowa that a raid into Texas to the Brazos River would be successful. There would be no white troops at Fort Belknap due to the Civil War in the east. Each warrior took an extra horse, and the party moved rapidly across the Red River, near present Burkburnett, Texas. They reached the Elm Creek junction of the Brazos River on October 13, 1864. A Joel Myers was killed near this point, and the Indians divided up into smaller groups for attacks on farms and ranches in the area. One of the ranches attacked was the Fitzpatrick ranch. There were no men at the ranch to defend it. Britt Johnson lived on the ranch and worked for Mrs. Fitzpatrick. Johnson was not at home when the Indians attacked. The women present were Grandma Fitzpatrick, her daughter Susie Durgan, two grandchildren—Lottie and Millie, and Mrs. Fitzpatrick's son by an earlier marriage, Joe Carter, aged fifteen. Of Johnson's family there was his wife Mary, three boys—Jimmy, Jube, John, and one daughter Lottie. One of his daughters was away from home during the attack. In the initial attack, Mary Johnson fired on the Indians to no avail. The Indians charged through the picket fence and killed Sue Durgan and Jimmy Johnson. The Indians then charged the house and looted it of any valuables. All who were not killed were taken captive. These included eighteen-month-old Millie Durgan, Lottie Durgan, Mrs. Fitzpatrick, Joe Carter, Mary Johnson, Jube Johnson, Lottie Johnson, and John Johnson. The Indians took their captives north across the Red River. Joe Carter was killed because he took ill and couldn't keep up.

On his return from getting supplies from the settlements, Johnson found a wrecked and burned farm house with dead bodies strewn about. Next, he discovered that his daughter Sallie, who had gone to try on a new dress, had survived the attack. Johnson vowed to get his family and friends back, whatever it took.

After some inquiry, Johnson found an old Mexican friend who had lived among these same Indians. The two men had punched cattle in Texas at an earlier time. The Mexican warned Johnson he would be killed if he went alone so he volunteered to help. The two men discussed their task. The Mexican gave Britt Johnson two horses and told him to go home and obtain blankets and any other items that could be used for barter with the Indians. Meanwhile, the Mexican would proceed to the friendly Peneteka Comanche to arrange the barter, then meet him later at his home. Johnson, in returning to the settlements, received ample help from many while gathering items for the ransom. The Mexican, Comanche Chief Asa-Harvey, and Johnson met and discussed, in earnest, trading for the captives. Britton, more commonly called "Britt," used all the tricks he had learned on the frontier to get his family back. He decided to use the ruse to wanting to join this hostile band once he found them. Johnson had learned the frontier art of sign language and convinced them he would make a worthy ally. Once he had gained their trust and alleviated their suspicions, Johnson put his plan into action. These talks took place near present Verden, Oklahoma. Johnson gave ten ears of corn for his boy, John, and blankets and other supplies for the rest. His wife, Mary, gave birth to a son while she was held captive. All received their freedom except the white toddler Millie Durgan, who lived among the Indians the rest of her life.

The group, Johnson, and the freed captives traveled to Pauls Valley, Chickasaw Nation, Indian Territory where settlers and government officials helped them get home. Two more children were born to Johnson and his wife. One, C. T. Johnson, was living in Dallas, Texas, in 1931.

The Kiowa consented to the trade through the intercession of the Penateka Comanche, who knew Johnson from their days in Texas. The Kiowa let Johnson leave with the captives, but threatened to kill him if they ever saw him again. They evidently made good on their threat. Johnson went into the business of hauling supplies on the West Texas frontier in hostile Indian country. His good luck with Kiowas ran out on January 24, 1871. On this day, Johnson and three other black men were hauling supplies from Fort Richardson to their homes near Fort Griffin. Twenty-five warriors met them on the famous Butterfield Trail two miles south of Flat Top Mountain on Salt Creek prairie. Although outnumbered, Johnson decided not to run; he told his men to listen to him if they wanted to live. The black men cut their horses' throats so they could use their dead bodies as shields. The battle became intense and deadly. Johnson's compatriots were killed early during the conflict. They were not as skilled as Johnson in fighting Indians and exposed themselves while trying to fire their weapons. Being the last one alive, Johnson gathered up his dead friends' weapons and ammunition and reloaded during lulls in the battle. The Indians charged his position again and again and became enraged at his resistance. After a lengthy battle they were finally able to subdue Johnson. In their intense anger, the Kiowa disemboweled and stuck a dead dog inside his corpse; they also scalped him. When Johnson's body was discovered, there were 173 empty rifle cartridge cases found. Britton Johnson had put up one great effort but came up short. His legacy will live on in the history of West Texas.

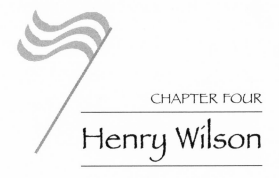

CHAPTER FOUR

Henry Wilson

One of the most interesting black scouts of the Civil War was Henry Wilson, who was a member of William C. Quantrill's Confederate guerrilla band during the rebellion. Wilson in later years reported that he was Quantrill's personal bodyguard and cook for the band.

Henry Wilson was born a slave of John Wilson, a large land and slave owner in Jackson County, Missouri. As a boy he said he witnessed the abolitionists known as "Red Legs" steal, plunder, and burn the homes of people in Jackson County. He said he was enticed to flee to a free Kansas, but he flatly refused, saying he didn't want to fall in with thieves and robbers. At the onset of the Civil War, Henry's master, John Wilson, fled to Texas. It was at this time that Henry joined Quantrill. Wilson said Quantrill trusted him because he didn't drink whiskey, was dependable, and could shoot straight. Plus, he had told John Wilson he would stick to the end with Quantrill. Henry became one of Quantrill's best spies; he could walk into a village without alarming the occupants and secure all the information needed for a raid.

The most famous raid Quantrill's band made during the Civil War was the sacking and burning of Lawrence, Kansas, which shocked the nation. This infamous raid took place on August 21, 1863. Not only did they burn the town to the ground, they killed 150 men in cold blood. Prior to this raid, Wilson was used to run the Union lines and bring much needed supplies to Quantrill. After the Lawrence raid was planned, Quantrill sent John Noland to learn the town's defenses. The information he came back with was inadequate. Quantrill sent his black spy and scout Henry Wilson to Lawrence for the critical surveillance needed for the raid. Wilson gave the following description: "I was really only a boy and small for my age when I went into Lawrence as a scout. I was barefoot and my pants rolled halfway to my knees. I begged cornbread for a poor nigger boy and got a good lay of things."

According to Wilson, when he got back to camp with information on Lawrence he cooked a ham for the raiders. During the course of the war Wilson stated he was shot seven times and dressed his own wounds on each occasion. Wilson was good to his word and stayed with Quantrill until the unit was defeated by the Union army. Wilson, after the war, ironically, moved to Lawrence, Kansas in 1874. He found employment with the wife of Governor Robinson and stayed until her death. There was some protest over Wilson's employment and some even asked for his execution because of his role in the Lawrence raid. The *Coffeyville Daily Journal* on August 20, 1931, reported that the Quantrill raiders who sacked Lawrence would probably not have a reunion again because there were only four known to be alive at the time. Of that four they only had an address for one of them. One of the four was reported to be Henry Smith (Wilson), Quantrill's black bodyguard and servant, last known address being Lawrence, Kansas.

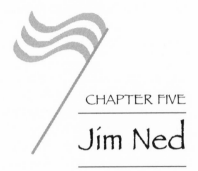

CHAPTER FIVE

Jim Ned

Jim Ned was a well known African Indian scout before and during the Civil War and a noted warrior. Ned lived among the Delawares from whom he was descended. His wife was also a Delaware. The Delaware had served as scouts and soldiers for the U.S. Army dating back to George Washington and the American Revolution. Prior to the Civil War, Ned was one of the leading scouts in the Trans-Mississippi West. Randolph Marcy, the explorer and general during the Civil War, wrote about the daring exploits of Ned. Marcy said Ned was a "remarkable specimen of humanity," a Delaware "united with a slight admixture of the African. Ned had a Delaware wife and adopted the habits of that tribe, but at the same time he possessed all the social vivacity and garrulity of the negro." Marcy went on to say that Ned was "exceedingly sensitive upon the subject of the African element in his composition, and resorted to a variety of expedients to conceal it from strangers...." He even went to the extremes of shaving off his kinky hair locks or wearing a turban on his head. Ned had accompanied Marcy on his expeditions across the Southwest as a scout. Marcy stated that Ned had spent a lot of time among the "wild tribes of the plains," principally with the Comanches. Marcy went on to say Ned was "one of the expert, daring and successful horse thieves among the southwestern tribes."

One of the principal leaders of the Delaware, Black Beaver, didn't like Ned. Marcy attributed Beaver's disposition partly to racial prejudice. Ned, in 1860, was living with the Absentee Delaware, so called because they lived briefly in Mexican controlled Texas, at the Wichita Indian Agency in the Indian Territory. They had settled on the north side of the Washita River on Sugar Tree Creek. In August of 1861, Jim Ned signed a treaty with the Confederacy which controlled the Wichita Agency. Mathew Leeper, the agent of the agency, flew into a rage when he found out Ned was encouraging Indians to flee. Leeper called him an "unmitigated scoundrel" and ordered the Confederate military "to kill Ned should they find him."

Confederate Gen. Alfred Pike had hoped to enlist from the Wichita Agency a Confederate mounted battalion of 350 men made up of Delaware, Kickapoo, and Shawnee Indians. Although the Delaware and Shawnee had signed a treaty, they fled north to Kansas, Jim Ned among them, to join the loyalist Indians under Creek Chief Opothleyahola. These Delawares formed the 2nd Indian Home Guard Regiment. Other Indians in the 2nd included Kickapoo, Osage, Shawnee, Seneca, and members of the Five Civilized Tribes. The 1st Indian Home Guard Regiment was primarily Creeks and Seminoles, and the 3rd Regiment was primarily Cherokee. All these units were mustered in Kansas.

In October 1862 Jim Ned was able to get revenge on the Confederates at the Wichita Agency. One hundred Kickapoo, seventy Delaware, and twenty-six Shawnee Union Cavalry left Fort Leavenworth on a 500 mile expedition to the Confederate held Indian agency. They were led by another Delaware, Captain Ben Simon. The Indian troops made a surprise attack on the Wichita Agency late in the evening of October 23. During the attack, Agent Leeper and four agency personnel were killed.

The Union troops had two wounded. They took a Confederate flag, $1,200 in rebel money, one hundred horses, and documents including General Pike's treaties with the Indians of the territory. The Indians proceeded to burn the Agency building to the ground.

The following morning, the Union Indian troops went after the Tonkawas who were allies of the Confederacy at the agency. The Tonkawas were tracked and trapped by mid-day in a blackjack thicket near the Washita River. One hundred and thirty-seven Tonkawas were killed including Chief Placido. In the official Confederate report of the battle it was said there was a deep hatred for the Tonkawa because they had "sided with the whites against the Indians some time ago in Texas." The Kickapoo had refused to sign a treaty with the Confederacy; they didn't like Texans.

Jim Ned had joined Company C of the 2nd Indian Home Guard Regiment. He was also used as a spy from time to time. Before the Wichita Expedition of 1862, Ned participated in the First Federal Indian Expedition made up of Indian troops in the Union Indian Brigade. On July 3 they defeated Missouri Confederate forces at Locust Grove. They killed one hundred, captured 110 Confederate soldiers, and secured sixty rebel ammunition wagons. After this battle, many Confederate Cherokee troops went over to the Union side. On July 16 the Expedition captured Tahlequah, the capital of Cherokee Nation, and on July 18 they captured Fort Gibson, their main objective.

As the war went on Jim Ned led "Jayhawking" expeditions out of Kansas into the Indian Territory. Ned would lead these guerrilla raids against Confederate positions, killing soldiers and stealing horses, mules, and cattle, until he was commanded by federal officials to cease his operations.

After the war Jim Ned lived the remainder of his years in the Anadarko community of the Delawares in what is now Oklahoma.

CHAPTER SIX

Alfred Wood

One of the most outstanding Union army scouts of the Civil War was a black man from Mississippi. Alfred Wood was an African American with Choctaw and European blood in his ancestry. It was said that Wood's Indian heritage was very prominent in his physical characteristics. He was the property of a large plantation owner named Doctor Wood in Mississippi. The doctor was famous for raising race horses which were put into competition in New Orleans. Alfred learned to ride as a youngster and became Dr. Wood's top jockey. Wood, by manhood, had grown to be six feet tall. Besides being an expert horseman he was also an expert with firearms. Although he was Dr. Wood's favorite slave and was given special privileges, including overseeing the plantation, Alfred Wood did not enjoy being a slave and was noted for arguing with Dr. Wood from time to time. The plantation was located in a remote area. With the Civil War becoming a major part of Mississippi life, Wood began to plot his escape to the Union army.

The plantation was bounded on the west by the Mississippi River, and on the south by the Yazoo River. The Confederate Cavalry stayed on constant alert for slaves trying to reach freedom with the Northern soldiers. Any type of escape attempt was dangerous for a slave. The Confederates had bloodhounds to assist in the capture of fugitive slaves. Bravely, Wood decided to take his wife Margaret with him on his run to freedom, despite the dangers inherent in such a task. On a moonless night, he took one of the Doctor's best horses and with Margaret seated behind him, they set out for freedom. After several close calls they had to abandon the horse and sought refuge in the swamps. Upon reaching the Mississippi River they were taken aboard a boat which took them safely to Vicksburg and Union headquarters.

After arriving in Vicksburg, Wood gained employment as a body servant for Captain E. D. Osband, who commanded General Grant's escort, Company A, Fourth Illinois Cavalry. In October of 1863 the U.S. War Department gave the authorization to recruit ex-slaves into the First Mississippi Cavalry Regiment (African Descent). Alfred Wood's name was one of the first on the rolls and he was detailed as an orderly at headquarters. Margaret was put in charge of the culinary department for the regiment and ministered to the sick and wounded. It was at this time that Alfred was given the nickname "Old Alf," even though he was only thirty years of age, and his wife was called "Aunt Margaret."

On March 11, 1864, the 1st Mississippi Cavalry (African Descent) was redesignated the 3rd United States Colored Cavalry. The regiment was organized by the officers of the 4th Illinois Cavalry Regiment. The first commander was Lt. Col. J. B. Cook. The black enlisted men were ex-slaves from Mississippi and Tennessee who showed a prowess for horsemanship. In the early days of the regiment Alfred Wood served as a recruiter. He could come and go at will and had a pass that was good anywhere within the army picket lines. His quick perception and keen insight into the motives of the people in the city proved rewarding. Alfred's skills led to the detection of spies and people trafficking contraband goods. While engaged in these duties, he gave evidence of those attributes that would later make him famous as an army scout. Being a superb horseman and a crack shot, quick to act and fearless, his skills were equal to, or better than, the best Union or Confederate scouts. Wood possessed another skill that was extremely useful; he had a thorough knowledge of the terrain and topography. This awareness was of great value to the African American regiment in its frequent raids into the interior of the state of Mississippi.

One of his first missions as a scout for the regiment occurred in December 1863. An expedition of Union forces was organized to scout territory across the Mississippi River in Louisiana and Arkansas. The force was composed of detachments of the 1st Mississippi Cavalry and the 4th Illinois Cavalry. The expedition began from Skipworth's landing on the east bank of the Mississippi and debarked from a steamer on the Louisiana side, about thirty miles south of the Arkansas border. Wood was sent out as a plantation slave, to move among the slaves in the vicinity, and find out as much as he could about troop movements, locations, and logistics. He slipped into the slave quarters of a large Louisiana plantation and learned from a couple of house slaves that the plantation owner was entertaining a group of Confederate officers from the Thirteenth Louisiana Cavalry. Wood also learned that the Confederates were aware of the Union troop's arrival at Skipworth's landing and were planning a trap to capture them by cutting off escape routes. He left very early the next morning for the Union lines on a fast horse. At one point he was pursued by a group of rebel cavalry, but he outran them and dodged their gunfire. Wood was able to alert the Union commander, Major Chapin, to the rebels' intentions.

On another occasion in the same vicinity, Wood was captured while trying to gain logistical information for the Union command. He pretended he was looking for a runaway slave from a nearby plantation. He was able to catch one of the guards looking away and knocked him out with a stick he was carrying. Spurring his mount to a fast gallop, Wood was soon closely pursued by mounted Confederate troops. He was able to outrun all of the rebel soldiers except one who was gaining on him fast.

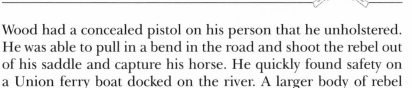

Wood had a concealed pistol on his person that he unholstered. He was able to pull in a bend in the road and shoot the rebel out of his saddle and capture his horse. He quickly found safety on a Union ferry boat docked on the river. A larger body of rebel cavalry was close behind, but could only hurl profanity with Wood secure on the other side of the river.

In September 1864 Wood was with a detachment of the black regiment numbering about 300 men. They were sent to break up some rebel camps not far from Vicksburg, up the Yazoo River. Wood was detailed as a guide on this expedition. In camp, at night, he got into an argument with one of the soldiers and in a fit of anger shot him. Fearing the consequences, he ran off into the woods. While wandering in the woods he was captured by rebel troops. He told the rebel troops that he had been captured by the black troops and had shot and killed one in making his escape. The rebel troops were so impressed that they took Wood to the Confederate commander who was anxious for any information on Union troop plans and movements. He told the colonel that he wanted to be his body servant and that the black troops would not fight. The commander, Colonel Montgomery, declared he was going to wipe the black troops out of existence the next day.

On the subsequent day, as planned, the colonel left camp with 400 rebel troops in pursuit of the black troops. He left Wood in camp to tend to his tent and extra thoroughbred horse. He secured two fine pistols and pretended to be grooming rebel horses while plotting his escape. He mounted a fine horse and rode out of camp in the opposite direction from which the rebel troops left. Being very familiar with the country, Wood felt by riding fast he would be able to cut off the rebel troops and warn the Union command. He was successful in reaching the black troops before the rebels. The Union commander was able to prepare for the attack. Although the rebel troops fought bravely, they were routed by the men of 3rd U.S. Colored Cavalry (U.S.C.C.)

By the fall of 1864 the 3rd U.S.C.C. was part of a force sent to scout the country between Vicksburg and Yazoo City. There were large numbers of rebel cavalry in this section of Mississippi. While doing so, the Union command was attacked leaving the

3rd cut off from the command for twenty-four hours. The black troops dismounted and took shelter in a small earthwork situated in a commanding position. They were able to hold this position for twenty-four hours, driving back several desperate rebel charges. In remembering that slaughter of black troops at Fort Pillow, the men of the 3rd resolved not to surrender. The enemy was very confident with superior numbers.

With the situation becoming more desperate by the hour, nightfall approached, and the Union forces came up with a plan. Three men were chosen to go for help, to reach Union lines through treacherous conditions. Wood was one of the three chosen and was the only one to succeed; the other two were captured and killed. He stated that after he left the fort he came upon dead rebel soldiers strewn across the nearby Mississippi fields. He decided to strip the uniform off a dead Confederate soldier and also the gun and accessories. Alfred Wood took on the appearance of being a Texas Ranger. With his long hair and light complexion, he was able to enter a rebel camp without being detected. Wood was able to secure a rebel horse and ride out of their camp, locate the Vicksburg road, find the Union camp, and give a description of the besieged position of the 3rd U.S.C.C. Soon thereafter, the Union troops were able to relieve the black troops from their tenable position.

Alfred Wood served out the war as a very important scout for the 3rd U.S.C.C. He was, without a doubt, one of the best military scouts during the Civil War. He is an unsung black hero who should be remembered for his contributions on the Western front of the Civil War.

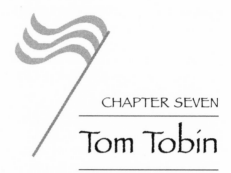

CHAPTER SEVEN

Tom Tobin

Noted frontier historian and National Park Ranger Bill Gwaltney has written that the southwestern traders Charles Autobees and Tom Tobin were half brothers and that the mother they had in common was a black woman who had been brought to the United States from the Caribbean. One newspaper account stated that Tobin's father was Irish and his mother Nova Scotian. Nova Scotia had a large population of former slaves who had escaped the southern U.S. via the Underground Railroad, or moved there after being freed in the Caribbean. Tobin, in appearance, looked to be of African ancestry. One of Tobin's daughters married the son of Kit Carson.

Tom Tobin was born in St. Louis on March 15, 1823. He served as a scout for Lieutenant Beale of the U.S. Army on the western frontier and then settled on land near Fort Garland in the San Luis Valley of Colorado. Tobin also worked as a scout on many occasions for Kit Carson and was hired out as a guide and tracker. He was noted as an Indian fighter, hunter, and trapper.

Tobin settled in Taos, New Mexico, in 1837 and trapped for Lancaster Lupton in the early 1840s. Tom almost lost his life in the Taos insurrection in January 1847. Being recognized as one of the best scouts and mountainmen of the western frontier, Tobin in 1853 led the Beale Expedition from the Gunnison River to California. The *Pueblo Chieftain* newspaper said Tobin was the most noted and successful trail man in western history. The paper stated:

> "It was claimed he could track a grasshopper through sage-brush. He had an uncanny ability to detect and follow 'the sign.' When on a hunt he would start at the most likely point and then make ever widening circles until he 'Cut Sign,' and then he clung to the sign until he overtook his quarry. He learned this from the Indians—only he probably improved on their techniques. He often dropped on all fours with his face close to the ground as he followed the sign that could not be detected by the average man."

The most famous incident in Tom Tobin's career was the subduing of the notorious Espinozas. The Espinozas were two Mexican brothers who were religious fanatics. Between 1860 and 1863, they were indicted for killing thirty-two white settlers in Ute Pass, South Park, and the San Luis Valley of southern Colorado. They lived in the La Veta Mountains and would travel as far east as Pueblo, Colorado, which was one hundred miles from their home base. The brothers told friends in New Mexico that during a dream, they had been inspired by the Virgin Mary to go out and kill all gringos.

The story of the phantom killers began one spring morning when William Bruce kissed his bride goodby and started from their log cabin near Cañon City for his sawmill twelve miles up Hardscrabble Creek. The horses returned home with an empty wagon that night, setting off a search that disclosed Bruce's body near the mill. He died without drawing his gun, shot through the heart. Bruce was well-liked and had no known enemy. There was no clue as to the murderer. The first people's and miner's courts had been established only four years previously. Justice

Scout, tracker, and bounty hunter Tom Tobin.
(Courtesy Denver Public Library, Western History Department.)

was interpreted largely by whose gun had been drawn first. The angry settlers of Pueblo, Cañon City, and the Hardscrabble were prepared to deal with the Bruce killers on the spot. They had no idea whom they were hunting nor where to hunt. This tragedy was only a couple of days past, when an old man named Harkins was found hacked to death with a hatchet near his sawmill on Little Fountain Creek in El Paso County. A short time later a man named Addelman was found shot through the head on his ranch on the Old Ute Pass Road leading from Old Colorado City to South Park. Again, as in the previous murders, there was no reason and no clue. In a few more days the bodies of two men named Binckley and Shoup were found in the Red Hills of South Park; both had been butchered. The next victim was a newcomer named Carter; he was fatally stabbed at Cottage Grove near Alma. Then the two murderous assassins butchered two more men, Lehmen and Seyga, in a Red Hills thicket.

Panic became the rule of the day. Any man moving along the Colorado trails had a double fear. First, that he might be set upon by the butchers; second, that posses might decide to nominate him as the killer and exact roadside justice.

More often than not, something happens that eventually exposes a criminal's deeds. As fate would have it, President Abraham Lincoln's Emancipation Proclamation brought about the identification of these phantom killers. A freighter, hauling a load of lumber behind an ox team, was ambushed as he was going from what is now Alma to Fairplay. A rifle barked, and the driver toppled over on his seat. Though hit, he had not been killed. The bullet struck his left breast pocket, and the impact stunned him momentarily. The aim had been perfect for the man's heart, but in his pocket he carried a copy of Lincoln's address and some other booklets. They stopped the bullet. Before the second shot could be fired, the oxen, frightened by the sound of the rifle, took off as fast as they could run. The freighter clung to his seat and found himself sheltered by the lumber. At first he believed his attackers were Indians because of their dark skin, but a second glance identified them as Mexicans. The brothers evidently thought the shot was fatal because it hit the freighter in the heart. They did not attempt to pursue the wagon, thereby allowing the victim to escape. When he reached the town of Fairplay, he made a report and gave a description of his attackers.

A posse had been assembled at Fairplay earlier to track the murderers. With fresh information and a description, they made haste in riding out to look for the Espinoza brothers. The posse was led by Capt. John McCannon of California Gulch. After several days and nights on the hunt, the posse sighted a couple of horses picketed outside a willow thicket at the mouth of Four-Mile Creek Canyon. One horse had his front legs hobbled. Suspecting their wanted men were in the thicket, Captain McCannon quickly laid the trap. As one of the Espinozas came out of the thicket he was hit by a barrage of rifle and shotgun fire. He was able to return fire, but was killed with a bullet between the eyes. The other Espinoza was able to elude the posse by leaping over into a ravine, where he must have had his horse ready. To their embarrassment, he made his way to New Mexico, picked up a nephew in his teens, and after a few weeks was back on the bloody trail in Southern Colorado.

The Colorado Territorial legislature and governor offered a $1,000 reward for Espinoza, dead or alive. Relatives of some of the victims raised another $500 for him, preferably dead. Soldiers were sent from Fort Garland to search for Espinoza. Tom Tobin was hired to assist the soldiers as a scout and guide. The army troops proved to be too clumsy and revealing to get close to the elusive Espinozas. Colonel Tappen at this point requested Tobin to apprehend the outlaws by himself. The Colonel insisted on providing a detachment of fifteen soldiers for his protection, but Tobin left them in camp and went ahead, accompanied only by a Mexican boy, whom he left behind when he actually located the Espinozas. A girl who had been captured by the Espinozas escaped and told her story to Tobin. With this information Tobin was able to ascertain the location of the Espinoza cabin. As Tobin reached the woods that surrounded it, he could see the smoke curling up from the fire where the outlaws were cooking their evening meal. Crawling upon his hands and knees, even wiggling along on his stomach, Tobin worked through the undergrowth in the thicket. As he came in view of the cabin, he saw one of the pair looking down the mountainside with his back toward the scout, as if on watch. One shot from

Tobin's Hawken rifle broke the back of the lookout, and another shot did exactly the same thing for the other as he was running to escape.

The Espinozas were still alive when Tobin reached them. They begged for mercy, but Tobin said they had shown no mercy to his friends. He then proceeded to take the elder Espinoza's knife out of its sheath and cut both of their heads off and hung them in a tree. Tobin then ventured to finish cooking the supper of the outlaws and ate it with great relish. On the elder man Tobin found a memorandum book, listing the various raids and the thirty-two murders.

There was bedlam when Tobin arrived in Fort Garland holding two heads by the hair and demanding his reward. Although he held up his end of the deal, Tobin initially didn't receive any reward money. The governor and legislature stalled the old scout, first for lack of funds and then for other various reasons. Nine years elapsed before any payment was made. Then the state treasurer issued a voucher for $500. There is no record that Tom Tobin ever received the remaining $1000. Tobin lived out the remainder of his days in his adobe house in the foothills of the Sangre de Christo Range in the San Luis Valley. Tom Tobin died May 16, 1904, and is buried at Fort Garland, Colorado.

The *Pueblo Star Journal* newspaper said: "Tobin will not be forgotten, for as long as the history of the eastern slope of the Rocky Mountains is preserved, just so long will Tobin have his chapter and it is an important one."

CHAPTER EIGHT

Isaiah Dorman

The Battle of the Little Bighorn is the most famous conflict of all the North American Indian Wars. It is also known as "Custer's Last Stand." What is not widely known is that a black man died with Custer and most of the 7th Cavalry on that fateful day. Isaiah Dorman has been listed as a scout in most accounts, but he was actually hired as an interpreter. The Sioux Indians called Dorman "Azimpi." Their oral history tells of a large black man who lived among them in the 1850s. He was known to ride a horse and trail a pack mule. For a living he trapped beaver and muskrat and never spent time around any white settlement. The reason may be obvious given the time and circumstances.

The wealthy D'Orman family of Louisiana and Alabama were searching for several escaped slaves, one of whom had the name of Isaiah. Dorman didn't surface in the white community in the Dakotas until the Civil War had ended. It was at this time that Dorman married a woman from Inkpudta's band of Santee Dakota. He built a cabin at Fort Rice, Dakota Territory, near the present city of Bismarck. He earned a living cutting wood for the fort. He soon was known to be trustworthy and reliable and was well liked by all the military personnel. In the fall of 1865 Dorman was hired as a woodcutter by the firm of Durfee and Peck, suppliers for the army forts in the territory. He became renowned for his ability to cut a cord of wood faster than a helper could stack or pile it. Army records reveal Dorman was hired as a courier to make trips between Fort Wadsworth and Fort Rice, Dakota Territory, a distance of 360 miles, on November 11, 1865, at one hundred dollars a month. It is interesting to note that army privates were only paid thirteen dollars a month; Dorman was getting a captain's pay. For an African-American on the frontier, it was an exceptional salary during this time in American history.

By 1871 Dorman had attained a job as a guide and interpreter for the Army column escorting the Northern Pacific Railroad survey team, also at a pay of a hundred dollars a month. In October of 1871 Dorman was hired as a Lakota Sioux interpreter for the Army at Fort Rice. This was a steady, full-time job up until May 1876, when he was ordered to accompany the Little Bighorn military expedition by Lieutenant Colonel George Armstrong Custer. It is interesting to note that, although Custer had forty Arikara Indian scouts and four renegade Lakota Indians, plus two white scouts and one white interpreter, he personally ordered Dorman to be attached to his command. Frederic F. Gerard and Dorman did all the interpreting between the Indians scouts and the 7th Cavalry. At the onset of the Battle of the Little Bighorn, Custer split his command up into three groups. Isaiah Dorman, along with the forty scouts, went with Major Marcus Reno and troops A, G, and M of the 7th Cavalry. Reno's battalion moved into the valley of the Little Bighorn River; when they got within view of the Indian Village they dismounted in preparation for battle. After the battle began, Reno retreated into a nearby thicket. But after Custer's favorite scout, Bloody Knife (who was standing next to Reno) had his brains blown out, some of which landed on Reno's face and shirt, Major Reno lost it. The Arikara scouts claim Reno became mad with fear and ordered a retreat with Reno in the front. Dorman mounted his horse in the retreat and shot and killed at least one attacking Indian. His horse was soon shot and fell with Dorman still in the saddle. This unfortunately left Dorman pinned to the ground with his horse on top of him; he became an easy target. The Lakota placed at least a dozen arrows in Dorman's chest, and a picket pin was placed through his testicles.

Isaiah Dorman, the interpreter for the 7th Cavalry, perished on that ill-fated trip up the Little Bighorn. The Lakota called Dorman "Wasicun Sapa," the "White man, black." He had lived and married into their nation. Undoubtedly, they felt betrayed by him helping the 7th Cavalry, and he died with Custer at the age of 55.

Frank Grouard, the most important U.S. Army scout in the history of the western frontier. His father was a black Creole and mother a Lakota Sioux.
(Courtesy Little Bighorn Battlefield National Monument)

CHAPTER NINE

Frank Grouard

The most famous army scout in the late 19th century was a black man named Frank Grouard. Of all the personalities that I have researched, his life was one of the most controversial and complex.

Frank Grouard was supposed to have been born on September 20, 1850. From there the story diverges on different paths. There was a book titled, *Life and Adventures of Frank Grouard* by Joe De Barthe in 1893. De Barthe interviewed Grouard late in his career and was told that Frank's mother was from the Paumoto Sandwich Islands in the South Pacific (today considered a part of the Hawaiian Islands) and that his father was a French-American missionary; the supposed father actually coming to visit Grouard in Buffalo, Wyoming, in the late 1890s. The interesting distinction today is that Pacific Islanders consider themselves black people or people of color and in the 19th century they were not remotely related to African Americans.

The flip side of the coin is that there are contradictory state-
ments from the turn of the century in the Ricker Interviews,
located in the library of the Nebraska State Historical Society. A
large number of White and Indian frontiersmen stated that
Grouard was part African and part Indian. They stated he was
the son of a man with African blood who came into the Northern
Plains by way of the Missouri River as a cook on a steamboat and
who later found work as a trader in the region. Probably the
most riveting testimony in the Ricker files comes from Mrs.
Nettie Elizabeth Goings who was interviewed on March 13, 1907:

> She and Frank Grouard are children of the same father by dif-
> ferent mothers. The brother of Frank Grouard's mother was
> named Black Lodge Pole. The name of her father and Frank's
> was John Brazeau. He was a French Creole. He was from
> St. Louis and worked for the American Fur Company. He came
> up and settled at Fort Pierre some twenty years; he and
> Papineau were companions and chums and he was an associate
> of the Picottes. [Brazeau worked in the fur trade in the upper
> Missouri region.] She says Frank got into some trouble on the
> Missouri and went off among the Indians. Mr. Brazeau was re-
> lated to the Choteaus and Picottes. Mrs. Goings is the mother
> of Frank Goings, Agency interpreter at Pine Ridge. She says
> that Frank and three other boys were in school and the four
> got into difficulty and she says that there was something said
> about a killing but she was young and does not know just how
> it was ... He got on a boat going up the river and the father
> boarded the same boat to bring him back, but did not succeed
> in doing so. His right Christian name was Walter Brazeau. His
> Indian name was Grabber. Mrs. Goings Indian name is Money.
> She does not doubt that he (Frank Grouard) may have been in
> the family of _____ Pratt in Salt Lake; she says that he told
> her that he lived in the family of some white man away off
> north or west, and he showed her a picture of the man. She
> says her family was acquainted with the Pratts of St. Louis.
> Choteau Pratt was killed at the Lower Brule Agency on the
> Missouri.

There is another interview in the Ricker files by a white man
named George Stover, which took place at Allen, South Dakota,
in 1906:

Mr. Stover speaking of Frank Grouard says that Grouard told him that he was a cousin to the mother of Frank Goings, who was a colored woman. He came from the Missouri River up near Apple River just below Bismark, North Dakota, when he went to the Indians. Mr. Stover heard that Grouard killed a man when he was 13 years old, and ran away and went to the Indians. Frank told Stover that he had trouble there. Grouard told Stover that he ran off with _____ from the Choteau family and went to the Indians. Mr. Stover thinks he was the first white man at Fort Robinson who made his acquaintance when he came down from the North with the Indians. He was painted like an Indian and his hair was braided. Grouard began his career as a scout at Fort Robinson. Mr. Stover let Col. Mackenzie know of him and his qualifications and his knowledge of the Powder River Country and his acquaintances with the Indians of that region, and the Colonel gave him employment.... Stover also says that the fact that Grouard had such good English is a point in favor of his having come from near the Choteau family where his early life was spent.

According to Mari Sandoz, Billy Garnett, an Indian scout, whose sister married Grouard, heard Gallino, a person of Indian-European descent from the banks of the Missouri River, call Grouard "Prazost" (Ricker's spelling) at Red Cloud Agency, saying that was Grouard's name when he lived up on the Missouri. Nick Janis told Garnett that he knew a former steamboat cook called "Brazo" (Ricker's later spelling), a black man with several Indian wives, working for the Missouri traders. John Brazeau was a black French Creole who was well known in the Dakotas and was employed many years for the American Fur Company at Fort Pierre. Brazeau also lived and worked for many years at Fort Union, North Dakota (Williston). Some of the pioneers remembered Brazeau as "a full-blooded Ethiopian, apparently of small stature and intelligent ... He enunciated his English well and had a good command of it for an uneducated man. He spoke French better than some Canadians; also Sioux and other Indian languages." Brazeau died around 1868 at Fort Stevenson in a destitute state.

The other story has Frank being born in the South Pacific to a missionary named Benjamin F. Grouard and a Polynesian woman named Nahina. The family relocated to California in

1852. While in California the weather proved to be too harsh on his wife, so Ben Grouard was forced to send her back to the islands. She took her eldest and youngest sons back with her, leaving young Frank in San Bernardino with his father. The elder Grouard, after a couple of years, placed Frank in the family of Addison Pratt, another missionary family, shortly after the Pratt family moved to Beaver, Utah. As a teenager, Frank began working as a teamster on wagons traveling between San Bernardino, California, and Montana. While on one of these trips he was kidnapped by Indians in Montana; thus began his life among the various bands of Indians in the far north country.

My belief is that Grouard found refuge in the home of the Pratts in Utah. While living in the Salt Lake City area the Pratts concocted a story to protect Frank from a murder charge in the Dakotas. Mrs.Pratt went to such extremes as to include Frank in a diary narrative that would bolster his South Sea Islands origins. I don't buy it, but I may be wrong. The people in the Dakotas, including the lady who says she was his sister, have no reason to lie. Native Americans are taught in their culture not to lie or tell mistruths.

By 1869 Grouard was living in Montana. He had secured a job breaking horses for Ben Holladay who owned a stagecoach station. Later he secured employment as a rider with the Pony Express between Diamond City and Fort Hall (Idaho). It was in this vocation that he was captured by the Blackfeet Indians. He claimed they stripped him naked, took his rifle and revolver, and then proceeded to beat him unmercifully. In terror he ran 75 miles to Fort Hall with no food or water. When he reached the fort he fell unconscious, remaining in this state for four days. It took Grouard three months to recuperate from this ordeal; his body had to recover from festering sores and his feet had swollen to twice their normal size. At the age of nineteen he went and lived among the Lakota Sioux Indians. In his biography he stated he was captured by the Lakota, and they adopted him after Sitting Bull took a liking to him. But if his mother was a Lakota, it would make sense for him to live among these Native Americans. In his biography, Grouard stated he was made a Lakota Sioux warrior and lived with them for six years.

It was during this time that he became good friends with the warrior Crazy Horse.

Grouard would state on several occasions that Crazy Horse was the bravest man he ever met. It was during this period that Frank fought as a Lakota warrior against the whites in the Dakotas. In 1874 Grouard left the Sioux and found his way to Fort Robinson where Gen. George Crook was headquartered. General Crook, impressed with Frank Grouard, asked him many questions about the country, the Indians, and the animals. Frank was a font of information. When he had problems with the English language, due to his length of stay with the Lakota, Baptiste "Big Bat" Pourier, would help Frank with the question. Grouard and Pourier became the best of friends, and Pourier also became a noted army scout. The Lakota name for Grouard was Standing Bear; some say when he had on a Buffalo coat, mittens, and leggings with moccasins that is what he looked like since he stood six feet tall and weighed 230 pounds. The Indian pronunciation of Standing Bear sounded like "Grabber" and that is what the Indians and other scouts called him. Frank Grouard joined Crook's other scouts who also included Bat Garnier, Lewis Shangreu, Speod Stanger, Buckskin Jack, Ben Clark, and Tom Reed. Initially Grouard was utilized as an interpreter's guide for Crook along with Big Bat and Louis Richard.

Frank Grouard became the principal scout for the U.S. Army in the Northern Plains. Grouard was given leadership of the thirty-four scouts with Crook's command. In an official correspondence in 1876, General Crook stated "I would rather lose a third of my command than Frank Grouard." As another measure of Grouard's worth to the U.S. Army we can look at his pay scale. After December 1877, he was paid $150 a month. At that time a private made $13 per month and a first sergeant made $22 per month. Gen. George Crook, Civil War veteran, was commander of the U.S. Army's Department of the Platte, and his command extended to the Northern Rockies and the Northern Plains area of the western frontier. Contrary to most military leaders, Crook had a good reputation with the Indians. Chief Red Cloud of the Lakota said of Crook, "He never lied to us. His words gave the people hope." After many years on the Plains, mountains, and deserts of the west, Crook died in March of 1890.

Given his status with Crook's command, Grouard was a major player in the Great Sioux War of 1876 and 1877. The exact dates for this war were fifteen months, between March 1876 and May 1877. The most famous engagement was the Battle of Little Bighorn, which cost Colonel Custer and his command their lives. Although it is called a Sioux war, the Northern Cheyenne were also very involved in the conflict. The first military engagement was the Battle of Powder River, Montana Territory, March 17, 1876. On the night of the 16th, Frank Grouard achieved a remarkable success and impressed officers and news correspondents accompanying the command. Grouard was given the orders to follow the trail of two hostile Indians seen earlier in the evening. The hope was that it would lead to their camp. Grouard picked up the trail at night, in a fog, over rugged bluffs and narrow valleys, sometimes having to get on his hands and knees in the deep snow. Sometimes he lost the trail, but would soon pick it up again with his keen skills; Crook and his command of troopers and scouts followed close behind. Grouard followed the trail until daylight. In a very short time it was said Grouard and his scouts had located the camp of Oglala Lakota war chief Crazy Horse, whom Grouard knew very well.

Col. James J. Reynolds led 400 troopers from the 2nd and 3rd Cavalry in an attack on this Indian village. The soldiers were able to drive out the Indians and capture 700 ponies. But Reynolds gave the command to destroy everything, including food supplies of buffalo meat and venison and other items, as well as ammunition. This was a mistake by Reynolds because Crook's troopers were low on supplies and food. Additionally, Reynolds didn't put a large enough detail on the horses, and the Indians were able to recapture them.

Casualties were four U.S. troopers killed and six wounded. The Indians suffered one killed and one wounded. Most of the Indians in the village had been Cheyenne.

The decisions made by Colonel Reynolds during this engagement cost him a court-martial and a military career that included duty during the Mexican War. But Grouard had proven how valuable his scouting skills and knowledge were to the military expedition.

Frank Grouard: scout, interpreter, trailblazer, tracker, and lawman
(Courtesy Wyoming State Museum)

Frank Grouard's next engagement against the Lakota (Sioux) and Cheyenne was at the Battle of Rosebud Creek on June 17, 1876. This was not a conclusive engagement. Both parties suffered some losses in the fighting. The Indians had initially held the high ground in this skirmish. Grouard stated that the Crows and Shoshones, allies of the U.S. troops, met the first charge of the Lakota and held them in check. He went on to say had it not been for the Crows, the Lakota would have killed half of the U.S. troopers before they could get in position to meet the attack. After this engagement, the Crows and Shoshones left Crook's expedition.

North of General Crook's command, Brig. Gen. Alfred H. Terry was leading a column of troops against the Lakota and Cheyennes. Included in Terry's command were the 7th Cavalry under the leadership of Lt. Col. George A. Custer. In mid-June Maj. Marcus A. Reno, a member of Custer's command, found a large trail of Indians leading westward. Reno reported his findings to Terry and Custer who were not knowledgeable of Crook's setback on June 17. Terry gave Custer orders to follow the trail and use discretion in moving toward a suspected major village in the Little Bighorn Valley. Terry, with Colonel John Gibbon's column, would proceed west along the Yellowstone River, then ascend the Bighorn and Little Bighorn Rivers where they would meet Custer's command. Crook's troops had been ordered to halt and wait on reinforcements from the 5th Cavalry. They were camped on the Little Goose Creek near the Bighorn Range. General Crook proceeded to go hunting in the mountains for game, and Grouard decided to see if he could pick up any signs of hostile Indians. According to Grouard, he saddled up his pony and headed in the direction of Indian smoke signals. He reached a trail which appeared to have been made by U.S. troops on the divide between Rosebud Creek and the Little Bighorn River on the evening of June 26. The trail led Grouard to the north of the creek, where it empties into the Little Bighorn, then turned off to the right, traveling along parallel to the creek, and back into the bluffs. Grouard found out later that this was the location where officers Custer and Reno split up their command. Grouard proceeded to follow the trail that Custer took. He kept riding into the night, cloudy and misting, until his jet black horse came to a spot and wouldn't go any further, which was unusual. Dismounting, Grouard checked the ground for objects that would cause his horse alarm, and he found the body of a scalped trooper. Realizing he had come across a battlefield, Grouard tried to extricate himself from the area by riding down a ridge lower than the one he had been on. By the movements of his horse, he said he rode through dead bodies for at least ten minutes.

That morning Grouard was able to locate the Indian trail which led to the warrior camps. Grouard was dressed as an Indian with a blanket around him as he came upon an elderly Indian herding his ponies. Grouard told the man in Lakota tongue that he was Sitting Bull's brother and that he was searching for his horse. He then proceeded to tell the man he missed the fight since he had been away scouting. The old man was very suspicious, then Grouard gave him his Indian nickname "Grabber." Evidently the old man recognized the name, and he rode his horse to the adjacent creek warning other Indians that troopers were nearby. It was apparently well-known by many Lakota that "Grabber" was the chief scout for the U.S. Army. The nearby camp was alerted, and Grouard had to put his horse to an instant gallop. They proceeded to follow Grouard for forty miles. But he was able to elude them since he had a good head start. By the time Frank Grouard got back to the command, the soldiers had received rumors of the Custer massacre.

The defeat of Custer and the total annihilation of five troops of the 7th U.S. Cavalry was the worst defeat of the U.S. forces during the Indian Wars on the western frontier.

The next episode in this campaign would seal the legacy of Frank Grouard as the greatest frontier army scout. While recuperating from the conflict on the Rosebud, General Crook wanted to find out where the Indians were and what was happening. One of the search parties included twenty-five troopers under Lt. Frederick W. Sibley of the 2nd Cavalry. A packer named John Becker, nicknamed "Trailer Jack" volunteered, and John F. Finnerty, a reporter from the *Chicago Times*, also joined the group. Scouting for Sibley was Grouard and his best friend "Big Bat" Pourier. This particular episode would become known in historical annals as "The Sibley Scout." The soldiers had been camped at Little Goose Creek at a location that is now Sheridan, Wyoming. Sibley and his small command left about noon on July 6, 1876, in a northwest direction toward the Bighorn Mountains. Each man had one hundred .45-.55 cartridges for his single-shot 1873 Springfield Trapdoor carbine. While crossing Beaver Creek the next morning, Grouard noticed an Indian sentinel who had spotted the troopers. Grouard tried to reach him but the Indian got away. The next morning, from their camp three miles north of the Tongue River, Grouard and Big Bat surveyed the surrounding countryside from a nearby butte with field glasses. Grouard noticed a large Lakota war party was on their trail and closing fast. Bat said he knew they were Lakota because they passed each other while mounted, whereas the Crow rode in order like the cavalry. Initially Grouard thought they might have been Crow, until Big Bat made his observation. John Finnerty, the reporter, stated that Sibley asked Grouard "What ... are we to do?" Grouard replied, "Well, we have but one chance of escape. Let us lead our horses into the mountains and try to cross them. But in the meantime, let us prepare for the worst." After taking in all the options, which were few, Grouard decided their only chance was to keep away from the Indians as best as possible. By the time the troops made it to the trail that led into the mountains, the Indians were within a mile, observing. The Lakota warriors made a decision not to follow Sibley's small command, but they would go to the upper trail at the head of Twin Creek and cut the troopers off. A large contingent of the warriors stopped at Tongue River at the mouth of the canyon, in case the troopers tried to come down off the mountains and escape that way. The troopers took the trail at a trot with Grouard going ahead to find out if they had been cut off. After reconnoitering Twin Creek to find out where the Indians were, Grouard saw no signs of the warriors or his troopers who were supposed to have been following.

Backtracking Grouard found Sibley and the soldiers resting because they were hungry and felt they weren't being followed. Grouard knew the Indians would be somewhere ahead and told Sibley to mount up and for every trooper to be ready. Sibley generally obeyed everything Grouard said. Crook had advised him that Grouard was the best scout in his command and to listen to

Frank Grouard (center) Chief of Scouts, with, left to right, Good Lance, Big Talk, Kicking Bear, Two Strike, and Major Burke on the far right

(Courtesy South Dakota Historical Society)

Grouard if an emergency arose. It was now an emergency. Sure enough, further up the trail, the Indians had set up an ambush. Grouard had the command ride to the right of the trail, not on it. The main trail ran right between two high buttes going to the right, and this saved the troopers from being ambushed. As they passed the buttes, about 200 warriors fired on them. Somehow the Indians missed everything except the horse that news correspondent Finnerty was riding. There was a timber line below their position, and Grouard told the soldiers to head for it. Once in the timber, they dismounted, putting the troopers in a position about a hundred yards from the tethered horses. Grouard instructed not to shoot unless absolutely necessary and to make every shot count. Frank Grouard was asked by some of the men if they had a chance of getting away alive, and he initially told them about the same chance as jumping over the moon. The best he could tell them was to fight as long as their ammunition held out and save the last bullet for themselves. Grouard had all intentions of saving his last bullet, for some of the Lakota warriors recognized him and had yelled threats of what they were going to do to him. Some of the troopers began to cry. As time went on, more and more Indians took to rocks surrounding the timber. The Indians began shooting, trying to draw the troopers' fire, but it didn't work. The only thing they hit were some of the soldiers' horses.

The stand in the timber began about 10:30 A.M. on July 7, 1876. By 3:00 P.M. there were only eight horses left; the rest had been shot by the Indians and killed. As time passed the Indians became more daring and kept riding closer and closer. The troopers had held their fire as Grouard had advised. There were two warriors who began to try to outdo one another. Grouard said the one who wore a large war bonnet was a Cheyenne chief named White Antelope. Grouard decided to shoot one of them, if not both. After a good deal of waiting, they rode straight by where Grouard was located. He took dead aim at the rider in front. He fired his Springfield, hit White Antelope, the bullet went through him (White Antelope), and hit the following rider who was five yards behind. The chief fell off his mount, and the other warrior in front fell on the neck of his horse. The shot that felled two warriors completely befuddled the Lakota and

Cheyenne. Grouard instructed Sibley to move the troopers out on their hands and knees. They were able to escape the entrapment by the pandemonium caused by Grouard's well-aimed shot.

The Indians evidently didn't feel the troopers would escape by leaving their horses behind. They kept firing into the trees where they thought the troopers were located. The troopers reached the Tongue River about a mile from where they had made their stand. They jumped in and crossed the river as quick as they could. The Indians had been leery of rushing into the thicket after the two warriors were killed, and the troopers had held their fire up to that one shot. The Indians didn't find out the troopers had escaped until the next morning. Grouard instructed Big Bat to tell the troopers not to step on the ground, but from rock to rock, and not to touch the trees or the limbs if possible. They traveled all the next day in this fashion. At the onset of the night a bad thunderstorm blew in so the command had to seek shelter under the mountain boulders. Grouard had removed his rope from his horse and was able to assist the troopers when their footing was not sure in climbing the rocks. He felt their only chance was to stay well up in the mountains where they couldn't be followed by men on horseback. After the storm the troopers traveled through the mountains for the remainder of the night. Grouard brought the troopers down off the mountains at the head of Soldier Creek, on the eastern end of the Bighorn Mountains. Here the soldiers were able to get some fresh drinking water. Moving out after a short morning rest, they went into the nearby timber at the foot of the mountain. As soon as they had done so, Grouard called out for silence. A large Lakota war party was approaching their position. The soldiers thought the Indians where looking for them; they were well positioned in the timber and ready for a fight. The Lakota warriors stopped about 500 yards from Sibley and his command. They got off their horses and took a rest by having a smoke and watering their mounts. The soldiers were surprised and relieved, but stayed silent in their positions until the Lakota rode on.

The warriors evidently were more interested in making an attack on General Crook's position. By the time the Indians left, it was sundown. Lieutenant Sibley was about twenty miles from Crook's camp at this time. The soldiers were totally exhausted, but they had to move. Grouard stated that the command couldn't walk a hundred yards without sitting down and resting. By the time the troops reached the Big Goose Creek, the water was swollen by the previous night's rain and moving fast. It would be difficult to cross. Two of the troopers, Sergeant Cornwall and Private Collins, refused to cross the creek. After much coaxing, but to no avail, Lieutenant Sibley decided to leave these soldiers. He told them to seek a good hiding spot, and troopers would be sent back for them. The command crossed the creek with the water reaching up to their necks. By daylight the next morning some of the men were so hungry they were catching small birds and eating them raw, feathers and all. Grouard and Big Bat were able to show the soldiers some Indian turnips. Most of the troopers were able to stave off their hunger by digging up and eating these wild turnips. It had taken the command four hours to cover six miles on flat land due to the condition of their hunger and exhaustion. At 5 A.M. a small group of Lakota appeared in the distance, but gave no evidence of noticing the troopers. At 6 A.M. they noticed a rider on a hill ahead of them. Grouard was able to see with his field glasses it was a trooper from Crook's command. In noticing the soldiers, the mounted trooper, being cautious, waited until the command walked up to him. He informed Sibley that he had been given permission to go out and hunt for game. They sent him to bring horses back due to the fact that many soldiers couldn't walk any further. At 10 A.M. on July 9, 1876, three days after their departure, everyone in Sibley's command returned safely to General Crook's camp at Little Goose Creek. This ended one of the greatest episodes in the history of the Indian Wars.

Frank Grouard was given most of the credit for his successful plan of escape and overall knowledge of Lakota habits and strategies. This was one of the narrowest escapes without casualties on record. Grouard's fame would only grow after this feat. It was stated by Big Bat and others that during this whole escapade, Grouard suffered from a bout of venereal infection he had picked up from a white prostitute. On the next morning, July 10, an official communique came in to Little Goose Creek from Fort Fetterman, Wyoming Territory, on the defeat of the 7th Cavalry on the Little Bighorn.

The next important fight in the Sioux War that Frank
Grouard participated in was the Battle of Slim Buttes which took
place in the Dakota Territory, on September 9, 1876. General
Crook, commander of the Bighorn and Yellowstone expedition,
had been reinforced after the Custer defeat and spent the summer looking for hostile Indians. His command consisted of
about 1,500 cavalry, 450 infantry, 45 volunteers, and 240 Snake
and Ute Indians, bringing his force to about 2,200 men. By early
September Crook's expedition had run out of food. They began
to kill abandoned horses for sustenance. General Crook decided
to send Capt. Anson Mills of the 3rd U.S. Cavalry with 150
handpicked men to go to Deadwood in the Black Hills for food
and supplies. Crook detailed Frank Grouard to be the head
scout for Mill's command. Big Bat also accompanied the command as a scout. The mission began after nightfall on September 7, 1876, near the Cannonball River. Along with Captain
Mills were Lts. Emmet Crawford, Frederick Schwatka, Adolphus
H. Von Luettwitz, and John W. Bubb—who had command of the
fifty-mule pack train that was to bring back provisions.

The night was rainy and foggy with very limited visibility.
The command could not travel quickly. After the rain stopped,
the fog lingered, but Grouard was able to see a little better. He
moved out about 300 yards in front of the troops. The fog lifted
somewhat, and Grouard was able to notice a large pony herd
about a mile ahead. He had noticed the tracks by striking a
match and scouring the ground. Grouard had the command
sequester themselves in a deep ravine while he located the exact
location of the Lakota village. The village was located on the
southeast side of Slim Buttes. Grouard kept an eye on the village
the whole day. At nightfall Grouard decided to go into the village and check it out, disguised as an Indian. He tried to find
the best location for the soldiers to attack. After his reconnaissance he decided the command was large enough to capture the
entire village. Before leaving the village he took two fine riding
ponies, a pinto and a black stallion. In returning to the command, Grouard informed Captain Mills that the best time to
attack the village would be at the break of dawn. At 3:00 A.M. the
command began preparations for the attack against the village.

Lieutenant Crawford was detailed to lead a mounted unit,

and Lieutenant Schwatka, with twenty mounted men, to drive Indian ponies away so they couldn't be used by the warriors. The rest of the command dismounted and moved toward the village on foot. As Lieutenant Schwatka tried to take control of the Indian ponies, they smelled the troopers and stampeded through the Indian village. Schwatka and his troopers followed the Indian ponies and used their revolvers to shoot into the Indian lodges. The majority of the Indians cut open the rear of the lodges and escaped as the troopers on foot attacked the village. Some Indians found shelter in a ravine, others got behind rocks and put up a good defense to the attack. The troopers took up positions on an incline that faced the slope the Lakota village was on. The Indians that were in the ravine, where a creek was located, let the troopers know there was a larger body of Indians nearby, and they were going to resist until they received reinforcements. The village was between the troopers' main position and the Indians in the creek ravine. Grouard knew if the Indians received assistance, it would be a very difficult spot for the troopers to hold. He got one of the mule packers to go back to General Crook's camp and bring relief as soon as possible.

The Indian village had about thirty-nine lodges and numbered over 200 people. In the initial attack on the village, Lieutenant Von Leuttwitz and a corporal both suffered leg wounds. In the charge, Pvt. W.V. McClinton of Troop C, 3rd Cavalry, discovered one of the guidons that belonged to the ill-fated Custer command. It was attached to the lodge of the Oglala Chief American Horse, who was the leader of this village. The guidon, by way of Captain Mills, found its way back to the 7th Cavalry. By this and other evidence (another soldier found $11,000), these Lakota had been some of the warriors that were involved in the Battle of the Little Bighorn. General Crook arrived on the scene at about 11 A.M. with reinforcements. Grouard met with General Crook and showed him where the village was located. The largest contingent of Indians were in the ravine. Crook had Grouard ask them to surrender; this was answered by a negative reply. Crook ordered a charge on the enemy position and army scout Jonathan White was killed. Finally two or three Indian women came out and gave them-

selves up. In seeing no harm come to them, the rest of the
Lakota surrendered. Chief American Horse was living, but badly
wounded, with a bullet wound to the stomach. There was no
chance for him to live. Two of the Indian women were also
wounded. There were eleven Lakota warriors killed in the battle
and three U.S. troopers, including the scout White. This
engagement was the first victory for the U.S. military in the
Sioux Wars during the summer of 1876.

The next engagement Frank Grouard took part in was the
Battle of the Red Fork which took place on November 24, 1876.
General Crook was very concerned about reports of depredations by Chief Dull Knife and his band of Cheyenne warriors.
The army, by this time, was employing a large number of Indian
scouts to help track the Lakota and Cheyenne. Grouard said that
there were now over 500 Indian scouts, including Shoshone,
Pawnee, and Lakota. For this engagement Grouard was serving
with Gen. Ranald S. Mackenzie of the 4th U.S. Cavalry. A trail
was picked up on the night of November 23 that would lead to
the hostile Indians. The column marched up the Crazy Woman
River on the Beaver Creek after leaving Fort Fetterman.
Grouard, after learning the exact location of Dull Knife's village,
suggested to General Mackenzie to make a night march for an
attack at daybreak. The General agreed with Grouard. The command, camped on the Crazy Woman River, was given orders to
break camp at sundown. The Indian village was about eighteen
miles from their location. The troopers attacked the village in
force at dawn and wiped it out. Many of the Indians fought a
retreating action into the nearby wooded hills; that continued
for the rest of the day. Grouard stated that in the heat of the battle, he shot and killed Chief Little Wolf. In this engagement Lt.
John A. McKinney, 4th U.S. Cavalry was killed, along with six
other troopers. They took twenty-seven casualties. The Cheyenne lost over thirty warriors in this fight. Dull Knife escaped,
but was given the cold shoulder by Crazy Horse, to whom he
went to for assistance.

Many articles were found in the village that came from the
ill-fated Custer command, giving irrefutable proof that the
Cheyenne were also at the Battle of the Little Bighorn. After this
battle Grouard, along with General Crook, tried to find a hostile

band of Indians under the leadership of Chief Lame Deer. The snow had become too deep, and the weather was intensely cold. The winter campaign came to an abrupt end. The soldiers pulled back to Fort Robinson near the Red Cloud Agency.

The most controversial episode in the life of Frank Grouard occurred in the spring of 1877. In May of 1877, Chief Crazy Horse, the greatest Oglala Lakota warrior, surrendered to the U.S. Army. Crazy Horse and his warriors turned their guns in at the Red Cloud Agency near Fort Robinson. They soon enlisted as scouts for the U.S. Army. Crazy Horse and Frank Grouard had been friends since their youth. Grouard stated Crazy Horse was the bravest person he had ever met, be they red, white, or black. Crazy Horse had been one of the principal leaders at the Battle of the Little Bighorn and always the proud warrior. Grouard was so well thought of by Crazy Horse's father that he was given the history of the Lakota Nation, which was preserved on buckskin. Crazy Horse's family kept the history of their people. This is a practice also found among the griots in West Africa. Grouard lost the precious document in a house fire that also burned up the scalp cape of Chief Sitting Bull. After surrendering at the Red Cloud Agency, Chief Crazy Horse took his first dinner at the agency with Frank Grouard. Afterwards Grouard took Capt. John G. Bourke to Crazy Horse's lodge so he could meet the venerated warrior. Bourke stated that the warrior chief would only "light up" in those first few days of being on the reservation by being in conversation with Grouard. Many of the Indians state that Frank Grouard was troubled by Crazy Horse being on the reservation. Why? Because Crazy Horse knew Frank Grouard's true identity; Grouard's mother was a Lakota Sioux and his father a black frontiersman who had worked with Missouri traders. Grouard's story of being captured in 1873 wouldn't hold up if Crazy Horse was questioned about what he knew about the "Grabber" as the Lakota called Grouard. They said he couldn't afford to let people know he was really Walter Brazeau, the Black Indian.

The Indian version of what occurred at the agency is that a big council was held to ascertain whether the Lakota were going to help the U.S. Army fight the Nez Perce, who were trying to flee to Canada. A meeting was held with the Lakota Sioux chiefs

Crazy Horse and Touch the Clouds at the office of Lt. William P. Clarke, whom the Indians called White Hat. Interpreting for Lieutenant Clarke was Grouard. Crazy Horse basically told Lieutenant Clarke that the warriors would rather go north to hunt versus going north to hunt the Nez Perce, but if the U.S. wanted them to serve as scouts, they would. Supposedly Grouard put a slant on Crazy Horse's words and said that Crazy Horse had said "We will go north and fight until not a white man is left." Grouard substituted "White man" for "Nez Perce" in the interpretation to Lieutenant Clarke. The young officer blew up over what he thought Crazy Horse had said. The Indians initially didn't understand the anger of the young white officer. There was another mixed-blood scout present, Louie Bordeaux, who knew what had happened and protested to Grouard. Grouard stomped out of the council after quarrelling with Bordeaux. Lieutenant Clarke sent for Billy Garnett, another interpreter, to finish the session. Crazy Horse continued the dialogue by saying he would only go north to fight if he could also take some women and lodges along for a hunt. Lieutenant Clarke was emphatic that there was to be no hunt and women and lodges couldn't be brought along. At this point Chief Crazy Horse stood up, gathered his blanket around him, and said, "These people don't know anything about fighting." The Chief and his men walked out of Lieutenant Clarke's abode feeling they had wasted a lot of time talking. But the damage by Grouard had been done. Rumor spread that Chief Crazy Horse would not go on the warpath. A detail was sent to arrest him. Chief Crazy Horse was told he was wanted at Fort Robinson. Upon arriving he was led unknowingly to the guard house. Realizing he was going to be arrested, Crazy Horse attempted to flee, but was bayonetted by a soldier on guard. Chief Crazy Horse died of his wound on September 7, 1877.

The Lakota believed the major cause of Crazy Horse's troubles were the words of Frank Grouard, which ultimately caused his death. Grouard, however, told a different story.

He stated that he had overheard some Indians, along with Crazy Horse, plotting to go on the warpath and kill him and Lieutenant Clarke during the council, then massacre everyone who was a foe at the Red Cloud Agency. Lieutenant Clarke was in charge of the Indians at the agency. Grouard stated that he told the Indians he had a dream that they intended to kill the whites at the post. He also stated he made sure there were plenty of armed soldiers nearby if anything happened. But after telling the Indians his dream, it threw them in a state of confusion whereby they didn't try anything. Grouard said that Crazy Horse had twenty warriors with him during the council, and they all had concealed weapons under their blankets. After Crazy Horse's death Grouard said that most of the troubles with the Lakota and Cheyenne were over, and many enlisted for service with the U.S. Army. Did Grouard really conspire to get Chief Crazy Horse, his old friend, out of the way? Did he really believe Crazy Horse would explain why Sitting Bull took Grouard into his lodge years earlier? Or that Grouard's father was a black trapper who had married a Lakota woman? This information would certainly contradict what Grouard had told all the whites in authority.

I believe we will never know for sure. But the Lakota definitely had their version of the story which can be heard today in the whispers of the Dakota winds.

Frank Grouard's work with the army took on another dimension in 1877. He was assigned to chase down horse thieves. These outlaws were a major nuisance in Nebraska, Wyoming, Oregon, Montana, and the Dakotas. Grouard was given orders to locate horse thieves and hold-up artists and to pursue and suppress them. He did so with detachments of U.S. cavalry units. They were assigned to the Indian agencies at Red Cloud and Spotted Tail. Forts that Grouard worked out of to run down outlaws included Laramie, Robinson, Fetterman, Reno (McKinney), and Sheridan. In 1877 horse thieves stole about one hundred ponies from the Indians at the Spotted Tail Agency. Grouard with M Troop of the U.S. 3rd Cavalry took the trail after the thieves. They were able to capture all the stolen horses, but in the ensuing gun battle with the outlaws, one of the troopers was killed. Grouard states that two of the outlaws rode off, but two fired on him; he killed one and captured the other. Being upset about the murdered soldier, Grouard and the accompanying soldiers left the outlaw dangling from the tree.

Also in 1877 road agents began to rob the Black Hills Stage. While stationed at Fort Laramie, Grouard was directed to assist in capturing these bandits. On one occasion he trailed two hold-up men from Bull's Bend on the Platte River to Green River, a little over 300 miles. Grouard made the arrest as they were preparing for breakfast.

In January 1878 Grouard made one of his best catches in pursuing outlaws. At the time he was stationed at Fort McKinney on the Powder River. There was a large gang of horse thieves sequestered in the famous Hole In The Wall. They had a regular trail running through Wyoming from Oregon to Minnesota. These particular outlaws had stolen some horses from the beef contractor for the fort. Grouard was given the assignment to track them. The morning following the crime he picked up their trail leading toward the Black Hills. He followed them for 400 miles and was successful in capturing one of the party. The one outlaw believed that Grouard was going to hang him and gladly told him everything he knew of the gang's operations. With information in hand, Grouard and federal authorities were able to locate and arrest twenty-eight members of this particular gang. All were sent to the penitentiary; their sentences were from fourteen to thirty years. For Grouard this was indeed a very good piece of law enforcement. This arrest put the gang completely out of commission.

In returning to Fort McKinney, post commander Capt. Edmond Pollack gave Grouard a new assignment. Pollack was to lead three companies of cavalry and two of infantry to intercept warriors from Lame Deer's band who were supposed to be making their way into the Little Powder River country. In Army circles this particular march became known as "Pollack's Sagebrush Expedition." In leading the expedition, near the forks of the Belle Fourche River and searching the surrounding country, Grouard came across no trail of the hostiles. Lame Deer had been killed earlier in 1877 by troops under General Miles. After finding no signs of the Indians, the command was ordered back to the post. En route the next morning back to the fort, the command being led by Grouard ran into a very bad blizzard. Many of the soldiers thought they were doomed. Not so, believed Grouard, who was familiar with the land. He was able to lead them safely through the storm. This was another of Grouard's outstanding examples of being able to track in awful conditions. His reputation was only enlarged by this episode of superior scouting.

Back on the trail of outlaws in the spring of 1878, Grouard had a communique that Jesse and Frank James were thought to be in the north country. After following up on a lead Grouard came close to arresting Frank James, but James was tipped off by a friend who lived in the area. Also in the spring of 1878 a store on Crazy Woman Creek which the Bozeman Trail ran past, was stuck up and Grouard was sent to investigate. Along with an undercover agent sent by the government named Llewelyn, they were able to establish evidence. At Fort McKinney there were several gambling dens. The worst one on the post was run by a black man who also ran a barber shop and cut the hair of many of the officers. In learning about shipments of money from the officers, this black man would pass the information on to his outlaw confederates. Grouard was able to also learn that the out-law who robbed the store on Crazy Woman Creek frequented the den. Grouard arrested the felon and closed up his gambling operation on post. The black man later tried to murder Grouard, but missed all five times he shot at him and made good his escape. Grouard never came across this man again.

In the fall of 1878 Grouard had a gun battle with an outlaw named McGlosky. Grouard was brought a note from an Indian from the Crow Reservation. The note was from Thomas H. Irvine, Sheriff of Custer County, Montana, informing him that two men had stolen a couple of race horses from a party on the Yellowstone River, and they might be headed south in his direction. That same night Grouard found the thieves at Ed O'Malley's dance house, which was two-and-a-half miles from the post. Grouard decided to effect the arrest the next morning at O'Malley's. Grouard reported that there were about a hundred people at 10:00 A.M. in front of the establishment. McGlosky came around the corner of the stable riding one of the stolen horses, and he recognized Grouard. McGlosky had threatened to kill Frank many times during the past year. McGlosky's part-ner, sensing trouble, put the spurs to his horse and rode in the direction of the Crazy Woman Creek. Grouard, standing his ground, carbine in hand, motioned for McGlosky to stop. McGlosky pulled his pistol at the same time he spurred his horse toward Grouard. He fired but missed. After riding out about a hundred yards, he turned to fire at Grouard again. He was too

Frank Grouard, deputy U.S. marshal, having fun with a colleague. Grouard's
gun and badge from his career as a lawman are in the Wyoming State Museum.
(Courtesy Wyoming State Museum)

late. Grouard spotted him in his carbine sights and blew McGlosky out of his saddle. Grouard mounted up and went after the other horse thief, but he escaped. McGlosky died later that night. He was wanted for murder in Fremont County, Wyoming, and in Kansas.

During the 1880s Grouard was kept busy by carrying dispatches between army posts when telegraph wires were downed or checking on the Native Americans. On several occasions he was sent to check on the Ghost Dance excitement among the Indians. On one of these trips he traveled from Fort Washakie, Wyoming, up into Idaho. On other occasions he was paid to supply game for the forts. Other times he was detailed to locate graves and bring bodies back to the military post. Prior to the Wounded Knee problems at the Pine Ridge Agency, Grouard was sent to investigate the problems. He reported back that there were whites who were trying to ferment problems so they could make money off an Indian uprising. No action was taken on his report. Before the "Battle of Wounded Knee" on December 29, Grouard was ordered to accompany Colonel Forsyth's command. But he was recalled by courier on the 28th. Therefore he wasn't present when the Indians were massacred by Forsyth's soldiers.

It is interesting to note that on April 4, 1892, Frank Grouard was commissioned a deputy U.S. marshal in Wyoming. This was a testament to his ability to hunt down outlaws. U.S. Marshal Joseph P. Rankin of Wyoming hired Grouard to assist with quelling the Johnson County War.

There is evidence that Grouard did not like Buffalo Bill Cody. He thought he was a "picture book scout and a picture book showman." On one occasion Grouard walked into the Sheridan Inn in Sheridan, Wyoming, to buy some cigars. Cody was in the barroom telling "Indian stories." Grouard faced off against Cody and told him what he thought of him in a low voice. Supposedly they faced each other until Cody dropped his eyes and turned away. Grouard purchased his cigars and left. Grouard detested Cody's tale of the killing of the Cheyenne warrior and chief, Yellow Hand. He felt it was a tragic death—not something to brag about. Furthermore, Cody did not have the years of service or experience on the frontier that Grouard, a truly important scout, had.

In 1893 while trying to find a mail route in northern Wyoming, Grouard's vision was impaired. Along with a companion, Grouard was on top of the range for eight days, three of which were spent in huge snowdrifts without food and fire. After finally finding a way off the mountains, Grouard's eyes were nearly closed from snow blindness. His face was swollen and frozen so badly he was unable to leave his house for two weeks. Even with the injuries, Grouard's trip was a success. The report he turned in was acted upon by the Postal authorities. The mail route was established as he had laid it out. Due to the damage done to his eyes, his service to the military was interrupted. He settled in St. Joseph, Missouri, for the last twelve years of his life. The *Wyoming Standard* newspaper, from Big Horn County, published the following story on Saturday, September 16, 1905:

FAMOUS SCOUT DEAD

Frank Grouard, a former plainsman and scout, who made his home in St. Joseph for ten or twelve years died at St. Joseph's hospital Tuesday, where he was a charity patient. Pneumonia was the direct cause of death, although he had not been in good health for several years. For many years he was chief of scouts at Fort Fetterman and Fort McKinney, making a number of trips through the Basin while acting in that capacity at the latter post. Grouard wrote a book of his life and experiences which had a limited sale and secured for him the animosity of a number of Army officers by reason of certain disclosures made therein. At the time of his death he was fifty-five years old and is survived by his widow, from whom he has been separated for a long time.

I will end this chapter with a quote from Margaret Brock Hanson, a researcher of Grouard's career on the frontier:

As he looked to the north, toward the land where he had roamed with his Indian brothers in his youth, was he longing for old friends? He had helped subdue the Indians and bring them into the white man's world, only to see them degraded and destroyed. He could never go back to his Indian friends, yet he did not feel too comfortable in the 'Civilized' world of the white man. Frank, like his beautiful (wife) Lallee, was a man of two cultures and not truly belonging in either.

Smokey Wilson and Yellow Bear Crane, Crow Indian Policemen at the the Crow Agency and Pryor, Montana. Wilson served as policeman, mailman, interpreter, and horse breaker for the Crow Indians.

(Courtesy of Nancy F. O'Connor, Fred E. Miller Collection)

CHAPTER TEN

Charles "Smokey" Wilson

One of the most interesting black men of the Northern Plains was a scout named Charles "Smokey" Wilson.

Wilson was born in St. Louis, Missouri, about 1860. He stated that his parents were African slaves, but he wasn't. Wilson was raised as a member of the family of Bud Howell, a white man, on Olive Street in St. Louis. In the summer of 1866 Wilson accompanied Howell and his family to Montana. They made the journey on steamboat to Fort Benton; its name was the *E. O. Standard.* At the mouth of the Milk River, the boat hit an obstruction and sank. Everyone was able to safely depart the boat before it went down. Wilson noted he was the only black person on the boat.

The Howell family took Wilson on to Bozeman, Montana. While in Bozeman, Wilson worked for a liveryman as a barn boy. It is believed this employer was General Wilson, the Bozeman pioneer. He took the last name of Wilson at this time. Wilson learned to grease harnesses, wash buggies, and do other livery chores. He also became an expert horseman and rider. In about a year's time Mr. Howell packed up his family and moved to California. Howell told General Wilson if Charles got lonesome, he would send the money for him to come to the West coast. Smokey stayed in Montana working the livery stable in Bozeman.

About two years later his employer died, and Wilson learned Howell had also expired in California. It was at this point in Smokey Wilson's life that he began to work for Montana cattleman Nelson Story. He learned to break wild horses and rode the cattle range that covered the areas encompassing the lower Madison, on the Gallatin, on the Shields River and the upper Yellowstone. It was while doing this work on the range that Smokey Wilson came into contact with the Crow Indians of the Deer Creek Agency, which was located near the present town of Livingston, Montana.

Early pioneers remember Wilson moving in with the Indians when the Agency was at Absaroka on the Stillwater River. He found work breaking horses that various Crow Indians couldn't break. His skill in this endeavor became legendary among the Crow. The Absaroka Agency was established in 1874 and was vacated in 1884.

The Crow Indians frequently visited nearby Fort Ellis. The Army officers noted that a black man was living with the Indians and fluent in conversation in both English and the Native American dialect. They gave Charles Wilson a job as a interpreter and a residence on the post.

When Fort Custer was built in 1877, Wilson was sent there as field interpreter under Lieutenant Robinson. On the post he was the principal interpreter working with the Army's Crow Indian scouts.

In regards to Custer and the Battle of the Little Bighorn, Wilson made the following remarks in the *Helena Independent* in 1916:

> At the time of the Custer massacre I was at the Stillwater Agency, and went to the Crow Agency about a week after the battle. At that time the men of Custer's command had not

been permanently buried, but had been given temporary burials by General Terry in shallow graves, each grave being
marked with a stone or brick. Just after reaching the Crow
Agency I talked to a number of men who were close enough to
witness the fighting. I asked one old warrior how long the battle had lasted and he replied, "As long as it would take a hungry man to eat a meal."

Many stories have been published blaming Colonel Reno
for not coming to the aid of his general, but Indian scouts of
Custer who were familiar with all the details of the battle told
me that Reno was attacked by the Indians before Custer was,
and Reno had his hands full in keeping his own command
together.

Three of Custer's scouts were the Crows, Goes-Ahead,
Harry Moxon and White-Man-Runs-Them. These Indians had
reconnoitered before the battle and warned Custer that the
Indians were in force and that it would be foolish to attack
them, but Custer evidently felt that he could fire a few volleys
into the Indians and cause them to quit. He told the Indian
scouts that they had done good work, and they could go to the
rear. This they did, and while they were close enough to see
the battle they were not actually in it, and so made their
escape.

As for the story of Curly, the Indian scout who claimed
that he made his escape from the scene of the battle by throwing a squaw's shawl over his head, the other scouts deny, and
claim that at no time was Curly ever in the battle, but when he
saw how the tide was turning he made off and carried the first
news of the massacre to General Terry....

The Indian warriors all fought on horseback and after
the carnage was over moved their own dead and wounded
from the field, while the women were killing the helpless
whites. The three tribes opposed to Custer included Sioux,
Cheyenne and Arapahos. The Crows took no part in the battle, and as long as I have been associated with them they have
always been friendly to the whites. They aided Custer in every
way possible, and in the past 40 years that I have spent among
them I have always found them friends of the Whites.

In later years, one of Charles "Smokey" Wilson's favorite
topics concerning the frontier was Custer's defeat on the Little
Bighorn. He gave the following comments to a newspaper writer
in 1935:

I was a young fellow then, acting as an interpreter at Crow reservation. I remember one night, the 25th of June it was, 1876, a lot of Crows were gathered around a camp fire and Chiefs Pretty Eagle and Plenty Coups and medicine men were talking about a big fight likely to take place between the Whites and the Sioux. Pretty Eagle was worried and Plenty Coups' face looked solemn. And while he was sitting there news came—I can't explain how—that day there had been an awful battle on Little Big Horn, and Custer's force had been wiped out. So me and some of the others saddled horses quick and rode as fast as we could from Absaroka to Little Big Horn. A three day trip it was. When we got there it seemed, at first, the rumor must have been a mistake, everything was so quiet. No soldiers, no Indians, no sign of battle. But we rode along and seen where the tepees had been. Then we went up the hill and, as long as I live, I can never forget what met our eyes. Bodies of horses—just a few—and bodies of men, hundreds, white soldiers, Custer's men, thick all over that hill. Folks tell now how the bodies of the were mutilated terrible but that ain't so. I was there just three days after the fight. I helped the soldiers bury the dead. The bodies, most of 'em, was stripped, but I didn't see any mutilated ones. Another thing, folks hint maybe Custer killed himself, at the last, least he be taken by the Indians. But I seen Custer, lying atop the hill with Tom Custer and Boss Custer close by, and I looked close at his body and I seen two bullet holes, one through his head, and one through his chest, and either shot would have caused his death. It was a Sioux bullet that got him, or maybe a Cheyenne, but never his own. All that hot June day we dug shallow graves in the hard baked earth with what few tools we had and laid the bodies in, and covered 'em, best we could with dirt, and we piled little mounds of rock besides each grave. I reckon there ain't many white men, besides the soldiers and myself, that seen that battlefield three days after the fight.

Wilson accompanied several of the military patrols that scattered and broke up the bands of hostile Cheyenne and Lakota warriors after the Custer defeat. For ten years Wilson served the U.S. military as an interpreter. In 1877 he worked with Lt. Hugh L. Scott who arrived in Montana shortly after the Battle of the Little Bighorn. Scott, in later years, attained the rank of general and had fond memories of working with Smokey Wilson.

While stationed at Fort Custer in 1887 as a field interpreter, Wilson was involved in the military action against the young warrior Wraps-Up-His-Tail, also known as Sword Bearer, who also had a reputation as a medicine man. Wraps-Up-His-Tail along with five companions evidently left the reservation to go after some Piegan Indians who had stolen some of their horses. They were able to recover the horses which caused much celebration on the reservation. The Indian agent, Major Wyman, threw Wraps-Up-His-Tail into jail at the Crow Agency for breaking rules about leaving the reservation.

Upon his release from jail, Wraps-Up-His-Tail and his companions shot up the agency, but didn't hurt anyone, just scared them. Bad feelings remained on the reservation at the Crow Agency, and troops were sent to take charge of the situation. General Ruger from Fort Keogh was given command of the military contingent.

Wilson was sent by General Ruger to Pryor to order all the Crows there to come to the agency. There were seventy lodges under Chief Plenty Coups and Bell Rock, the head men of the Pryor band. Then he went on to Clark's Fork, where there was another band of twenty to twenty-five lodges. The men came in first on horseback and the women on foot followed later.

Wraps-Up-His-Tail came in with the other Indians, but remained aloof from the main contingent. At a later date Wilson witnessed the shooting of Wraps-Up-His-Tail, which occurred close to the Little Bighorn River when there was an attempt to arrest him and his followers. He was killed by Fire Bear, an Indian policeman. Medicine Tail, another policeman, also shot him during the melee.

After his stint with the military Wilson lived and worked on the Crow Agency in Montana as a policeman, interpreter, and messenger. In 1891 the black 10th U.S. Cavalry was stationed in Montana. Wilson became acquainted with these troopers at this time. They were stationed at Fort Custer, Fort Assinniboine, and Fort Keogh, Montana. Wilson held a commission of deputy U.S. marshal for the Crow Agency. One of his exploits as a policeman was told by historian and photographer of Bighorn Country, Fred Miller, former chief clerk of the Crow Agency:

... Smokey was an Indian policeman in the Pryor Creek country. Two white men intruded themselves unlawfully upon Indian lands there or committed some sort of act justifying their prompt expulsion from the reservation. Smokey escorted them to the boundary line. "Now you two men go on across that line, and don't ever come back to this side of it," the policeman sternly admonished them. The two did as they were ordered—crossed the line. They stopped 40 or 50 feet away and took a stand. There they declared their feelings.

"You dirty black___ ____ ____," they opened up, "get off your reservation and come to this side of the line if you dare," they challenged accompanying their fiery invitation with flourishings of fists, Smokey simply listened, or paid no heed at all. He stood there on guard. They continued their barrage of verbal abuse. Finally the policeman lost his patience. He went out of his official bounds and walked straight into encounter with the two challengers. Mr. Miller tells of the outcome in these terms:

By jinks, Smokey licked the hell out of both of 'em. One of 'em had to go to the hospital in Billings.

The above passage came from a newspaper article written by Dr. Thomas B. Marquis in 1932.

Charles "Smokey" Wilson lived in the Crow Reservation for over sixty years. He was noted by Dr. Marquis as a "full-blood Negro, his entire makeup being such as to indicate clearly an unmixed ancestry running back to Africa." His one unique distinction was that on the census reports he was the only full blood African-descended "Black Crow Indian" ever officially recognized.

Wilson was loved by the Crow Indians and proved invaluable to them. If they came to the agency to see a doctor, to complain about their women, to seek shelter or medicine for their stock, they would go to Smokey Wilson. If it was midnight they would rouse him, if it was mealtime they would interrupt him. Wilson gave the Crows consolation, advice, and took them to the authorities who could assist them. He was an asset to both the U.S. government and the Crow nation. Wilson married a Crow lady named Pine Fire, the daughter of Goes Ahead who was one of the Crow scouts at the Battle of the Little Bighorn. Goes Ahead was with Major Reno's command. She was a deaf mute and they had three children, the oldest surviving child being

John Edward Wilson, whom I had an opportunity to speak to before he died.

Smokey in later years married a black woman. For many years a picture of Smokey Wilson hung in the Crow tribal headquarters.

Wilson was quoted as saying:

> I was never abused by any white man. Most colored men get into trouble by talking too much. But I always remember what my mother told me: "When folks ask you questions, give them a civil answer to what they ask, but don't tell them more than they ask." I have found that this kept me out of a lot of trouble.

A Montana newspaper in 1932 stated that Charles "Smokey" Wilson was the only full blood African descended "Black Crow Indian" ever officially recognized on the U.S. census rolls. Wilson was a truly unique and special individual of frontier Montana.

Sam Bowman, Chief of Apache Scouts (top of picture), with Lt. Charles B. Gatewood and Apache Scouts. Bowman's interpretations were trusted by the Apaches more than any of the other U.S. Army scouts. (Courtesy National Archives)

CHAPTER ELEVEN

Sam Bowman

There is not much information available on black army scouts in the Apache campaigns in Arizona and New Mexico.

The most famous was Sam Bowman, a noted black frontier figure in Arizona during the last Apache Wars. He was part African and part Choctaw. He was from the Indian Territory (Oklahoma). Bowman was noted for being brave and reliable in the face of adversity in various military campaigns against the Apaches.

As a scout and interpreter Bowman had a very good reputation among the Indians. The Apaches trusted him to interpret for them much more than they would the more well-known scouts Tom Horn, Mickey Free, or Al Sieber.

Bowman served as chief of scouts, and assistant chief of scouts, to Al Sieber. He worked with famous officers such as Lt. Britton Davis and Lt. Charles B. Gatewood.

In 1871 Bowman joined an Indian scout company at Fort

Whipple, Arizona Territory. At that time he was an assistant to Al Sieber who headed the company. The unit moved to Fort Verde and Fort Reno before moving to San Carlos. The Indian Agency was established in 1872.

At San Carlos, Bowman served under Britton Davis as an interpreter and accompanied him to Turkey Creek. Bowman had thirty Apache scouts under his command. Prior to working with Britton, Bowman worked under General Crook. While Bowman was at Turkey Creek, Geronimo was there with his contingent of followers.

General Stoneman commended Bowman and others for their part in the 1883 campaign against Geronimo in Mexico.

Bowman was sent to Washington D.C. as an interpreter with Chatto, Loco, and other captured Apaches in 1886. From there the delegation and interpreters were sent to Fort Marion, Florida, where some of the Indians captured with Geronimo had been interned. Bowman stayed in Florida for a while with the Apaches, whom they trusted, while Mickey Free was sent back to Arizona.

It was reported by Al Sieber that Sam Bowman retired from military service around 1890. After receiving his accumulated pay, Bowman was shot from an ambush and robbed of his money by unknown parties near Fort Apache. Very little information is known of this black scout and many feel that little was written about him due to Bowman's illiteracy.

CHAPTER TWELVE

Wash Robinson

Wash Robinson was a black man who was born in Mexico around 1840. While he was a little boy, he was kidnapped by the Navajos. In his late teens Robinson was sold by the Navajos to the Pueblos. At a later date Washington left the Pueblos and traveled east to the Wichita Mountains. He was befriended by the Indians who lived in this locality, which today is southwest Oklahoma.

In combat with the Indians against the U.S. military, Robinson was taken prisoner at the Battle of Big Frame on the Santa Fe Trail. From there he was transported to Washington D.C. After being incarcerated as a prisoner of war, Robinson was given parole. At this time he could speak Spanish and several Indian languages and was given the name George Washington. Robinson enlisted in the U.S. Army, probably the 10th U.S. Cavalry. While in the army he learned to speak English. Four

George Washingtons were enlisted in his company, and his name was changed to Wash Robinson.

In 1869 Robinson was with the 10th Cavalry Regiment at Fort Sill, Indian Territory, and took part in numerous raids against hostile Indians. Being familiar with the Wichita Mountains and surrounding vicinity, plus his knowledge of Indian languages and customs, Robinson was given the position of scout with the military.

In the early 1880s Robinson was assigned to Fort Reno, Indian Territory, with the black 9th U.S. Cavalry Regiment. At this time in Indian Territory, the government was having a severe problem with white settlers, called boomers, who were illegally setting up camp on Indian lands. The 9th Cavalry was very active in arresting and escorting boomers back to the Kansas border.

Robinson met the well-known "Captain" David Payne, leader of the boomers, during one of the altercations. He said that Payne had come into the territory with about fifty families from Kansas and settled on the south side of the Cimarron River in Indian Territory. Payne and his contingent of illegal settlers threw up breastworks and were prepared to battle the army soldiers. They had let it be known that they would die before they would leave the territory.

Two black companies of cavalry from Fort Reno were ordered to escort Payne and his conspirators out of the area. The boomers were alerted to the troop movement by cowboys working on ranches in the area who had befriended them.

The boomers were prepared for battle and felt confident in their make-shift fort. According to Robinson, Payne said, "All right, let them come." When black troopers of the 9th Cavalry arrived on the scene, they pitched camp near the boomers' breastwork. The white commanding officer of the 9th went over to talk to Payne. The officer was informed that the boomers were ready for a fight. The officer laughed and told Payne he wasn't quite ready for a fight; that he didn't propose to cause any bloodshed unless it was absolutely necessary.

For several days the soldiers didn't take any action against the boomers. They actually became friendly with Payne and his followers. Robinson says the commanding officer made the

Scout Wash Robinson of the Indian Territory (Oklahoma)
(Author's collection)

remark, "There isn't any use hurting these people; it's bad enough to be forced to put them out. I hate to have to do it, but I'm not responsible for my orders, and all I can do is to obey."

On one of the following mornings, the troopers found most of the boomers away doing various tasks. Payne was alone in camp with only five or six followers. The 9th's officer, along with Wash Robinson and six or seven other troopers, decided to pay Payne a visit. The officer informed Payne, "Now, captain, you had better give up; I have to put you out."

At this point an all-out fist fight took place between the soldiers and settlers. They proceeded to knock over tables, benches, tents, and anything else in the path of the brawl. At the conclusion of the fight the boomers were roped and hogtied well enough to be sent to the market. There were several bloody noses and black eyes among Payne's men.

Shortly thereafter a signal was given and the whole camp was surrounded by the buffalo soldiers. The soldiers quickly secured the camp, gathered up the illegal squatters, and proceeded to escort them to the Kansas border.

The Oklahoma Indians told a story about Wash Robinson, which he would not admit had happened.

According to the story, a Cheyenne chief took a lot of buffalo skin pouches, filled them with water, and tied them to the ponies of his men. The warriors then proceeded to leave the reservation whereupon U.S. troops were assigned to follow. This was not a difficult task because the Cheyenne made a broad trail easy to read. In order to prevent the soldiers from overtaking them, however, they avoided every water hole. The troopers had neglected to bring adequate water; they thought they could do without water as long as the Indians. The soldiers passed numerous camps used by the fleeing Indians but found no water holes. After many miles, the troopers found themselves on the plains, and at this point the Cheyenne tracks scattered in many directions.

According to the Oklahoma Indians, the only true scout with the soldiers was Wash Robinson. The soldiers attempted to follow, but had to soon change their course for the South Canadian River. The soldiers' horses had begun to die from thirst, and many of them became faint and weak. Robinson, however, could follow a trail and decided to continue to track the Indians.

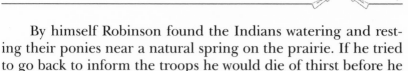

By himself Robinson found the Indians watering and resting their ponies near a natural spring on the prairie. If he tried to go back to inform the troops he would die of thirst before he made it. Therefore, Robinson surrendered to the Cheyenne who gave him something to eat and drink.

The Indians knew Robinson. If he had been a white man they would have killed him. They proceeded to remove all of Robinson's clothes, tied him face down across a log, and the women whipped him with switches. After this punishment the Indians turned Robinson loose, naked as a jaybird. He therefore had to walk two hundred miles back to the fort, thoroughly humiliated and shamed.

In the 1880s, Robinson married a woman from the Arapaho tribe and raised a family. He had two sons who were noted for being nice and attentive. The oldest was named George; he had black features with straight hair. It was said that George could beat anyone in the tribe at throwing a rope, playing ball, or running foot races. By 1906 Robinson had retired from government service and owned a farm on the Washita River at the mouth of Boggy Creek. He also owned a livery stable in Colony, Oklahoma. It was said that Robinson was the only black man allowed to live in Washita County, Oklahoma, the main population being white Texans, Russians, and Germans. Wash Robinson was definitely a colorful figure in the history of western Oklahoma.

Early photo of Seminole Negro Indian Scouts in the field
(Courtesy Sul Ross State University)

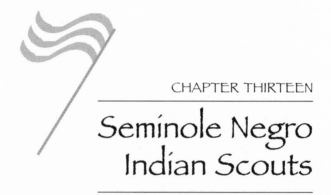

CHAPTER THIRTEEN

Seminole Negro Indian Scouts

Undoubtedly, the most extraordinary unit of scouts that served with the U.S. Army on the western frontier was the unit officially named the Seminole Negro Indian Scouts.

These scouts' ancestors had been runaway African slaves who found refuge and freedom among the Seminole Indians in Florida. The fugitive African slaves called maroons became allies of the Seminoles in battles against the U.S. military. They lived in separate villages; had their own fields, flocks, and herds; habitually carried arms; went into battle under their own chiefs; and, except for an annual tribute in corn to the Indian chiefs who were their protectors, were as free as the Indians themselves according to historian Kenneth W. Porter.

Some whites of the time (1830s) felt that the Africans' knowledge of the English language and of the white man's ways, coupled with their agricultural and industrial knowledge, made them the real rulers of the Seminole nation.

The Black Seminoles spoke a language that has been termed, Afro-Seminole; a creole related to Gullah, the main base being English sounding words, but also included some Spanish, African, and Muskogean (Creek) expression. The main body of the Seminoles were Creek, therefore they spoke Muskogean or Hitchiti.

The Africans became major strategists and warriors in the Seminole Wars. The Second Seminole War was the costliest Indian war in U.S. history.

The United States paid out over $30,000,000 and lost over 1,500 soldiers in the war. The war came to an end in August of 1842. The Africans were a major reason for the length of the war which began in December of 1835.

Researchers have discovered that the famous Seminole war chief Osceola was of African-Indian heritage. The African maroons, in addition to being warriors in this conflict, also served as spies, guides, interpreters, and intermediaries. This was the conflict that James Beckwourth couldn't wait to get away from.

The last maroon leader to surrender in Florida was John Coballo, Gopher John, or John Horse. In 1842 John Horse and about one hundred of his followers made the successful trek to the Indian Territory (Oklahoma). The Seminoles were originally settled in the Creek Nation which didn't sit well with the maroons. There were many mixed-blood Creeks who wanted to kidnap the free African-Seminoles and place them in bondage. For this reason many Seminoles lived close to Fort Gibson in the Cherokee Nation.

John Horse built a home on the Deep Fork of the North Canadian River. Shortly thereafter a Black Seminole community was established at this location. John Horse made several trips to Washington D.C. to complain about the treaty with the Creeks and living conditions for the maroons in the Indian Territory.

In 1845 John Horse led a large group of former maroons deeper into the territory where they settled on Wewoka Creek. This would later become the principal site for the Seminole Nation, which became known as Wewoka. Slave raids into the Seminole Nation became more pronounced by mixed-blood Creeks and Seminoles in 1848.

In November of 1849 about 200 Seminoles left the Indian

Territory under the leadership of Chief Wild Cat and maroon chief John Horse; their destination, Mexico. Slavery was abolished in Mexico in 1829, which was attractive to the Seminoles, and Mexico was trying to colonize the land adjacent to the Rio Grande. One of the reasons for the Mexican colonization of this area was that the border region was in a state of chaos. Many hostile Indian groups were ravaging towns, killing, and plundering the populace in the vicinity.

On June 27, 1850, the Seminoles signed an agreement with the Mexican government. They were to receive 70,000 acres in Coahuila in exchange for their military service against the Comanche, Lipan, and Mescalero Apache who were raiding into Mexico. The government also agreed to give the Seminole a small food subsidy and tools for building and farming. The Black Seminoles were called Mascogan Negroes by the Mexicans, undoubtedly meaning Muscogee Negroes. Unofficially, the Mexicans would come to call the maroons "Los Mascogos."

In July 1850, 309 Seminoles, maroons, and Kickapoos arrived at their new home in Mexico. The Seminole Indians settled at Zaragoza; the blacks, whose group also included Creek and Cherokee maroons, settled at El Moral near Piedras Negras; and the Kickapoos at Tuillo. The blacks were under the leadership of John Horse. The Mexican government dealt with the blacks as a separate entity from the Indians. Other leaders of the Black Seminoles were John Kibbetts, Dembo and Hardy Factor, along with Sampson July. The blacks held Chief Wild Cat in high esteem because he had been the undisputed champion of their cause in the Indian Territory. Wild Cat had also built up friendships with many of the Indians on the southern plains.

A group of Black Creeks had preceded the Seminoles to Mexico. Their surnames were mostly Wilson and Warrior; there was also a family of Biloxis with them. These groups became part of the Black Seminole family in Mexico. It is interesting to note that there was another group among the Seminoles which didn't have any Indian connection. Their last name was Shields; they were free mulatto settlers from South Carolina.

After repeated incursions by Texas slave hunters, the Black Seminoles in 1851 moved deeper into Mexico. The community became known as Nacimiento de los Negros, Coahuila, where some descendants can be found today. The leaders of the community in Coahuila were John Horse, John Kibbetts, Cuffy, Hardy, Thomas and Dembo Factor, Sampson July, and Jim Bowlegs. John Horse was the leader and the Mexicans called him Capitan; Kibbetts was second in command.

After Wild Cat's death in 1857, the Seminoles left Mexico by the fall of 1861 and traveled to the Indian Territory. The Seminoles had been given their own land that they didn't have to share with the Creeks. The Black Seminoles in Mexico decided to stay put because slavery was still practiced in the United States.

For his service against hostile Indians, John Horse was given a silver-mounted saddle with a gold-plated pommel in the shape of a horse's head. He used this saddle when he rode his horse, "American." By the 1860s, the Mexicans were calling John Horse, El Coronel (Colonel) Juan Caballo.

By the end of the American Civil War, the Black Seminole community in Mexico had splintered. The largest contingent was led by John Horse. Elijah Daniels had led a smaller group of Black Creeks into Uvalde County, Texas, and John Kibbetts had taken a group of Black Seminoles to Nacimiento. John Horse had earlier moved to Laguna de Parras in southwestern Coahuila with 350 followers. Some Black Seminoles also settled in Matamoros across the Rio Grande from Brownsville, Texas.

The Comanches and Apaches had made West Texas almost unlivable for white people during the Civil War via incessant raids. The U.S. Army, who had deserted the frontier posts at the beginning of the war, had now reoccupied them. This still did not stop the Indian raids. The army could not detect the movements of the raiders either coming or going. There was a real need for Indian scouts, but only a very few Tonkawas and Lipans were available.

In the interim, the Black Seminoles under John Kibbetts at Nacimiento had become discontented with Mexico. Additionally, Kibbetts had journeyed to the Indian Territory and observed the improved status of Black Freedmen in the Seminole Nation. After several meetings between Kibbetts and U.S. Col. Jacob De Gress concerning the return of the Blacks to U.S. soil, Maj. Zenas R. Bliss, 25th Infantry, brokered an agreement with Kibbetts. The Black Seminoles called it both "de treaty" and "de treatment."

The Black Seminoles were invited to return to the United States to serve as Indian scouts. Bliss was authorized to enlist twenty men for six months. Their pay would be the equal of cavalry privates, except Kibbetts who received a sergeant's wage. In addition, the U.S. would provide for their families and give them land in Texas in return for their services as Indian scouts. The Seminole maroons were allowed to settle at Fort Duncan where they were given land for crops and grazing their livestock. Due to the fact they were enrolled as Indian scouts, the blacks had as their official title, Seminole Negro Indian Scouts. The Indian moniker caused great confusion, for some people always thought of them as Indians and not Africans.

On August 16, 1870, John Kibbetts and ten privates were mustered into service with the U.S. Army. Kibbetts enrolled under his Indian name Chitto Tustenuggee or Snake Warrior. At Fort Duncan the black scouts were given guns, ammunition, and food. Most of their horses eventually came from horses captured from hostile Indians. The blacks initially were not required to wear uniforms and dressed in frontier fashion buckskin. Some dressed more like Indians with feathers in hats and even a buffalo horn war bonnet. At a later date, they would wear regulation U.S. Army scout uniforms.

Kibbetts mustered in as a sergeant and was elected as Chief of Black Seminoles at military reservations until his death in 1878.

There were also scouts recruited from Elijah Daniels' band from Matamoros; these numbered about twenty. They were transferred to Fort Clark, near Brackettville, Texas. In 1872 and 1873 there were more than a dozen Black Seminoles recruited from John Horse's Laguna band; they were mustered in at Fort Duncan. Some of these scouts were blacks who had intermarried with Seminole and Creek women. There were also some Mexicans who had either intermarried or became associated with the Black Seminoles and joined the scouts. Some former black cavalry troopers or infantrymen, along with a few border Indians, also joined the Seminole scouts at a later date.

John Horse's main group came to Texas at a later date. He

never did enlist in the scouts, probably due to his age, although he did serve as an interpreter and mediator for the U.S. Army in negotiations with the Kickapoo and other Indians on the border.

The Seminole scouts mainly patrolled West Texas from 1870 to 1872, but things changed in 1873. On March 6, 1873, Lt. John Lapham Bullis of the 24th Infantry (Colored) was given command of the Black Seminole scouts. From March 1873 to June 1881, the Black Seminole scouts would take part in twenty-six campaigns, twelve of which would be major. They would not receive one fatality or serious wound in combat! Four of the men would receive the Medal of Honor. There would never be more than fifty scouts serving at any one time during their long tenure with the U.S. Army.

Major Bliss described the Black Seminoles as "excellent hunters and trailers and brave scouts ... splendid fighters." Their trailing skills have been particularly pointed out as having been almost uncanny. Their ability for being multi-lingual also was an asset. Lieutenant Bullis said of them, "fine trailers and good marksmen and very useful in the frontier."

Lieutenant Bullis was born in Wayne County, New York, in 1841. During the Civil War he enlisted as a corporal in the 126th New York Volunteer Infantry. He was captured by Confederate troops at the Battle of Gettysburg, but released three months later in a prisoner exchange. Bullis was able to work himself up to the rank of captain. After the war he entered the army as a second lieutenant in the 41st Infantry (colored) and was stationed in Texas. The 41st was later combined with the Black 38th Infantry thereby creating the famous 24th Infantry Regiment. Bullis's reputation as an outstanding frontier officer began with his service in the 24th Infantry.

Bullis gained a reputation for working well with black troopers. While stationed with the 24th in Texas during 1871, he had one of his first skirmishes. Bullis was riding in advance of a military command from Fort McKavett; with him were four troopers from the Black 9th U.S. Cavalry. They came upon three Indians with a small herd of cattle. They immediately attacked and gained possession of the herd. The Indians were reinforced by more warriors, but Bullis and the troopers were able to repulse them and keep control of the herd.

Closeup view of Seminole Negro Indian Scouts
(Courtesy Sul Ross State University)

The scouts under Elijah Daniel at Fort Clark were the first to encounter serious military action. On May 18, 1873, thirty-four scouts, eighteen from Fort Clark and sixteen from Fort Duncan under Lieutenant Bullis accompanied six troops of the 4th Cavalry under Col. R. S. Mackenzie. The objective was the Lipan and Kickapoo camps at Remolino, Mexico. The ensuing battle resulted in the destruction of three villages, the deaths of nineteen Indian warriors, and the capture of forty prisoners. One of the captives, Chief Costillitto, was lassoed by black scout Renty Grayson. Costillitto's daughter later married Seminole scout James Perryman, the wedding being officiated by Lieu-tenant Bullis.

Kickapoos had a hatred for white Texans because they had been attacked several times in the 1860s in their journey from Indian Territory (Oklahoma) to Mexico. By raiding into Texas for retribution from their Coahuila base, the Kickapoos had cost the Texans $48,000,000 by the early 1870s. The raid at Remolino put an end to Kickapoo raids into West Texas.

In the spring of 1874 more than 600 Kiowa, Comanche, and Cheyenne warriors and their families left their reservations in the Indian Territory; they were headed for West Texas. They joined up with other Indians to do battle and redress old losses of life and land. There was an attack by those Indians at an encampment called Adobe Walls on June 27, 1874. Two hun-dred warriors were led by Comanche Chief Quanah Parker on a small group of well-armed buffalo hunters that included a young Bat Masterson. The hunters were able to repulse the Indians with their long gun sharp shooting. One of the interesting aspects of this battle was that the Comanche had a black warrior who gave signals with a bugle. The black man was killed during the battle, and the supposition was that he was a deserter from the army who went over and joined the Indians. Masterson gave a report on this black man's role in the battle after the hunters were rescued. This battle marked the beginning of the Red River War.

By the summer the U.S. Army made a move to defeat these Indians in the Texas Panhandle. There were three columns of troopers from the Department of Texas trying to encircle the adversary. The largest column was led by Colonel Mackenzie. A group of twenty-one Black Seminole scouts were with him under the command of Lt. W. A. "Hurricane Bill" Thompson. Their destination was the Staked Plains. Joining the Seminoles as scouts were twelve Tonkawas and a few Lipans. These men served as advanced scouts and trailers for the Mackenzie column.

The U.S. troopers pushed the Comanche onto the Staked Plains of the Texas Panhandle. They later found evidence that the hostiles had taken up refuge in the Palo Duro Canyon near the present city of Amarillo. The upcoming Battle of Palo Duro Canyon would be the most decisive and important conflict in the Red River War.

On September 19 the Seminole Negro scouts discovered fresh Comanche tracks in the area of the headwaters of the Pease River. Mackenzie directed his column northward with scouts in advance early the following morning. Later in the day four of the scouts returned to camp with the news they had been attacked by twenty-five Comanche, and they were able to make a hasty retreat after a short skirmish.

Of these four scouts, one, Adam (Paine) Payne, won a Medal of Honor for his actions during this skirmish with the Comanche on September 20. Adam Payne was noted for being a "Bad Man" with no fear in battle; he was also noted for wearing a headdress of buffalo horns. Payne was born in Florida. Mackenzie said in a letter of commendation that Payne (he spelled it Paine) was a man of "habitual courage" and "more daring than any scout I have ever known."

Adam Payne was later killed on New Year's Day, 1877, in the Seminole village at Fort Clark. By this time he had been discharged and suspected of stealing horses and cattle in Texas, then running them to Mexico. He had a more serious charge of stabbing a white private in the 8th Cavalry in Brownsville. Deputy Sheriff Claron Windus snuck up on him at the dance and shot him at point-blank range with a shotgun. He died instantly. It was reported that the blast set his clothes on fire. This deed did not sit well in the Black Seminole community.

Returning to the Battle of Palo Duro Canyon, the Seminole scouts on the 25th of September informed Mackenzie about a large number of fresh Indian tracks near Tule Canyon. The next day the scouts reported that Comanches were very near to the southern column. Forewarned, the U.S. troops were able to push back an attack by 250 warriors. The next day Lieutenant Thompson with the Seminoles and Capt. Peter Boehm with the Tonkawa scouts led a counterattack that drove the Comanches out of the vicinity. During the engagement, one Comanche was fleeing up the side of a wash. One of the Seminole scouts swung casually from his saddle, aimed, and fired his rifle, killing the Comanche's pony. Then a Tonkawa scout rode up and killed the warrior with his pistol. Not long after this skirmish the Seminole scouts found a large number of Comanche tepees on the floor of the nearby Palo Duro Canyon. Mackenzie decided to launch a surprise attack the following morning.

On the morning of September 28 the troopers found in the canyon five large villages of Kiowa, Comanche, and Southern Cheyenne which stretched for three miles. They also noticed a huge herd of horses. This was discovered by one of the Black Seminoles.

Thompson and his black scouts were ordered to lead the attack. It took an hour to descend onto the canyon floor by following a narrow trail. The attack caught the Indians by surprise and most fled for a pass at the western end of the canyon. All the tepees were destroyed as were tons of supplies. Some hostiles took up positions in the rocks and sniped at the troopers. Mackenzie had his troopers regroup back at the rim of the canyon. They did this by driving the large Indian horse herd in front of their advance. After gaining high ground the scouts and troopers were allowed to eat and rest, something they hadn't done in thirty-one hours. Only one trooper was wounded during the entire engagement. The black and Indian scouts chose the best horses for themselves; then the troopers proceeded to shoot the remainder, numbering over 1,000 ponies. This was done to prevent the hostiles from recapturing them. This engagement was the last major conflict of the Red River War. The Comanche, Kiowa, and Southern Cheyenne would never again mount a sizable action against the U.S. government. In April of 1875 Lt. Bullis and three scouts, Sergeant John Ward, Isaac Payne, and Pompey Factor, were riding near the Pecos River in Texas, and found a fresh trail of Indians with seventy-five horses leading north from some white settlements. They followed the trail for an hour and discovered about thirty Comanche warriors getting ready to herd the horses across the Pecos. Bullis and the scouts dismounted and crept through the brush until they were about seventy-five yards from the Indians. From this position the soldiers opened fire; the firefight lasted forty-five minutes. Twice, Bullis and his scouts captured the horses and twice, the Comanches regained them. The scouts were far outnumbered, and the Indians were using Winchester repeating rifles while the scouts had the single-shot Springfield rifle. The Seminoles killed three of the Comanches and wounded a fourth. But the scouts had to make a mad dash for their horses before they were cut-off from escape.

The three black scouts were able to reach their mounts and were prepared to retreat when Sergeant Ward, looking back, noticed Bullis had been cut-off from his horse with no chance for escape. "We can't leave the lieutenant, boys," Sergeant Ward cried. He immediately rode back toward Bullis with bullets flying everywhere. Payne and Factor dismounted and provided as much cover as they could, firing left and right. A bullet cut John Ward's carbine sling; as he reached Bullis and pulled him up on his mount, a bullet shattered the gunstock. The other two scouts mounted up, and fighting off the Comanches, made good their escape without suffering any injuries.

For their valor in battle the three Black Seminole scouts received the Medal of Honor.

In the spring of 1875 the Comanche were causing quite a bit of trouble for the white settlements in West Texas. Col. William Shafter led an expedition out of Fort Concho on July 14 to suppress and remove the Indians to the reservation. Shafter's command was the largest ever mounted in West Texas. The command included African-Seminole and Tonkawa scouts, along with six companies of the 10th Cavalry, two of the 24th Infantry (mounted), and one of the 25th Infantry (mounted). All the troopers and scouts were African or Indian except the officers who were white.

The Seminole scouts came into serious action again with Indians on October 18. They came upon a camp at Sabrinas, destroyed all their supplies, and captured twenty-five Indian ponies. This attack by the Seminoles was Shafter's best victory

Color Guard, Seminole Negro Indian Scouts, Fort Clark, Texas, 1910
(Courtesy U.S. Army Military History Institute)

during his expedition. Shafter brought his expedition to an end in late November. He had been successful in pushing the hostiles deep into Mexico.

On the evening of October 16, 1875, Lieutenant Bullis and Sgt. William Miller, a mulatto, crept into an Indian camp at Laguna Sabrinas, Mexico, and stole thirty horses and mules. In January 1876 Miller, disguised as an Indian, went into a camp of Comanches and Apaches in Mexico. He stayed five days gathering intelligence for Lieutenant Bullis.

During the spring and summer of 1876 the Lipan and Mexican Kickapoos made a few raids on white settlements in West Texas. In July Shafter took a large group of black scouts and troops into Mexico to attack a large Lipan village near Zaragoza. In the expedition were three troops of the 10th Cavalry, detachments of the 24th and 25th Infantry (mounted), and a group of African-Seminole Scouts under Lieutenant Bullis.

Bullis was told by Shafter, after traveling deep into Mexico, to take his twenty scouts and twenty men from Company B, 10th Cavalry and find and destroy the Lipan village. Shafter stayed in camp and guarded against any attacks from Mexican troops who might cut them off from returning to United States soil. The small force led by Bullis found the Lipan village the next day, July 30, after leaving camp. The Indian village was located on the San Antonio River, five miles from Zaragoza. The Seminoles attacked at dawn; the fighting was very intense. The battle lasted all of fifteen minutes before the Lipans broke and ran. The American soldiers killed fourteen of the Indian warriors and captured four women and one hundred horses. The black soldiers received only slight wounds from Lipan lances. The soldiers destroyed the village and rejoined the main column which returned safely to Texas. For this action in Mexico, Bullis was brevetted to Major.

The Seminole scouts, along with U.S. Army units, were successful in their efforts in suppressing Indian raids which originated on the Mexican side of the border. The Black Seminoles in the late 1870s spent a good deal of their time in West Texas as escorts, guides, explorers, and fort and road builders.

On January 31, 1879, Lieutenant Bullis with thirty-nine Seminole scouts, fifteen cavalry troopers, three Lipan scouts, and the famous former Comanchero outlaw Jose Tafoya gave pursuit to a group of Mescalero Apache raiders. (Comancheros were unsavory individuals of various ethnicity in Texas who traded with the Comanches.) They trailed the Indians across the Texas desert for thirty-four days. Bullis' command almost perished from thirst, but Seminole Sergeant David Bowlegs discovered a "Sleeping Spring" which the Apaches had stopped up and hidden. By using his consumate scouting skills, Bowlegs was able to make the spring flow freely again. Lieutenant Bullis' command trailed the Apaches to within two miles of the Fort Stanton, New Mexico, reservation. The Indian agent refused to give the Apaches up for arrest, and the Seminoles were forced to return to Texas empty-handed. Bullis and his scouts had been gone eighty days and traveled 1,266 miles.

The Seminole scouts' last Indian battle followed the last important Indian raid into Texas from Mexico. On April 14, 1881, a small band of Lipan Apaches crossed the Rio Grande and attacked the McLauren Ranch at the head of the Rio Frio in Real County. They killed Mrs. McLauren and a boy named Allen Reiss, robbed the ranch and other homes in the nearby area, and made their escape with the plunder and stolen ponies. At Fort Clark, Texas, Lieutenant Bullis was given the order to capture or kill the Lipan Apaches responsible for the crimes. Two weeks after the raid Bullis rode out with thirty-four black scouts at which time they proceeded to cross the Rio Grande in pursuit. The Lipans had wrapped their horses' hooves in rawhide, but the Seminoles were still able to pick up the trail. They soon found a location near the Devil's River where the Lipan Apaches had killed thirty of the horses because they proved too difficult to drive over the rugged terrain.

Bullis was using Teresita (daughter of Lipan Chief Costil-litto), who had been captured by the scouts in the battle in 1873, as the lead scout. Teresita had two children by the Seminole scout James Perryman. In recognition of signs picked up on the trail, Teresita realized the Lipan Apaches they were after were from her own band. With this knowledge, she tried to give some wrong readings of trail sign. One of the Seminole scouts was able to see through her designs and kept the command on the right trail. Teresita became violent at this point, and the scouts tied her to her horse. After six days trailing the Lipan Apaches through the Sierra del Burro Mountains, the scouts located the camp on May 2. Bullis made the decision was made to attack at daybreak. Leaving seven men to watch the horses and Teresita, Bullis and twenty-seven scouts made a rousing charge at sunrise on the unsuspecting Lipan raiders. In the fight, five Lipan Apaches were killed, the scouts rescued a wounded woman and a little boy, and recaptured twenty-one horses. The Lipan leader San-Da-Ve, suffered a mortal wound and died shortly after the battle. The Seminoles suffered no casualties in the conflict and crossed safely across the Rio Grande back into Texas.

It is important to reiterate that in a dozen or more military actions with hostile Indians, covering a period of eight years, not a single Seminole scout was killed or seriously wounded in action in U.S. service.

After 1873, the Indian attacks on the West Texas frontier decreased dramatically. Lieutenant Bullis was released from his command of the scouts and transferred to Fort Supply, Indian Territory.

Although the Seminoles suffered no casualties in a military action against the Indians, they had worse luck with the white citizens of Texas. In 1874 when the Seminole scouts were stationed at Fort Duncan, Texas, there were problems that occurred at Eagle Pass during the Christmas season.

Eagle Pass was controlled by gunslinger King Fisher and his gang. The trouble occurred in the Old Blue saloon of that town. A gun battle broke out, King Fisher shot Corporal George Washington in the stomach, and one of the Seminoles creased King Fisher's scalp with a bullet. George Washington was the nephew of the great Seminole Chief John Horse. The army decided to diffuse the situation by moving the Seminoles to Fort Clark, Texas. Washington died a couple months later from his gunshot wound.

After being transferred to Fort Clark, Chief John Horse and Titus Payne were shot in an ambush near the post hospital. The chief was badly wounded, and Payne was killed instantly. The chief's horse American, which was also wounded, took the chief back to the Seminole camp. Many people felt King Fisher was behind the ambush.

The next serious trouble came on New Year's Day, 1877, shortly after midnight. After Adam Payne had been shot at point-blank range, anger broke out. Five scouts and former scouts, including Pompey Factor, were so incensed over this incident and others, they decided to go back to Mexico and never come back to the United States. These scouts re-enlisted with the Mexican army and served under Colonel Pedro Avincular Valdez, known as "Colonel Winker." Major Bliss called Valdez, "one of the bravest men I ever knew."

As stated earlier, John Kibbetts was Chief of Seminole scouts at U.S. military reservations until his death. He was replaced by Elijah Daniels, leader of the Black Creek Seminole scouts. Daniels, thereafter, was the Chief of the Seminoles at Fort Clark until his death on January 12, 1908.

The Seminole Negro Indian Scouts remained a unit of the U.S. Army until September, 1914. The Assistant Secretary of War, Henry Breckenridge, in 1914 asked for land for the Black Seminoles, but the Interior Department informed him that the enrollment books for the Seminoles in Oklahoma were closed. Consequently, there would be no rights for these Black Seminoles as Indians, or Indian Freedmen, regardless of their history. Breckenridge replied with another question: Could the 225 acres the Seminoles lived on at Fort Clark be set aside as a reservation seeing that they had cultivated the land since 1874? The Interior Department replied that no allotments could be made to them as Seminoles, and there was no provision of law allowing for allotments to them as blacks. The Black Seminoles were slowly moved into the nearby small towns of Brackettville, Texas, or Nacimiento, Mexico.

The African Seminole scouts who served the U.S. Army on the Texas frontier in the late nineteenth century were one of the most outstanding, elite units in the history of the United States military. It's a shameful disgrace they were never treated as citizens or veterans by the U.S. government, even to this day. Their descendants still live in Brackettville, Texas, and Nacimiento, Mexico; keeping the history of the Seminole Negro Indian Scouts alive for all who are willing to listen.

Section 2: Civil War in the West

CHAPTER FOURTEEN

1st Kansas Colored Volunteer Infantry Regiment

The people of the mid-19th century considered the area west of and including the Mississippi River as America's frontier. During the Civil War the area was known as the Trans-Mississippi by both the Union and Confederate armies.

An interesting aspect of black troops mustered into the Union army in the Trans-Mississippi theater was the fact they were used as fighting men versus the East, where many black troops were used for labor details. The use of black men as army troopers and infantry continued into the twentieth century.

The initial locale, during the War of the Rebellion, where black men were armed for fighting was in the highly volatile border state of Kansas. Jim Lane, a senator, and general in the state militia of Kansas, as Commissioner of Recruiting in Leaven-worth City, Kansas, issued General Order No. 2 on August 6, 1862. This particular order instructed recruiting officers to make sure persons of African descent who entered the service of the United States in that department fully understood the terms and conditions upon which they would be received in the service.

Senator Lane, although warned by Secretary of War Stanton, went ahead with raising black troops in Kansas without War Department approval. The First Kansas Colored Volunteer Infantry Regiment was raised at Fort Scott, Kansas, in August of 1862. Lane appointed Capt. James M. Williams, Co. F, 5th Kansas Cavalry as the commanding officer. The black men who comprised the regiment were mostly fugitive slaves from Arkansas, Missouri, and the Indian Territory. The black troops were initially issued blue jackets, grey pants, and forage caps.

The black soldiers of the 1st Kansas Colored were the first Africans to see battle during the Civil War. On October 29, 1862, detachments of the 1st were attacked by Confederate troops at Island Mound, Missouri. There were 225 black soldiers under command of Capt. H. C. Seaman. The Confederates numbered about 500 and were commanded by Colonel Cockrell. The black troops repulsed the Confederate forces and inflicted heavy casualties in doing so. The 1st lost ten men and twelve were wounded. The next morning the black troops were reinforced with new recruits by Capt. J. M. Williams; they pursued the enemy for quite a distance, but the Confederates didn't show any fight. A most important and pivotal point was established with this small engagement; black men would fight.

The Emancipation Proclamation, signed by President Abraham Lincoln, took effect on January 1, 1863. On January 13, the 1st Regiment Kansas Colored Volunteer Infantry was officially mustered into federal service. James M. Williams, the commanding officer, was made a Lieutenant Colonel. By this time three other black regiments had preceded them as being officially mustered into the Union army.

The first major battles for African-American soldiers occurred during the spring and summer of 1863; all in the Trans-Mississippi region except one, the attack on Battery Wagner outside Charleston, South Carolina.

The first of these engagements was the Union attack on Port Hudson, Louisiana, the last Confederate obstacle to the capture of Vicksburg. Port Hudson was located thirty miles north of Baton Rouge, on the banks of the Mississippi River. Leading the attack on Port Hudson were the black soldiers of the 1st and 3rd Louisiana Native Guards on May 27, 1863.

The Louisiana Native Guards were the first black soldiers to be officially mustered into the Union Army during the Civil War; outside of those enlisted earlier in the 1st Indian Home Guard Regiment in Kansas. The 1st Regiment of Louisiana Native Guards were mustered into service on September 27, 1862. The 2nd and 3rd Regiments were sworn in during October and November, respectively.

During the Battle of Port Hudson, the black soldiers made six suicidal charges on the entrenched Confederate positions. The attack was led by Captain Andre Cailloux, a prominent Creole from New Orleans who liked to boast of his blackness. While on the battlefield, Cailloux spoke in French and English urging his men to fight. Cailloux's left arm was shattered by a bullet, but he continued to repeatedly lead his men against the enemy positions. He was mortally wounded fifty yards from the Confederate fort. The Black Louisianians failed in capturing the fort, but received well-earned praise. On June 13, 1863, the *New York Times* made the following comments on the black troops at Port Hudson: "... no body of troops Western, Eastern or Rebel has fought better in the war."

Of the 111 African Americans who were commissioned officers in the Union army, ninety served in combat units. Of the black officers in combat regiments, just about all served in the Louisiana Native Guards. One, Octive Rey, 2nd Lieutenant, resigned for reasons of prejudice. Rey went on to become a legendary police officer in New Orleans in the late nineteenth century.

The next major battle for black soldiers was Milliken's Bend, about twenty miles up the river from Vicksburg on the Mississippi River. In June 1863 General Ulysses Grant was forced to pull Union troops out of the Milliken Bend Fort to aid with the attack on Vicksburg. Milliken's Bend was left with black troops of the 9th and 11th Louisiana Regiments and of the 1st Mississippi, totalling 840 men. There was also a small detachment of white soldiers who totaled 160 men; these men were from the 23rd Iowa Cavalry.

The battle at Milliken's Bend occurred ten days after the

battle at Port Hudson. Brigadier General Dennis of the 9th Louisiana was in command of the Union forces at Milliken's Bend. He was attacked on the morning of June 7th at 3:00 A.M. The Confederates were led by General Henry McCulloch who had 3,000 Texas men in his command. The Texans had expected to slaughter the small garrison. They shouted as they charged the Union positions, "No quarter! No quarter to Negros or their officers!" This meant the black troops would not be taken as prisoners, but killed on the field, whether they surrendered or not. The Texans had driven the federal soldiers to the banks of the river the day before, murdering captured black soldiers as they advanced and I am sure they expected to annihilate the Union garrison. The black troops received some help of no small measure by two Union Navy gunboats the *Choctaw* and *Lexington*.

Captain Miller of Company I, 9th Louisiana gave a personal account of the conflict:

> We had about fifty men killed in the regiment and eighty wounded; so you can judge of what part of the fight my company sustained. I never felt more grieved and sick at heart, than when I saw how my brave soldiers were slaughtered, one with six wounds, all the rest with two or three, none less than two wounds. Two of my colored sergeants were killed; both brave men, always prompt, vigilant, and ready for the fray. I never more wish to hear the expression, "The niggers won't fight." Come with me, a hundred yards from where I sit, and I can show you the wounds that cover the bodies of sixteen as brave, loyal, and patriotic soldiers as ever drew bead on a rebel.
>
> The enemy charged us so close that we fought with our bayonets, hand to hand. I have six broken bayonets to show how bravely my men fought....
>
> Under the command of Colonel Page, I led the 9th and 11th Louisiana when the rifle-pits were retaken and held by our troops, our two regiments doing the work.
>
> I narrowly escaped death once. A rebel took deliberate aim at me with both barrels of his gun; and the bullets passed so close to me that the powder that remained on them burnt my cheek. Three of my men, who saw him aim and fire, thought that bullets wounded me each fire. One of them was killed by my side, and he fell on me covering my clothes with

his blood; and before the rebel could fire again, I blew his brains out with my gun.

It was the most horrible fight, the worst I was ever engaged in, not even excepting Shiloh. The enemy cried, "No quarter!" but some of them were very glad to take it when made prisoners.

Colonel Allen of the 16th Texas, was killed in front of our regiment, and Brigadier General Walker was wounded. We killed about 180 of the enemy. The gunboat "Choctaw" did good service shelling them. I stood on the breastworks after we took them, and gave the elevations and directions for the gunboat by pointing my sword; and they sent a shell right into their midst, which sent them in all directions. Three shells fell there, and sixty-two rebels lay there when the fight was over.

This battle satisfied the slave-masters of the South that their claim was gone; and that the Negro as a slave was lost forever. Yet there was one fact connected with the Battle of Milliken's Bend which will descend to posterity, as testimony against the humanity of slave holders; and that is, that no Negro was ever found alive that was taken a prisoner by the rebels in this fight.

Concerning the battle, historian Lerone Bennett wrote, "The black and white soldiers stood toe to toe, clubbing each other, baseball fashion, with the butts of muskets and gouging with bayonets. Finally, after a ten or fifteen minute struggle, the Texans broke and fled."

The most important engagements for black troops during the summer of 1863 took place in the Indian Territory, later to become the state of Oklahoma.

The 1st Kansas Colored Volunteer Infantry Regiment had trained and was anxious to see some major action by the summer of 1863. They left Baxter Springs, Kansas, with a supply train from Fort Scott for Fort Gibson, Indian Territory, on June 25. They were accompanied by other detachments of white artillery, cavalry, and infantry units. But the 1st Kansas' 800 soldiers was regimentally strong. The train which consisted of 300 wagons traveled the "Military Road" which connected Fort Scott to Fort Gibson in this frontier setting.

Colonel Phillips, the commander at Fort Gibson, had sent out several hundred troops to intercept and help guard the wagon train. This unit was made up of detachments from the 6th Kansas Cavalry and the three Indian Home Guard Regiments, under the command of the 3rd Indian Home Guards' Maj. John Foreman. This was the first time in the Civil War that black soldiers would be fighting along with whites and Indians in organized units. Earlier, on May 18, 1863, due to the reluctance of white cavalrymen to serve with a detachment of the 1st Kansas, Colonel Williams suffered a setback. About twenty-five black infantrymen, along with white troops numbering about twenty, were surprised by 300 rebels. The Confederates massacred about twenty of the black soldiers and later killed one they had taken prisoner. After this debacle Colonel Williams always made sure his cavalry was in support of his black infantry. The cavalry was indispensable in reporting troop movements.

The famous Cherokee soldier Col. Stand Watie of the Confederate army decided to make a raid on the wagon train. Watie decided the best place to hit the supply train was at the ford of Cabin Creek, now located in Mayes County, Oklahoma. Watie had about 2,000 Confederates in his command. On June 26, Union Cherokee scouts, riding well ahead of the long train, picked up numerous horse tracks that alerted them to the danger ahead. The Union supplies were now crossing the Grand River moving slowly toward Watie's position. The Union scouts were able to locate Watie's position, and after skirmishing with confederate pickets, they captured two. With their rebel prisoners the scouts made it back to the supply train.

Colonel Williams was told of Watie's troop strength and location and that Brig. Gen. William L. Cabell with 1,500 soldiers was on his way to reinforce Watie, but couldn't cross the Grand River because of high water. Due to heavy rains, the supply train moved slowly through the mud toward Cabin Creek. The Union officers were given ample time to plan their battle strategy when they reached it.

The Union forces were joined on June 28th by the 300 men under Major Foreman. The Union train arrived at Cabin Creek on July 1,1863. The Confederates were dug in well on the south side. The water was high, and the federal troops couldn't cross to engage the enemy. There were some light fire fights and sniping across the creek. The Union officers made a decision to ford the creek the following morning; the recent rain water would subside enough for crossing. The train was parked and corralled two miles from the creek, guarded by three companies of the 2nd Colorado and a detachment of one hundred men of the 1st Kansas Colored.

The next morning, July 2, 1863, the Union command moved forward. It consisted of the 1st Kansas Volunteer Colored Infantry, three companies of the 2nd Colorado Infantry, and detachments of cavalry and mounted Indian troops, along with four pieces of artillery. The Union forces numbered about 1,200 men.

The battle began with the federal artillery opening up a barrage on the south side of Cabin Creek. This went on for half an hour. Then Major Foreman and his mounted Indian troops made a mad dash across the creek; Foreman was seriously wounded. Foreman's men retreated back across the creek to the north side. The initial assault hadn't been successful, but it did expose the Confederate soldiers in their well-dug rifle pits on the south side of the creek. Williams had artillery fire along with rifle sniping directed on the rebel positions. This was followed by a charge by the 9th Kansas Cavalry which gained a foothold on the south side of the creek. Then the black troops of the 1st Kansas forwarded the creek, all the while holding their rifles and cartridge boxes above their heads to keep them dry. Once on the opposite side, the black soldiers rapidly formed battle lines and attacked the Confederate positions. The rebels couldn't stand up to the pressure mounted by the black soldiers; they broke and ran. Again the men under Stand Watie attempted to regroup about a quarter mile away, but broke and ran again. Some of the Confederates, in trying to retreat across the Grand River, drowned along with their horses; the river was high and swift. The black soldiers chased Cherokee Col. Stand Watie's rebel soldiers for five miles. This engagement at Cabin Creek was one of the worst losses Stand Watie suffered during the war. Watie would later be commissioned a general, the only Indian general of the war, and the last Confederate general to surrender.

The casualties at Cabin Creek were one hundred killed and wounded and eight prisoners for the Confederates. The Union forces suffered eight killed and twenty-five wounded. This engagement served as a prelude for the next major engagement.

On learning of the serious action at Cabin Creek and the Confederate army concentration near Fort Gibson, Gen. James Blunt, commander of Union forces, Department of the Frontier, took to the field. Blunt arrived with additional reinforcements at Fort Gibson that brought troop strength up to 3,000 with twelve artillery pieces.

It was learned from scouting parties that Gen. Douglas Cooper, commander of the Confederate forces in the Indian Territory, had 6,000 troops with four artillery pieces at the rebel base located at Honey Springs. There were an additional 3,000 rebels coming up to reinforce Cooper. Honey Springs was only twenty-five miles from Fort Gibson, and Blunt was forced to make quick decisions on strategies to defend Fort Gibson.

Blunt decided he would attack Cooper before the rebel reinforcements arrived from Fort Smith, Arkansas. Due to the severe rains, Blunt's command had to cross the high Arkansas River on rafts. The Union forces assembled on the south bank of the Arkansas River on the evening of July 16. From this location Blunt resumed his march toward Honey Springs. By 8:00 in the morning some of Blunt's advance elements clashed with rebel soldiers near Chimney Mountain. The Union troops were able to dislodge the Texan and Choctaw soldiers in a heavy rain.

The main body of the federal forces stopped about a half-a-mile from the rebel lines; they took an hour's rest and ate a meal. After their respite, Blunt's forces moved up to a quarter-of-a-mile from the Confederate line. This location was one-and-a-half miles north of Elk Creek timber with the Texas Road running through the center.

Union forces consisted of the Indian Brigade; the 1st Indian Home Guard Regiment and the 2nd Indian Home Guard Regiment; 1st Kansas Colored Volunteer Infantry Regiment; 2nd Kansas Battery; 3rd Wisconsin Cavalry Battalion; 6th Kansas Cavalry Battalion; 2nd Colorado Infantry, six companies; and Hopkin's Kansas Battery. The Indian regiments were dismounted as infantry for this engagement. Otherwise, they served mostly as mounted units.

There were quite a few African Americans who served with the 1st Indian Home Guard Regiment. They were either former slaves of the Seminole or Creek Nations, or had lived as free men among the Indians. Interestingly, the interpreters in the Indian regiments, especially the Creek, were almost exclusively native blacks of the Indian Territory. Many of the noncommissioned officers (Sergeants) of these units were black.

In May 1862 when the 1st Indian Home Guard was mustered there were nearly thirty African Creeks in the regiment. Twenty or more African Creeks fought at the Battle of Prairie Grove on December 7, 1862, which made them the first regularly mustered blacks in the Federal Army to participate in a major battle.

The African and Indian troops had earlier defeated Confederate Indians at the Battle of Maysville in Arkansas. This engagement greatly affected the morale of the Confederate Creeks.

African Creek scouts from the Home Guard supplied vital information to General Blunt on Confederate troop positions prior to the Battle of Honey Springs. By the war's end, more than one hundred black soldiers were enlisted in the Indian Home Guard. Almost a third of the men in Companies D, E and I, 1st Regiment, were black. Black veterans of the 1st Regiment Indian Home Guard who were leaders in the Creek Nation after the war included Sugar T. George, Harry Island, Pickett Rentie, Simon Brown, Tally Lewis, and Jacob Perryman.

The Confederate forces at Honey Springs consisted of the 1st and 2nd Cherokee Regiments; 1st and 2nd Creek Regiments; 20th Texas Cavalry Regiment, (dismounted); 29th Texas Cavalry Regiment; 5th Texas Partisan Rangers; 1st Choctaw and Chickasaw Regiment, and Captain Lee's Battery. There were some African Indians serving with the Confederate Indian units.

Around 9:30 A.M. General Blunt formed his total command into two columns: the First Brigade under Colonel Judson on the right of the Texas Road and the Second Brigade under Colonel Phillips on the left of the road. Blunt moved forward, the infantry in columns of companies, the cavalry by platoons, and the artillery by sections.

By advancing in close formation, Blunt hoped to deceive the Confederates as to his strength. When the Union forces had come within a quarter of a mile of the rebel army, they deployed to the left and right into a battle line. The Confederate front that was now facing the forces of liberation appeared to be more than a mile in length to the soldiers in blue.

It was said that the black soldiers of the 1st Kansas were spectacular, as if they were drilling on a parade ground. While the federal artillery were getting into position to fire their weapons, Colonel Williams rode to the front of the black regiment. Williams called his men to attention and gave the following oration:

> This is the day we have been patiently waiting for; the enemy at Cabin Creek did not wait to give you an opportunity of showing them what men can do fighting for their natural rights and for their recently acquired freedom and the freedom of their children and children's children. I am proud of your soldierly appearance; and it is especially gratifying to know that it has been my strenuous efforts in drilling you, in handling you, and providing for you for the last months, that I find you in such splendid condition, physically and in morale. We are going to engage the enemy in a few moments and I am going to lead you. We are engaged in a holy war; in the history of the world, soldiers never fought for a holier cause than the cause for which the Union soldiers are fighting, the preservation of the Union and the equal rights of all men. You know what the soldiers of the Southern army are fighting for; you know that they are fighting for the continued existence and extension of slavery on this continent, and if they are successful, to take you and your wives and children back to slavery. You know it is common report that the confederate troops boast that they will not give quarters to colored troops and their officers, and you know they did not give quarters to your comrades in the fight with the forage detachment near Sherwood last May. Show the enemy this day you are not asking for quarter, and that you know how and are eager to fight for your freedom and finally, keep cool and do not fire until you receive the order, and then aim deliberately below the waist belt. The people of the whole country will read the reports of your conduct in this engagement; let it be of brave, disciplined men.

The rebel soldiers opened the battle with their artillery shelling the Union artillery position. Each side was able to knock out a cannon. After nearly two hours of skirmishing which had been an even stand off, General Blunt gave an order that changed the course of the battle.

Blunt ordered Colonel Williams to take his black troops which were located near the center of Union line, to capture the four artillery guns supporting the 20th and 29th Texas Cavalry Regiments. The black soldiers fixed bayonets and moved in formation to within forty paces of the rebel line. At this juncture, Colonel Williams gave the command to fire. At the same instance the Texas soldiers also fired. Colonel Williams' horse was shot out from under him, and he was severely wounded; Col. Charles DeMorse, the Confederate commander of this sector, was also severely wounded. Lt. Col. John Bowles took over command of the black soldiers; he ordered them to fall upon the ground and continue firing at the rebel line. During this volley between the armies, the 2nd Indian Regiment (dismounted) passed between the right of the black infantry and the Confederates. Lieutenant Colonel Bowles ordered the Indian troops to fall back to their original positions. Colonel DeMorse commanding the Texas regiment heard the federal order and thought it was for the black regiment to retire. He ordered his men to advance; this was a fatal mistake. The federal soldiers had held their fire while the Indian regiment fell back to position. The black troops were partially hidden in the tall grass and gunsmoke. As the rebel soldiers advanced within twenty-five paces of the federal position, the black regiment raised up and fired a volley of rifle shots into the advancing rebel soldiers. This one volley turned the tide of the battle for the federal troops at Honey Springs.

In this volley the color bearer of the Texas regiment was shot down; another rebel soldier picked up the colors and he was shot down; soon thereafter some Union Indian soldiers picked up the colors of the Texas regiment. The black soldiers fought with conspicuous gallantry and completely routed the Confederate soldiers from Texas. Their demeanor inspired the white and Indian federal troops. Cooper could no longer hold his troops north of Elk Creek. He decided to try to hold the bridge across the creek and entrench on the south bank of the stream. But this was not possible with the deadly rifle and artillery fire pouring in from the Union troops. The Confederates had to retreat. They decided to burn their supplies and buildings at Honey Springs so they wouldn't fall into Union hands. They were not completely successful; the Federal forces did capture food supplies. The rebels were pushed three miles, ending up one mile south of Honey Springs.

By two in the afternoon the battle was over, four hours after it had started. The Confederate forces retreated to the east. They were met too late by the 3,000 men from Fort Smith to reinforce their positions. Cooper felt his defeat was due to superior Federal arms, munitions, and artillery and not being reinforced in a timely manner by General Cabell from Fort Smith. General Blunt detailed his losses of seventeen men killed and sixty wounded. Additionally, his men buried 150 Confederates, wounded 400, and took seventy-seven prisoners.

One interesting discovery occurred after the war was over. In looking over the Confederate headquarters, the black soldiers found 400 handcuffs in one of the depot buildings. The rebel soldiers had planned on putting the handcuffs on captured black soldiers after the battle. Thereafter they would transport them to Texas for slave labor. But the black soldiers had other plans, as evidenced by the outcome of the battle.

The history of the handcuffs was obtained from David Griffith, a bodyservant of Maj. J. A. Carroll of Coopers' Texas regiment. Griffith left his master after the battle and joined the black regiment at Fort Smith in September, enlisting in Company G. Griffith stated that he frequently heard Confederate officers saying they did not believe black soldiers would fight. All the Southern troops would have to do would be to march up to the black men and take them in, as they would a herd of cattle in a pasture.

Colonel Williams, commander of the black regiment, said, "I had long been of the opinion that this race had a right to kill rebels, and this day proved their capacity for the work. Forty prisoners and one battle flag fell into the hands of my regiment on this field."

The black regiment in the battle at Honey Springs sustained five killed and thirty-two wounded. The 1st Kansas Colored returned to Fort Gibson after the battle. In his official report General Blunt stated, "The 1st Kansas (colored) particularly distinguished itself; they fought like veterans, and preserved their line unbroken throughout the engagement. Their coolness and bravery I have never seen surpassed; they were in the hottest of the fight, and opposed to Texas troops twice their number, whom they completely routed. One Texas regiment (the 20th Cavalry) that fought against them went into the fight with 300 men and came out with only sixty. It would be invidious to make particular mention of any one where all did their duty so well."

The Battle of Honey Springs was the Gettysburg of the Indian Territory. It opened the way for the capture of Fort Smith and much of Arkansas. After Honey Springs the Confederacy never again fought for control of the Indian Territory. The 1st Kansas Colored Regiment served until the end of the war seeing duty primarily in Arkansas and the Indian Territory (Oklahoma). In April of 1864 the 1st Kansas received a terrible defeat at the Battle of Poison Springs in Arkansas. Outmanned by the rebel army, most of the black wounded soldiers were killed by the Confederates after they surrendered. In this battle the 1st lost half of its troops, either killed or wounded. They were avenged later by the 2nd Kansas Colored. The 1st was mustered out of service on October 30, 1865, after seeing garrison duty at Pine Bluff and Little Rock. Before they were mustered out they were redesignated as the 79th U.S. Colored Troops (U.S.C.T.).

CHAPTER FIFTEEN

Remember Poison Springs

After the 1st Kansas was defeated, then indiscriminately murdered after surrendering, the battle cry for all black soldiers in the west became "Remember Poison Springs!" They vowed not to take any prisoners. The unit most affected by Poison Springs was the 1st Kansas' "brother unit," the 2nd Kansas Colored Volunteer Infantry Regiment.

The 2nd Kansas began the process of being mustered into service in August 1863, and was finished by October 1863 at Fort Scott, Kansas. Col. S. J. Crawford of the 2nd Kansas Cavalry was the commanding officer, and he was assisted by Lt. Col. Horatio Knowles of the 4th Indian Home Guards. The regiment left on the 19th of October for Fort Smith, Arkansas, as an escort to a large supply train from Fort Scott under command of Maj. J. H. Gilpatrick.

By November 1, at Fort Smith, Arkansas, the organization

of the regiment had been completed. Assisting Crawford were Lt. Col. Horatio Knowles and Maj. James H. Gilpatrick.

On March 24, 1864, the 2nd Kansas Colored left Fort Smith as part of the Camden Expedition. The 2nd Kansas Colored formed a part of Colonel Williams' Brigade of General Thayer's Division. Maj. Gen. Fred Steele's command left Little Rock near the same time that General Thayer's Division left Fort Smith. The two commands met on the Little Missouri River, and together they pushed toward the Red River.

The Confederate army met the Federal force on April 10, but fell back after a slight engagement. The Federals moved southward until April 15 when General Thayer's rear guard was attacked. The enemy was repulsed, but the Union was ordered to abandon the engagement and proceed toward Camden which they reached on the 16th.

A shortage of supplies for his army at Camden forced Maj. Gen. Fred Steele to send out a foraging party to gather food that the Confederates had stored about twenty miles up the prairie on D'An Camden Road by White Oak Creek. The Federal troops were able to load the corn into wagons, and on April 18 Col. James M. Williams and the 1st Kansas Colored Regiment started on the return to Camden.

Also part of Williams' command for the escort were 195 cavalry troops of the 2nd, 6th, and 14th Kansas Regiments and two ten-pounder artillery pieces of the 2nd Indiana Battery. On the return to Camden, Williams was further reinforced by 383 of the 18th Iowa Infantry, 90 cavalry troopers of the 2nd, 6th, and 14th Kansas Regiments, and two twelve-pounder mountain howitzers attached to the 6th Kansas. This brought William's brigade up to about 1,100 men. These soldiers had to guard upwards of one hundred wagons loaded with corn.

After scouting the movements of the Union supply train, Confederate Brig. Gen. John S. Marmaduke decided he would capture the train before it could be further reinforced by Union soldiers. Marmaduke's division was joined by Brig. Gen. W. L. Cabell's division and Brig. Gen. Samuel B. Maxey's division for a combined Confederate force of 3,700 men and twelve pieces of artillery under Maxey's command. The rebel army decided to attack at the Lee Plantation which was fifteen miles from Camden.

The morning of April 18, 1864, the Confederates surprised the supply train and struck with full force. Some of the Texas troops had been defeated by the black Federal soldiers at Honey Springs. The Confederate forces made three assaults on the Federal positions, but were beaten back. The fourth assault forced the black soldiers from their positions. Due to the superior numbers and the artillery barrage, the Union soldiers retreated into the timber.

Most of the wounded black soldiers who were left on the field were shot and bayoneted by the Confederate soldiers; many of the wounded black soldiers feigned death so they wouldn't be killed. The Confederate soldiers went over the field after the battle shouting at one another saying "Where is the 1st Kansas Nigger now? All cut to pieces and gone to hell by bad management."

The Union soldiers sustained 122 men and officers killed, ninety-seven wounded, and eighty-one missing. Of those, the 1st Kansas Colored had 117 men and officers killed and sixty-five wounded. Many of the black soldiers had been shot down while trying to surrender. This was the largest massacre of black soldiers in the Civil War, second only to the attack on Fort Pillow, Tennessee. The black soldiers had fought valiantly against superior numbers.

The Confederates captured the Union supply train and reported they had only seventeen men killed and eighty-eight wounded. Additionally, the Confederate forces had a large contingent of Choctaw and Chickasaw soldiers.

After this battle, the survivors of the 1st Kansas Colored and their counterparts in the 2nd Kansas Colored Infantry made a commitment not to take Confederate prisoners in future battles. All black troops west of the Mississippi used the battle cry "Remember Poison Springs," until the end of the war.

CHAPTER SIXTEEN

2nd Kansas Colored Volunteer Infantry

The permission to organize the 2nd Kansas Colored Volunteer Infantry was received in June of 1863. The initial work of assembling the regiment began at Fort Scott, Kansas. By mid-October ten companies had been mustered into service. Major James H. Gilpatrick was placed in command. The regiment left Fort Scott on the 19th of October for Fort Smith, Arkansas, as escort to a very large Union supply train.

On November 1, at Fort Smith, the regiment received new commanding officers, Col. S. J. Crawford, formerly of the 2nd Kansas Cavalry and Lt. Col. Horatio Knowles, formerly of the 4th Indian Home Guards.

The 2nd Kansas Colored was camped on the Poteau River, about two miles south of Fort Smith. In the official records it was stated the regiment practiced and drilled until it attained a degree of proficiency second to none in the Army of the Frontier.

Its main duties, around Fort Smith, at this time were escort, fatigue, and garrison duty.

The regiment was part of the fateful Camden Expedition which left Fort Smith on March 24, 1864. The 2nd Kansas Colored was attached to Colonel Williams' Brigade of General Thayer's Division. Major General Steele's forces left Little Rock to meet up with Thayer's forces for a push on Confederate armies near the Red River.

They met the Confederates on April 10th at Prairie de Anne, Arkansas. Although the two armies massed, making the most spectacular military formation west of the Mississippi, nothing transpired, except a brief skirmish late at night.

For the next few days, the opposing armies skirmished. The Union Army was ordered to Camden after repulsing several rebel advances. They reached Camden on April 16.

On April 18, the 1st Kansas lost nearly one-half of its regiment to a force of rebels ten times its size. This was the engagement known as Poison Springs. While sequestered at Camden, the 2nd Kansas was constantly engaged on forage or picket duty.

On April 26 the 2nd Kansas along with the other Union army at Camden abandoned their fortifications on account of General Banks' defeat and retreat on Red River. Gen. Fred Steele's command at Camden drew the attention of Confederate Gen. Kirby Smith who had been pursuing Banks. Now, the rebel army decided to focus their attention on the Yanks at Camden.

On April 30 the 2nd Kansas arrived at the pontoon boats at Jenkins' Ferry on the Saline River. The regiment was informed that the rear of General Steele's command was under heavy attack by the rebel army. The Union commander of the rear was General Rice.

At this point Col. S. J. Crawford ordered his regiment to march one-and-one-half-miles to the battle scene. When Crawford arrived he asked General Rice where he wanted his men deployed. General Rice asked Crawford which regiment he commanded, at which time Crawford said "Second Kansas Colored Infantry." General Rice quickly responded, "They won't fight." Crawford immediately said his men would go as far as it was possible for any others to go, only in more emphatic, unstatesman-like terms.

Rice ordered the 2nd Kansas to relieve the 15th Indiana. As soon as the black troops were in position they were engaged in fierce combat with rebel soldiers for two solid hours, at which time the southern soldiers aimed three cannons on the 2nd Kansas. The Union soldiers had no artillery to engage the rebel battery. Colonel Crawford had to either retreat or try to attack the battery and kill or capture the rebel artillerymen.

Up to this time in the Civil War no black troops had been permitted to charge upon a Confederate battery. General Rice was hesitant in giving Crawford permission. But the rebel army was gaining ground and almost in position to encircle the Union command. Under pressure General Rice relented and gave permission for the attack.

Colonel Crawford wasted no time in telling his men to fix bayonets and gave the order "Charge." As the men of the 2nd Kansas rushed toward the battery they chanted and hollered "Remember Poison Springs."

The black soldiers charged into positions three times their number, but gave no quarter as they dashed across 300 yards of open field. The black soldiers shot and killed all the horses with the rebel battery, except two. The Confederates fought with great determination, but it wasn't enough. The black soldiers overran the rebel battery and killed or wounded over 150 Confederates supporting the artillery. The 2nd Kansas lost an officer and seventy men killed in this heroic action.

The Union army was able to cross the Saline River and regroup. Although it was a defensive action by the Union forces, it would have been a defeat had not the 2nd Kansas Colored captured the battery and inflicted such heavy damage on the Confederate advance. It was the first time in the war that black soldiers had successfully charged and captured an enemy battery. The 2nd had made history and avenged their brother regiment, the 1st Kansas Colored. It is said that the black troops showed no hostility toward the captured rebel soldiers, but in the Confederate hospital, a Texas soldier, in the presence of one of their officers, killed nine wounded men of the 2nd Kansas Colored Infantry. The total casualties for the Battle of Jenkins' Ferry were 521 Union soldiers and 443 Confederate soldiers.

After this battle the 2nd Kansas was ordered to garrison duty at Little Rock, Arkansas. Remaining in Little Rock long enough to draw rations, the 2nd Kansas was ordered to force march to Fort Smith, Arkansas. They would be part of a black brigade.

Fort Smith was under threat of attack by a large Confederate force and had been unoccupied by any army soldiers, North or South, for a while. Many southern sympathizers were hoping rebel troops would get to Fort Smith first. But that was not to be; the black brigade marched in and took control of the important river city. James M. Williams commanded them. Units in the brigade were the 1st Kansas Colored, commanded by Major Ward; 2nd Kansas Colored, commanded by Col. S. J. Crawford; the 11th U.S. Colored, commanded by Lt. Col. James M. Steele; and the 54th U.S. Colored Infantry.

In the summer of 1864 the 2nd Kansas was part of an expedition into the Indian Territory. This expedition was led by Crawford; they covered approximately seventy-five miles, south and west, as far as the Canadian River. The black soldiers on this campaign convinced their skeptics of their bravery, discipline, and powers of endurance.

During the month of December 1864, the 2nd Kansas made a force march to Hudson's Crossing, Indian Territory, on the Neosho River, by way of Fort Gibson. They travelled on quarter rations for a distance of 150 miles, returning as the escort to a large supply train.

After the black regiment returned from this expedition, it was ordered to Little Rock, with all the other black troops at the post of Fort Smith. They escorted a large wagon train of white refugees from Fort Smith. At first the whites showed bias and prejudice toward the soldiers, but by the end of the trip, the black soldiers were shown respect for doing their duty well. The 2nd Kansas had left Fort Smith on January 15, 1865, and arrived at Little Rock on February 4, 1865.

In Little Rock the 2nd Kansas had set up headquarters on the north side of the river. The 2nd was now a part of the 7th Army Corps. The regiment would drill for six hours a day. The black regiment was considered to be the best in the Corps in discipline and general efficiency. There were some health problems contracted by the soldiers due to the camp being located in the Cypress Swamps, two miles north of Little Rock.

Lt. Col. J.H. Gilpatrick, the commanding officer, in the spring of 1865 led the regiment in an expedition south of Little Rock. They located a large band of rebel guerrilla fighters on the Saline River, capturing twenty-five, killing and wounding several, routing the group completely, and driving them from their stronghold.

This was believed to be the last offensive movement on the part of Union troops in this Department prior to the surrender of the Confederate Trans-Mississippi Army.

The 2nd Kansas Colored was ordered to Camden, Arkansas, arriving on August 10, 1865. They remained on duty in this town until they were mustered out on October 9, 1865.

The 2nd Kansas Colored Infantry was officially redesignated the 83rd United States Colored Troops before the end of the war. Their principal weapon was the Enfield .577 rifle. The 2nd Kansas Colored Volunteer Infantry left a record as one of the best Union army regiments west of the Mississippi during the Civil War. The discipline of the regiment was considered excellent at all times.

CHAPTER SEVENTEEN

1st Iowa Regiment of African Descent

In August 1863 the authorities of the State of Iowa began the enlistment of blacks. Keokuk, Iowa, was chosen as the enlistment site and blacks principally from Iowa and Missouri were the main recruits.

By October 11, 1863, there were nine full companies of black recruits under the command of Colonel John G. Hudson. The regiment was designated the 1st African Descent Regiment Iowa Volunteers. It was later redesignated the 60th Regiment of United States Colored Troops (U.S.C.T.) and was mustered for the duration of the war.

Leaving Keokuk barracks the regiment departed for St. Louis, Missouri. They were headquartered in Bounden Barracks. Another company joined them there, bringing the troop strength up to ten full companies. While in St. Louis, Mrs. I. N. Triplet, on behalf of the ladies of the State of Iowa and the city of Muscatine, presented the 60th with a well-constructed, silk national flag. The black soldiers carried the flag throughout the war and were able to return the flag to the state.

In January, 1864, the 60th U.S.C.T. was ordered to report to General Beaufort at Helena, Arkansas. While at Helena the 60th took part in several skirmishes and captured a number of prisoners.

In July Col. W. S. Brooks, in command of the 56th U.S.C.T., the 60th U.S.C.T., and a detachment of the 3rd Regiment U.S. Colored Heavy Artillery with two field guns, sailed out of Helena on troop transport boats, then down the Mississippi River, to the mouth of the White River. After disembarking there, the black troops marched inland all night. At breakfast they were allowed to rest and eat, then scattered over the nearby fields after stacking their rifles.

Without warning, a superior Confederate force under General Dobbins attacked their position with the intention of annihilating the black soldiers. The Union soldiers were able to recover their rifles, but their commander, Colonel Brooks, was killed. At this point, Captain Ransey of Company C, 60th U.S.C.T., took command.

The black artillerymen were able to get their two field guns into action and did considerable damage to the rebel attack. The Confederate attack was blistering; they outnumbered the black troops two to one. Every line officer of the black regiments was either dead or wounded during the intense fighting. Black non-commissioned officers had to step up and take command positions.

Sergeant Triplet led his men in Company C against the repeated rebel charges, holding their position firm. A black artillery sergeant was in charge of the field guns; his leadership was exemplary for well over two long hours of battle.

The conflict lasted from six in the morning until noon. Charge, after repeated charge, the black soldiers were able to spurn the Confederate Army. As the battle moved into the afternoon, the situation looked bleak for the Union soldiers due to a short supply of ammunition.

These soldiers were well aware of the massacre of black

soldiers at Fort Pillow, Tennessee. They were mentally prepared to fight to the last, with bayonets, if they had to.

The Confederate Army began massing for a final charge that would obliterate the black soldiers; they were going to sweep the field clean.

Just as the Confederates began their movement, a sound could be heard coming from the rebel rear. It was the charge of a detachment of the 15th Illinois Cavalry Regiment under the command of Major Carmichael. After five long hours of fighting, the black troops got much needed support and would live to fight another day.

The Union soldiers were able to begin a retreat that would be successful in gathering their dead and wounded and reaching safety. They were joined by reinforcements, but the Confederates didn't pursue the retreating column. The black soldiers lost fifty men and the rebels lost 150 in the conflict.

Two days later, Colonel Hudson, with the two same regiments, the 56th and 60th and the artillery contingent, rode up to the White River, disembarked, and marched three days across land until they found the enemy entrenched. The black soldiers attacked and drove the rebels out of their works, burned their store, captured a few Texas Rangers, and returned to Helena.

The 60th U.S.C.T. was ordered to join Brigadier General Reynolds' command at Little Rock, Arkansas, in March of 1865. Here they were brigaded with the 57th, 59th, and 83rd U.S.C.T. Regiments. This "Black" brigade was ordered to Texas overland, but the events in the East (General Lee surrendering to General Grant) made this movement moot.

The courageous 60th U.S.C.T. was mustered out at Davenport, Iowa, on November 2, 1865, where they were greeted by thousands of Iowans, after a job well done.

CHAPTER EIGHTEEN

Other Units in the West

Although the 3rd Regiment, United States Colored Cavalry (U.S.C.C.) fought primarily in Mississippi, it did have skirmishes in Arkansas and Louisiana. The 3rd U.S.C.C. may have been the best military unit in the Union Army, bar none. They were never defeated in battle and had preeminent *esprit de corps*. The 3rd was mounted, and all the men had to be expert riders to join the regiment.

The final battle with the Confederates took place at Palmetto Ranch, Brazos Island, Texas, on May 12 and 13, 1865. Black soldiers played a pivotal role in this final conflict. The 62nd U.S. Colored Infantry (originally the 1st Regiment Missouri Volunteer Infantry—Colored) was organized at Bounden Barracks, St. Louis, Missouri. The 62nd would engage a Texas contingent that included Mexican Americans. The Union soldiers were repulsed and suffered one wounded in the action. The small conflict was considered a Confederate victory. Louis

Henry Carpenter, a lieutenant colonel of the 5th United States Colored Cavalry, wrote of duty on the western frontier in Arkansas and Indian Territory. According to Carpenter, who later became a hero in the Indian Wars, the 5th U.S.C.C. was sent west after April 1865 to run down outlaw fugitives from the Indian Territory and subdue unreconstructed Confederate rebels.

The 5th U.S.C.C. had earlier distinguished themselves in battle at Saltville, West Virginia. The 3rd U.S.C.C. and the 5th and 6th U.S.C.C. were also outstanding black cavalry regiments during the Civil War. The 5th U.S. Colored Cavalry became a part of the Department of Arkansas in August 1865, until it was mustered out March 20, 1866. The 6th U.S. Colored Cavalry had earlier distinguished themselves in southwestern Virginia in Stoneman's Raid, December 10–29, 1864. The 6th was also sent to the Department of Arkansas in December, 1865. They were stationed at Helena, Arkansas, in January 1866, then Duvall's Bluff, Arkansas, until April 15, 1866, when they were mustered out.

Some black cavalry regiments in the Civil War did not receive horses. The 3rd, 5th, and 6th U.S.C.C. were all mounted and known for their horsemanship.

In 1865 there was an official communique concerning the 6th U.S.C.C. and the Confederate raiders who served under Gen. John Hunt Morgan:

> Lexington, Ky., Jan. 2, 1865
> Hon. E. M. Stanton
> Secretary of War:
>
> Major General Burbrige, with his command, has just returned from a most successful expedition. Five hundred negroes accompanied his command and Gillem. A battalion of the Sixth U.S. Colored Cavalry, 300 strong, attacked and whipped Duke's Brigade, of 350—the last remnant of Morgan's force. The rebels were driven half a mile, with a loss on their side of thirty men killed and wounded. They were on the crest of a hill at Marion, and the negroes charged over open ground, and did not fire a gun until within thirty yards of the rebels. This is the first time that any of these men were under fire. Three full

regiments of colored troops will leave the for the Army of the
James about the end of the week ...

L. Thomas
Adjutant General

On May 24, 1865, the 25th Corps set sail for Texas by way
of Mobile Bay. The 25th Corps was the only predominantly
black Corps in the Union Army and had played a pivotal role in
the surrender of General Lee at Appomattox. The 25th Corps
was made up of three army divisions. The black soldiers briefly
were stationed at Brownsville, Texas. The Confederate Army in
Texas, shortly after the Corps' arrival, surrendered and the
black soldiers were sent back East. The 25th Corps was the last
active Corps in the Union Army during the Civil War. Immediately after war's end, black troops were sent to the New Mexico
Territory. They were part of three different black regiments.

In August of 1866 Companies A, B, and D of the 57th Infantry Regiment, U.S.C.T., were sent to Fort Union, New Mexico
Territory, and Companies C, E, and G from the same regiment
were sent to Fort Bascom, New Mexico Territory. The 57th was
organized in March 1864 and up until August of that year did
garrison duty at Little Rock and Helena. They were involved in
three skirmishes around Little Rock. Between August 1864 and
June 1865, the regiment was stationed at Little Rock, Brownsville, and Duvall's Bluff. For the remainder of the year they did
guard duty at various locations in Arkansas, primarily protecting
property. This went on until portions of the regiment, as noted,
were sent west to New Mexico Territory. The 57th Infantry was
mustered out of service on December 31, 1866.

The 125th Infantry, U.S.C.T., was mustered in Louisville,
Kentucky, in 1865. They did garrison and guard duty in Kentucky,
Illinois, and Ohio. In August 1866, eight companies of the 125th
were sent to the New Mexico Territory and occupied seven dif-
ferent forts. All these companies were ordered to Fort Union in
October of 1867 to prepare for their movement to Fort Riley,
Kansas, where they were discharged on December 20, 1867.

Section 3:
Buffalo Soldiers

CHAPTER NINETEEN

Inception

By 1866 there was a call for regular army troops to relieve the volunteer units in the west. Some of the volunteers were on the verge of mutiny. The regular U.S. Army was occupying the south; Gen. Philip H. Sheridan was with a contingent of regulars on the Rio Grande to show force to the French and Maximillian who were occupying Mexico. To increase the numbers of regular army members, the Congress of 1866 authorized a troop strength of 54,304 officers and men. These numbers were never met during the Indian Wars and during the late 19th century, the U.S. Army never numbered more than 25,000 even with congressional authorization. Many officers who were in the regular army at the beginning of the Civil War reverted back to their originally designated rank at the end of the civil rebellion.

The legislation of 1866 mandated an enrollment of six African American regiments in the regular army: two cavalry and four infantry. Of the four black infantry regiments, two were to be stationed in the South, and two on the western frontier. The 38th Infantry Regiment—Colonel Williams, Commander; and the 41st Infantry Regiment—Col. Ranald S. Mackenzie, Commander; were the two black infantry regiments in the South. In 1869 they were sent to Louisiana, consolidated, and given the designation as the 25th U.S. Infantry.

The 39th Infantry Regiment and the 40th Infantry Regiments, also black, were assigned to Texas and were consolidated there as the 24th U.S. Infantry in 1869. In 1870 both the 24th and 25th Infantry Regiments were ordered to garrison posts protecting the western settlers on the Texas frontier.

Of the two African-American cavalry regiments, the 9th was organized on September 21, 1866, at Greenville, Louisiana, under the leadership of Col. Edward Hatch, a Civil War veteran, and assigned to the Division of the Gulf under the command of Gen. Philip Sheridan.

Recruitment for the 9th was concentrated in New Orleans, but recruits came from Louisiana, Virginia, South Carolina, Mississippi, and Kentucky. Enlistment would be for five years, and they would be paid sixteen dollars a month. Hatch would have all twelve companies of his regiment organized by February 1867. The next month Hatch was ordered with his regiment to Texas. The 10th was organized on September 21, 1866, at Fort Leavenworth, Kansas, under the leadership of Col. Benjamin H. Grierson, a Civil War hero who had led two successful cavalry raids across the state of Mississippi. The 10th was assigned to the Military Division of Missouri under the command of Gen. William T. Sherman. Recruitment for the 10th was conducted in Philadelphia, Boston, New York, Pittsburgh, Memphis, and St. Louis. Capt. V. W. Walsh on recruiting duty at Little Rock, Arkansas, was ordered by Grierson to organize Company D at Fort Gibson, Indian Territory. Companies E and L were also organized in the Indian Territory and they (Companies D, E, and L) were posted in the Indian Territory. The remaining companies were stationed at posts and camps along the Kansas Pacific Railroad under construction in Kansas. All the officers in the black regiments were white, many of them having served with black troops during the Civil War. Although the opportunity for greater rank and quicker promotions existed in the black regiments, many white officers refused to serve with black troops. The infamous George A. Custer turned down a lieutenant colonel position with the 9th Cavalry and served the same rank with the white 7th Cavalry. The highest rank a black trooper could reach was as a non-commissioned officer or a sergeant.

While on the western frontier, the immediate task for the black troopers, or as they sometimes were called by the Cheyenne and Comanche, Buffalo Soldiers, was the subduing and subjugation of the Plains Indians. According to historian Bennie V. McRae, Jr., the black troopers' duties included:

1) Controlling hostile forces, escorting wagon trains and stagecoaches, building forts and roads, and installing telegraph lines;
2) Guarding water holes, railroad construction workers, and horses and cattle;
3) Protecting and escorting settlers, travelers, immigrants, workers, farmers, miners, and cattlemen; and
4) Mapping areas of uncharted country.

Besides hostile Indian warriors, the black troopers also had to contend with:

1) Horse thieves and cattle rustlers
2) Scheming and murderous politicians
3) Greedy land and cattle barons
4) Crooked government contractors
5) Heartless Indian agents
6) Land-hungry homesteaders
7) Mexican revolutionaries
8) Train and stagecoach robbers
9) Law and Criminal Justice System (especially in Texas and Indian Territory)
10) Certain hostile and prejudiced white commanders
11) The white press and sometimes hostile white public.

Despite all the adversity the black regiments had to contend with, they were known for getting their task accomplished. The black regiments had the highest *esprit de corps* and lowest desertion rates of all military units on the Western frontier. They served from 1866 to 1898, first in the central and southern plains and later in the northern plains.

During the Spanish-American War all of the four black regiments served in Cuba. After the Spanish-American War elements of the 9th Cavalry and other units were assigned to the Philippines. Later the 9th and 10th Cavalry, along with the 24th Infantry, would spend time hunting for Pancho Villa during the Mexican Expedition of 1916.

CHAPTER TWENTY

The Black Infantry

The 24th Infantry Regiment under the command of Col. Ranald S. Mackenzie and Lt. Col. William R. Shafter was in Texas from 1869 to 1880. On December 15, 1870, Colonel Mackenzie was assigned to the 4th Cavalry, and Col. Abner Doubleday succeeded him. Doubleday commanded the 24th until December 1873 (his retirement), and was replaced by Col. Joseph H. Potter.

In the autumn of 1880 the 24th Regiment relocated to the Indian Territory, and several companies were stationed at Fort Supply, Fort Reno, Fort Sill, and Post Cantonment on the north fork of the Canadian River. A detachment was also stationed at Fort Elliot, Texas.

In April 1886 Colonel Potter was appointed a brigadier general; Col. Zenas R. Bliss succeeded him as commander of the 24th.

In June 1888 the 24th Regiment moved to the Department

of Arizona with headquarters and three companies at Fort Bayard, New Mexico; the remainder of the companies were distributed in Arizona at San Carlos and Forts Grant and Thomas. The duty at San Carlos was primarily in conjunction with an Apache reservation located there. In 1892 Companies D, E, F, and G of the 24th were headquartered at Fort Bayard, while Companies A, B, C, and H at Fort Huachuca in Arizona.

In 1869 the 25th Infantry Regiment had a full complement of officers and 1,045 men. Colonel Mower was commanding and had charge of the Department of Louisiana with headquarters at New Orleans. Companies D, G, and K, were under command of Lieutenant Colonel Hinks at Jackson Barracks, Louisiana. Companies E, F, and I were under command of Major Bliss at Ship Island, Mississippi. Company A was at Fort Pike, Louisiana; Companies B and H at Fort Jackson, Louisiana; Company C at Fort St. Philip, Louisiana.

On January 6, 1870, Colonel Mower died and was succeeded by Col. J. J. Reynolds who was placed in command of the Department of Texas. In May, 1870, the 25th Regiment left by steamer for Indianola, Texas, then marched over land to San Antonio. The march to military posts began on June 22nd. Companies C and H went to Fort McKavett, and Companies E and I to Fort Duncan, under Colonel Bliss. Companies D and F were stationed at Fort Clark; Company K at Fort Stockton; Companies A and G at Fort Davis; Company B did not reach its distant station, Fort Quitman, until August.

In May 1872 the 25th Regiment marched to western Texas and established its headquarters at Fort Davis. Some of the conflicts they were engaged in included, but are not limited to: Company I, Captain Lawson commanding, participated in an engagement with hostile Indians at the Wichita Indian Agency, Indian Territory, on August 22 and 23, 1873, sustaining one man wounded in the conflict; and Company B, Captain Bentzoni commanding, was with General Mackenzie's expedition into Mexico in June 1878. The 25th Infantry spent ten years in Texas doing all types of tasks and duties.

In April 1880 the 25th was ordered to the Department of Dakota, exchanging with the 1st Infantry. Headquarters and four companies took station at Fort Randall, South Dakota. In

November of 1882 they were transferred to Fort Snelling, Minnesota, relieving the 7th Infantry. During this period four companies were stationed at Fort Meade, South Dakota, and two at Fort Hale, South Dakota. The latter post was abandoned in May 1884, and the garrison transferred to Fort Sisseton, South Dakota. In May of 1888 the 25th Infantry Regiment made a headquarters change with a move to Montana. The headquarters was at Fort Missoula, while four companies went to Fort Shaw and two to Fort Custer.

Companies I and K were skeletonized on orders of the War Department in September of 1890. When matters got tense at Wounded Knee, Companies C, E, F, and H were sent to Fort Keogh, under Lt. Col. Van Horn. They remained there from November 1890 to February 5, 1891. Later, they returned to their regular stations in Montana.

By the late 1890s there were still some black veterans in the infantry who had served in the Civil War or had been members of the 38th or 41st Infantry Regiments at the close of the War.

The Indian Wars were primarily fought on horseback; yet the infantry did participate in many battles. The infantry performed the preponderate share of garrison duty. On some instances when the cavalry was not available, the infantry units performed scouting duties. On many occasions when infantry was ordered to perform scouting duties, they did so mounted. Many times on the frontier the cavalry would be assisted by mounted infantry for scouting patrols. On one such occasion in October of 1871, mounted infantry and cavalry left Fort Davis on patrol and covered 500 miles in twenty-nine days.

Another important task for the black infantry was escort duty for survey parties, stagecoaches, contract trains, supply trains, and wagon trains. Work off-post for the infantry also included road building and repair, and detail for military wagon roads that connected posts and forts to frontier towns.

A common practice after the Civil War was for stagecoach companies to request military protection for their remount stations. This assignment was given to the infantry. Where requested, two or three infantrymen would be assigned to a stagecoach station on the frontier. The remount stations were basically a location for stagecoaches to change horses and let the passengers rest and eat. The main threats were of outlaws or hostile Indians stealing the horses, or an attempt to rob either the mail or freight carried by the stagecoaches.

During the campaign against the Apache Indians in the Southwest, the black infantry was used to guard strategic water-holes and mountain passes frequented by the Indians. This strategy was used very effectively against Chief Victorio in 1880 when he was forced into Mexico.

On the Texas frontier black infantry erected telegraph poles and strung telegraph wire over a vast area. Sometimes this duty took months to complete.

It is interesting to note that the 24th Infantry Regiment had the lowest desertion rate of any regiment in the U.S. Army during the years 1880 to 1886. Desertion was the biggest problem of the frontier army. The regiment during those years was stationed at Fort Reno, Fort Sill, and Fort Supply in the Indian Territory. In 1885, the 3rd Cavalry (white) had 104 desertions, the 5th Cavalry (white) had 99 desertions, while the 24th (black) had only 3 desertions. At this time all three regiments were stationed in the Indian Territory (Oklahoma).

According to Buffalo Soldier researcher Anthony Powell, the Silent Drill Team, which is very popular today in the U.S. Marine Corps, was actually started by the black frontier infantry. Around 1902 and 1903 the 24th Infantry started silent drilling; later the 25th also began this drill. The black regiments would perform the silent drill with an entire battalion.

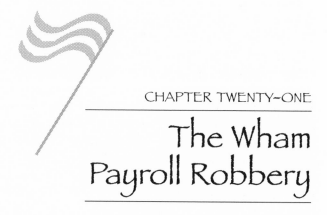

CHAPTER TWENTY ONE

The Wham Payroll Robbery

The most celebrated event in Wild West history involving the black infantry was the Wham Payroll Robbery of May 11, 1889. This event took place in southern Arizona Territory and is named for Maj. Joseph Washington Wham.

Major Wham was an army paymaster in charge of delivering wages to troops at Forts Thomas, Grant, Apache, and at the San Carlos Apache Indian Reservation. Major Wham picked up $45,000, mostly in gold pieces, at Willcox, Arizona Territory, delivered by the Southern Pacific Railroad. Wham's first stop was to pay about $17,000 to the black troops stationed at Fort Grant. The next stop would be Fort Thomas; Wham set out on May 11 with $28,000.

The escort with Wham included eleven black troopers. Of these men, Sgt. Benjamin Brown of C Company, and Cpl. Isaiah Mays, B Company, 24th Infantry, were the top two noncommissioned officers of the escort. Of the remaining men, all were from the 24th, except two men who were from the 10th Cavalry.

Major Wham led a two wagon convoy, his ambulance with strongbox in the lead, followed by the escort vehicle. The road to Fort Thomas had many curves through the rugged terrain of the Graham Mountains, although the two forts lay in a direct line.

About fifteen miles from their destination, the soldiers rode through a narrow gorge; to the east was a rock wall about fifty feet high and to the west, a low ledge. As they began to enter the gorge, an African American female on horseback passed the escort and rode out of sight around a bend in the road.

As the escort reached the bend in the road they found a huge boulder obstructing the way. Sergeant Brown was ordered by Major Wham to remove the boulder. As the soldiers were preparing the huge rock, they noticed it had been wedged in place by stones and dirt so it wouldn't roll. Just as the alarm was to be given to Major Wham that something was amiss, gunfire rang out from the high ledge above their position. Then they took incoming shots from a rear position, and they were caught in a crossfire. Initially, Pvt. Hamilton Lewis was wounded and several of the twelve mules on the ambulance were hit. Lewis was the driver on the ambulance. Three of the black troopers were wounded by the gunfire coming from the rear. Major Wham ordered his men to retreat to a dry creek bed about 300 yards away that ran perpendicular to the cliff line. This offered the soldiers only minimum cover; they were sitting ducks for the outlaws. The soldiers returned fire as best they could under the circumstances.

Major Wham estimated the outlaws numbered a dozen or more white men. He figured the gunfight lasted for more than thirty minutes with the outlaws firing about 480 shots. Of the eleven black troopers in the escort, eight were wounded. Sergeant Brown was wounded twice, in the abdomen and arm.

Cpl. Isaiah Mays, without Wham's approval, decided to go for help. He crawled to avoid detection and then ran three miles to Barney Norton's ranch. Once there, ranch hands took Mays to nearby Cedar Springs where a message was sent to Fort Grant for help.

Being badly wounded and in an unstable defensive position, the soldiers couldn't prevent the outlaws from taking the strongbox of gold coins.

Barney Norton and his cowboys arrived after the outlaws had made their getaway. They hitched four mules to the ambulance and carried the wounded men to the hospital at Fort Thomas.

Before twelve hours went past, there were 1,700 armed men out looking for the desperados. This contingent included soldiers, Indian scouts, deputy U.S. marshals, sheriffs, and detectives. They searched the entire Southeast Arizona Territory, but came up empty handed.

Maggie Campbell, the black woman who passed the escort before the shooting started, was a suspect. Later she testified that as soon as the shooting started, she was thrown by her horse. After the robbery, Major Wham gave her a ride to Fort Thomas. It was never proven whether she was a conspirator in the robbery.

In writing his report after the robbery, Major Wham gave glowing testimony to the conduct of the black troopers. Wham, who was a veteran of the Civil War wrote, "never witnessed better courage or better fighting than shown by these colored soldiers, on May 11, 1889, as the bullet marks on the robber positions today abundantly attest."

In September of 1889 Major Wham requested that troopers Brown and Mays receive Medals of Honor and asked for Certificates of Merit for eight others. The awards were approved by Secretary of War Redfield Proctor on February 1, 1890.

Sergeant Benjamin Brown's citation read, "Although shot in the abdomen, in a fight between a paymaster's escort and robbers, did not leave the field until again wounded through both arms." Brown qualified as a distinguished marksman and represented the 24th Regiment in 1893 at the Department of Arizona rifle competition. He later became the senior enlisted soldier in the regiment. At Fort Assiniboine, Montana, in 1904 Brown served as the 24th's drum major. At that time he was ranked fifty-fourth in the entire U.S. Army for rifle accuracy. In 1905 Brown was admitted to the U.S. Soldiers Home in Washington, D.C., after suffering a stroke. He died there in 1910, the third black Medal of Honor recipient to be buried in the home's soldier cemetery.

Regarding the robbery, two weeks after the event, seven men, all members of the Mormon Church, were arrested. The trial lasted thirty-three days with 165 witnesses testifying. Although there was incriminating evidence against the defendants, a jury found them not guilty. The youngest of the defendants, Wilfred Webb, became a successful rancher in Arizona. He was elected to the territorial legislature three times and in 1905 was Speaker of the House.

For the remainder of the 19th century, the 25th Infantry Regiment was assigned to posts in the Dakota Territory, Montana, and Minnesota. During the labor unrest in Idaho and Montana, black infantrymen from the 25th were sent to maintain peace, which they did successfully. Detachments from the 25th also took part in the Pine Ridge Campaign of 1890–91 in the Dakotas.

The 25th also served in the Spanish-American War in 1898. They fought in Cuba during the assault of Santiago and San Juan Hill in July 1898 during which American forces were victorious. After the war the 25th was assigned to posts in Colorado, New Mexico, and Arizona.

In 1899 the 25th took part in suppressing the Philippine Insurrection. They returned from this mission in 1902.

CHAPTER TWENTY-TWO

9th U.S. Cavalry

On August 3, 1866, Maj. Gen. Philip H. Sheridan, Commander of the Military Division of the Gulf at New Orleans, Louisiana, was authorized to raise, among others, one regiment of colored cavalry (African American) to be designated the 9th Regiment of U.S. Cavalry. Men serving in volunteer colored regiments who desired to enlist in regular regiments were authorized to be discharged from the volunteer organizations. These volunteer units were former combat-tested black Civil War veterans. Many men of this class took advantage of the opportunity to join the regular service, and many would later serve as non-commissioned officers.

The mustering of men for the 9th was assumed by Maj. Francis Moore, 65th U.S. Colored Infantry in New Orleans. The initial nucleus of the recruitment came from the vicinity of New Orleans. In the autumn of 1866 a recruiting station was established in Kentucky. During the Civil War there had been two mounted regiments of black cavalry from Kentucky, the 5th and 6th United States Colored Cavalry. All the men for the 9th Cavalry Regiment initially came from either Kentucky or Louisiana. They were able to acquire excellent horses for the regiment from St. Louis.

While in New Orleans empty cotton presses were used as barracks, and the rations were cooked over open campfires. Later, due to cholera outbreaks, the camp was moved to Greenville and later Carrollton, both suburbs of New Orleans.

By the spring of 1867 the regiment had a total of 885 enlisted men for an average of over seventy to a troop. Shortly thereafter, the regiment was ordered to Texas. The majority of the regiment set up camp at San Antonio. Troops L and M, under the command of 1st Lt. J. M. Hamilton, took station at Brownsville, Texas.

By the summer of 1867 the 9th had its officers in place; these included the commander, Col. Edward Hatch, Lt. Col. Wesley Merritt, and Majs. James F. Wade, George A. Forsyth, and Albert P. Morrow.

After extensive drilling and organizing it was felt by the military brass that the 9th was disciplined and well-equipped for its next mission. They would be sent into the extreme Texas frontier to do battle with the land, the elements, and the hostiles.

The principal duties of the 9th in western Texas were to open up and protect the mail and stagecoach route from San Antonio to El Paso; to establish law and order in the country contiguous to the Rio Grande, which was open to attacks by both Mexicans and Indians since the Civil War; to prevent depredations by hostile Indians; and to capture and confine to their reservations all roving Indian bands.

In July 1867 Headquarters and Companies A, B, E, and K, with Colonel Hatch commanding, were sent to re-activate Fort Stockton, Texas. The old fort had been vacated during the Civil War and was deemed unusable. A new fort was built one-half mile northeast of the old fort on 960 acres, leased from civilian landowners. The mission of the post was to protect the many roads in the area and the water supply at Comanche Springs.

Companies C, D, F, G, H, and I, under the command of Lt. Col. Wesley Merritt, were sent to Fort Davis, Texas. This area had been traumatized by numerous Indian raids. Out of the Guadalupe Mountains, the Mescalero Apaches had waged havoc with stagecoaches, wagon trains, cattle herds, and travelers. From south of the border, Mexican Kickapoos and Lipans had come north on numerous raids, striking fear into Texas frontiersmen. From the north, Comanche and Kiowa raiders, some of the best horsemen in the world, raided the length of West Texas and into Mexico. Like Fort Stockton, a new post had to be built, and black troopers accomplished much of the work. The post was built near the mouth of Limpia Canyon, with defense of the fort the prime consideration.

The mission of the troopers of the 9th at Fort Davis was more varied than those at Fort Stockton. At Davis they scouted and mapped the surrounding territory and guarded railroad surveyors. Protecting the San Antonio-El Paso Road, which included stagecoach travel and wagon trains, was very important. The 9th was also the only line of defense for white settlers who lived in that portion of west Texas from hostile Indians.

Everyday post life for the black troopers in West Texas included drilling, stable duty, and parading. Troops at Fort Davis would have a dress parade every evening, except Saturday, that included the post band. There were logging teams for the sawmill and special details for the garden. Also, troopers were prohibited from leaving the grounds of the post, except in small parties, at which time they were ordered to always carry their carbines. Whenever the horses and mules were grazed, there would be a number of guards with lookouts posted on high ground.

The only amusement the troopers had was horseback riding on a nice day, rare opportunities to shoot a wolf or coyote, a rarer chance to chat with a visitor, and the much anticipated mail call.

The 9th remained in Texas for eight years and made a name for itself during that period that would rival any regiment in the U.S. Army. The earliest test for the Buffalo Soldiers of the 9th Cavalry's mettle was the Battle of Fort Lancaster. This engagement took place on December 26, 1867. Fort Lancaster, located on the Pecos River in West Texas, was considered a subpost of Fort Stockton. Colonel Hatch had stated on the record

9th Cavalry Band, performing in the Plaza, Santa Fe, New Mexico Territory, 1880.
(Courtesy Fort Davis National Historic Site)

Baseball team, Troop L, 9th Cavalry, Fort Wingate, New Mexico Territory, 1899
(Courtesy Museum of New Mexico)

that Fort Lancaster was as important as any post in West Texas, more so than Fort Davis. Part of Hatch's reasoning was that one of the few good crossings of the Pecos River was at Fort Lancaster.

The U.S. Army had abandoned Fort Lancaster in 1861 during the Civil War. The Confederacy didn't assign any troops to the fort, therefore hostile Indians controlled the area until the end of the war. Fort Lancaster became part of the Buffalo Soldiers' domain to patrol and protect in 1867.

On December 26, 1867, Brevet Lt. Col. William Frohock and Company K, 9th Cavalry were camped at Fort Lancaster with a herd of horses for the military. That same afternoon Frohock and his men would be attacked by a "Comanchero" type of outlaw confederacy. The enemy strength was estimated at between 900 and 1,500 insurgents. The objective of the attack appeared to be the horse herd the soldiers were guarding.

The most interesting aspect of the attackers was that many of them were white men wearing Confederate gray uniforms. The leader of the Indian insurgents appeared to be a white man. Others in the attacking party were said to have been Comanche, Kickapoos, and Mexicans. The white renegades were undoubtedly former Texas soldiers still trying to fight the Civil War. Later this same mix of ethnic groups would make up the group known as "Comancheros," a land based pirate outfit that terrorized West Texas and the Indian Territory into the 1870s.

The attack began when a small detachment of Company K were moving a portion of the horse herd from pasture to water. From the north, riding hard, were 200 horsemen who surprised the troopers and stampeded the herd. The troopers opened fire, but were overwhelmed by the superior numbers. Very shortly thereafter, an attack on Company K's position came from the west. The troopers took up defensive positions on the north, south, and west. The troopers tried to put the horse herd in the post corral, but there was too much confusion and the horses couldn't be controlled.

The troopers moved their main position to the ruins of a settler's store that had been at the post. In actuality, the old fort was in bad condition, having not been occupied for the last five years.

The black troopers repulsed the attack coming from the north. But the desperados attacking from the west were able to breech camp security and stampede the horse herd. Ironically, the horses which stampeded southward through the camp ran right into another contingent of mounted renegades, numbering about 400, who were attacking from that position. The horses dissipated this attack.

This stampede of the horse herd saved the army command, according to Frohock. He felt they wouldn't have been able to defend a charge from the third front. Now the renegades had complete control of the horse herd, but not of the fort.

Frohock was now able to leave some men in the camp and with the larger portion of troopers, he advanced on foot toward enemy positions. The renegades moved back, away from rifle fire, several times while keeping control of the horses which were in their rear. Frohock heard intense gunfire at the camp and sent a sergeant and ten men to reinforce the troopers at that position. Frohock moved his skirmish line to repel an attack from the north for a second time. The troopers, after intense fighting, were successful in breaking this attack.

The troopers at this point noticed large groups of unmounted renegades in the hills and a nearby canyon surrounding the fort. Frohock thought they might try to attack the fort from all four sides. But there were no further attacks on the 9th Cavalry that day. It appeared the renegade's main objective was to get control of the horse herd, which for the most part they did. Frohock had sent a detachment of mounted troopers after the horse herd, but they came back later that night after a four mile chase, low on ammunition, and without the herd.

After an examination of the battlefield, Commander Hatch from Fort Stockton stated that the black troopers had killed twenty of their attackers on December 26. Hatch also took note of the large amount of white men with the renegades and the military style attack. There was one private's Confederate coat retrieved from the battlefield.

Frohock counted his losses; there were two troopers and a teamster killed. The teamster and his crew had been out gathering wood and water near the fort when they noticed the renegades and gave warning that an attack was imminent. The loss of horses was put at thirty-two with six mules and five horses killed. Not all of the horse herd was captured. On the night of December 28 a smaller war party attacked the fort in hopes of capturing the remaining horses and were repulsed.

The attackers fled down the Pecos and headed south toward Mexico. They were never heard from again in the numbers they mustered at Fort Lancaster. The battle did establish the fact that the black troopers of the 9th would fight like tigers if they had to. This engagement helped to establish their credentials in the "wilds" of West Texas.

Other actions of the 9th Cavalry in Texas included a fight on September 12, 1868, when Lieutenant Cusak with sixty troopers, surprised a large party of hostile Indians, killing twenty-five and capturing all of their horses, ponies, and supplies. Only one trooper was wounded during the engagement, which was noted as a brilliant military operation.

In 1869, on October 28 and 29, Troops B, E, F, G, L, and M had a running fight of forty miles at the headwaters of the Brazos River, where a number of Indians were killed. On December 25 five men of Troop E defeated a band of twenty Indians who had attempted to surprise the U.S. mail coach.

In 1870, January 16, Troop G and a detachment of Troop L, 9th Cavalry, under Captain Bacon, attacked and surprised an entire Indian village. In doing so, they captured eighty-three horses and all the provisions. On April 25, at Crow Springs, Texas, fifty troopers from Troops C and K, under Major Morrow captured thirty horses and all the supplies of an Indian village.

On May 20, 1870, at Kickapoo Springs, Texas, Sgt. Emanuel Stance of Troop F was leading ten privates on a scout expedition to locate Kickapoo Indians who had committed depredations. About fourteen miles out from Fort McKavett, Stance spotted a small party of Kickapoo with nine ponies. The sergeant ordered a charge on the Indians. After a brief gun battle the Indians abandoned the horses and fled into the hills. The troopers gathered up the Indian ponies and made camp for the night at Kickapoo Springs, a stagecoach stop.

The next morning, May 21, Stance and his command with their captured ponies started back to Fort McKavett to report to Capt. Henry Carroll, commander of Troop F. On their way back

Noncommissioned officers, Troop L, 9th Cavalry, Fort Wingate, New Mexico Territory, 1899.
(Courtesy Museum of New Mexico)

to the fort, Stance and his men spotted a band of twenty Kickapoo preparing to attack two army wagons with extra horses defended by a small guard. Stance immediately attacked the Indians, firing a blistering carbine barrage into their positions; the Indians fought, then broke, and ran leaving five ponies behind. Now with a captured herd of fourteen ponies, Stance continued on his way to Carroll's encampment. Shortly thereafter, Stance and his detachment were attacked from the rear. He coolly halted his men, ordered an about-face, and poured a withering volley into the Indians who broke and ran. Stance was not attacked again and continued on his way back to camp. Stance reached Carroll's camp on May 21, about 2:00 p.m. with the fifteen Kickapoo horses and one rescued white boy. The Kickapoos suffered four wounded during the skirmishes; the only casualty the black troopers had was one slightly wounded horse. For his actions at Kickapoo Springs, Sergeant Stance became the first trooper of the 9th Cavalry to win the Medal of Honor on July 24, 1870, at Fort McKavett, Texas.

By the end of their eight year stay in West Texas, the 9th had made that particular frontier hospitable for white settlers. Most of the time the black troopers were on scout patrol, guard duty, and long marches. While doing these tasks, they covered thousands of miles of territory.

In 1875 the 9th Cavalry Regiment was transferred to the New Mexico Territory with their headquarters at Santa Fe. The white 8th Cavalry Regiment was ordered out of New Mexico; they had been there five-and-a-half years and were being replaced by the 9th. Various units were sent to nine forts and one camp in the New Mexico Territory. These posts included Fort Bayard, Fort Stanton, Fort Union, Fort Wingate, Fort Selden, Fort McRae, Fort Craig, Fort Cummings, Fort Tularosa, and Camp Ojo Caliente.

The 9th Cavalry's main objective in New Mexico was to subdue the Apache who were constantly raiding the southern portion of the territory. The most important Apache leaders were Nana, Victorio, Juh, and Geronimo. They were rebelling against the U.S. government's policy of placing Indians on reservations, which were not conducive to growing crops. The main Apache reservation was located at San Carlos in the southeast Arizona

Territory; a virtual desert wasteland that the Apaches passionately hated. The Indians were allowed to keep their weapons on the reservations, but on numerous occasions would go on raiding parties outside reservation land, or retaliate against white settlers who had stolen their livestock. Often, the Apache raiding parties were small in number and very elusive. Moreover, some Apaches refused to live on reservation land.

Many Medal of Honor winners from the 9th won their recognition in the Apache campaigns of New Mexico and Arizona Territories.

In late January 1877 the Chiricahua Apache began a series of raids in New Mexico Territory. Some young men from the Warm Springs and Mescalero tribes left their reservations to join the Chiricahua raiders. A communique was received at Fort Bayard that fifty Chiricahua warriors had battled with a detachment of six cavalry units in Arizona Territory and were moving toward New Mexico Territory. At once Lt. Henry H. Wright, along with six troopers of Company C of the 9th Cavalry and three Navajo scouts, set out to locate the raiding party.

On the morning of January 24 in the Florida Mountains, the Apaches were located. Although outnumbered, Lieutenant Wright tried to talk the Indians into giving up their weapons and surrendering. By the time Wright noticed that talk was fruitless, his small command was completely surrounded by the Apaches. Wright gave an order for his men to break out of the encirclement. In doing so a vicious fight ensued. The troopers fired their carbines, then used them as clubs. Cpl. Clinton Greaves fought like a man possessed of a demon; he alone opened up a hole in the Apaches' formation. Greaves' actions made it possible for the other troopers and scouts to escape certain death. After the troopers were clear of the immediate danger, the Apaches broke off the fight and fled. The Apaches lost five of their warriors while the troopers only suffered superficial wounds. After the Apaches ran the troopers captured eleven Indian ponies. Cpl. Clinton Greaves won the Medal of Honor for his action during this engagement.

Capt. Charles D. Beyer, Lt. Henry H. Wright with thirty-one men of Company C, along with a detachment of fifteen men of Company I from Fort Wingate, two Navajo scouts, and a volunteer guide named John R. Foster left Fort Bayard on May 25, 1879, near Silver City, riding north into the mountains searching for Victorio. On May 29 after cresting the summit of the Mimbres Mountains, Beyer and his troopers found Victorio. On a nearby summit the Apaches had built a defensive position out of brush and rocks. Victorio stood on a ledge and waved a white flag indicating that he wanted to talk. Beyer refused to go into Victorio's camp unarmed to parley. Beyer suggested to Victorio that they meet halfway, which Victorio refused. Victorio became visibly upset and in Apache launched into a tirade to the effect that he and his people were poor, that they didn't want to fight the soldiers, and all they wanted was to be left alone.

In response, Beyer sent Sgt. Delaware Penn and some men from Company I forward and to the right to outflank the hostiles. Victorio positioned his women and children in a more secure location. Victorio then waved a lance over his head and took down his flag of truce. Captain Beyer gave the order for his men to advance. The battle began. Sergeant Penn and his men were able to get behind the Apaches and force them to retreat from their position. After a thirty minute gun fight the Apaches gave up their positions and fled. The troopers captured the Apaches' supplies and burned their camp. Of the casualties one trooper of the 9th was killed, Pvt. Frank Dorsey of C Troop, and two wounded, Pvts. George H. Moore of C Troop and John Scott of I Troop. One was singled out for gallantry, Sgt. Thomas Boyne.

Boyne had an interesting background. He was originally a native of Prince George's County, Maryland. During the Civil War Boyne was mustered into Battery B of the 2nd Colored Light Artillery in 1864. He took part in critical battles around Richmond, Wilson's Wharf, and City Point, Virginia, in May and June 1864. At the conclusion of the war Boyne and his unit were sent to Texas. He was discharged at Brownsville in March 1866. Ten months later Boyne enlisted in the 40th Infantry Regiment which was consolidated into the 25th Infantry Regiment (black) where he served until 1875. At that time Boyne transferred to the 9th Cavalry Regiment.

In September 1879 Sergeant Boyne, with Lt. Henry Wright and a small detachment, was escorting a wounded soldier to Fort Stanton. While riding beside the Cuchillo Negro Creek they were attacked by Apaches. The troopers were caught totally by surprise; victory appeared to be at hand for the Indians. Lieutenant Wright's horse was shot and fell dead. The Apaches moved in quickly on Wright. Suddenly Sergeant Boyne and a few troopers flanked the attacking party and charged with such ferocity and precision of riding and shooting that the Apaches were driven off. Congress presented Sergeant Boyne the Medal of Honor. The inscription stated: "The Congress to Sergeant Thomas Boyne, Troop C, 9th Cavalry, for bravery in action at Mimbres Mountain, N.M., May 29, 1879 and at Cuchillo Negro, N.M., September 27, 1879." Boyne received his medal on January 6, 1882, and stayed in the army until 1889. He lived his last days at the U.S. Soldiers Home where he died on April 21, 1896.

On September 18, 1879, a column led by Lt. Col. N.A.M. Dudley, consisting of Troop B, led by Lt. Byron Dawson, and Troop E, led by Capt. Ambrose E. Hooker found Victorio and his band in a canyon at the headwaters of Las Animas Creek. Victorio had about 150 warriors firmly entrenched in the canyon walls. Dudley's command was caught in a withering crossfire from the Apache rifles. Not far away were Troops C and G led by Captain Beyer and Lt. William H. Hugo. Hearing the gunfire, they came to assist Dudley. Even with superior numbers, the four troops were unable to dislodge the Apaches.

Dudley decided to pull back under the cover of darkness. Pvt. A. Freeland of B Troop was wounded and pinned down about 400 yards from Captain Beyer's position. As Freeland was trying to crawl to his comrades, Sgt. John Denny dashed through a hail of bullets. When he reached Freeland, Denny put the wounded man on his back, then raced to the safety of the rocks. Lieutenant Day said, "The act was one of most conspicuous gallantry, and one deserving of a Certificate of Merit, more than simply a Medal of Honor." The Certificate of Merit, unlike the Medal of Honor, held monetary value as well (a soldier received $1 more a month).

In this particular engagement the U.S. Army lost five troopers, three Indian scouts, and thirty-two horses. Lt. Matthias Day and Sgt. John Denny both received the Medal of Honor for their actions during the Battle of Las Animas.

Dudley was relieved of command of southern New Mexico Territory after this battle.

Denny finally received the actual medal fifteen years later in 1895 while stationed at Fort Robinson, Nebraska. He spent thirty years in the army, five years early on with the 10th Cavalry and the balance with the 9th. Denny lived his last days at the U.S. Soldiers Home in Washington, D.C., where he died on November 28, 1901.

On May 11, 1880, Sgt. George Jordon, Troop K, with a detachment of twenty-five men, was ordered to the abandoned Old Fort Tularosa to protect the adjacent town of Tularosa. Troop K had been stationed at the Barlow and Sanderson stagecoach station. It was learned that Victorio and his warriors might attack the town. Jordon and the troopers rode all night to reach Tularosa and were thoroughly exhausted upon arrival. They found out that a few hostile Apaches had come through before they got there and killed an old man in a cornfield. After resting, the troopers built a stockade the next day and moved all the townspeople inside for protection.

On May 14 Victorio attacked Tularosa with more than one hundred warriors. During the initial attack, according to Jordon, the Apaches fired at least one hundred shots before they could gain the shelter of the stockade. All the civilians and soldiers made it to safety, except the troopers serving as teamsters, two who were herding the mules, and about 500 head of cattle.

Victorio's warriors made repeated attacks, but were repulsed numerous times by the small detachment of troopers. Realizing the futility of attacking the stockade, the Apaches turned their attention to the stock herd. Jordon, keenly aware of what was going on, sent ten men to assist the cowboys. Traveling by cover of the nearby timber, the troopers made their way to the cowboys and drove the Apaches away, saving the men and stock. The Indians were surprised by the troopers' presence. The Apaches broke off the engagement and left as swiftly as they had arrived. Jordon felt the Apaches left because they thought there were more soldiers in the vicinity. The townspeople thanked the black troopers for saving their hamlet. The remainder of the 9th Regiment arrived the next day.

Next year Sergeant Jordon was in an engagement known

as the Battle of Carrizo Canyon. It began in July of 1881 when Apache Chief Nana led fifteen warriors north across the Rio Grande into New Mexico Territory. At this time Nana was seventy years old. He was later joined by twenty-two Mescalero Apaches who jumped the reservation to join him on his raids against settlements and ranches.

The 9th Cavalry clashed with Nana twelve times between July 17 and August 19. On August 12 there was a fierce fight between nineteen men in Troop K, under the leadership of Lt. Charles Parker and Nana's band. This engagement took place in Carrizo Canyon, twenty-five miles west of Sabinal. The troopers were outnumbered more than two to one. Even so Parker ordered an attack and the fight lasted for an hour-and-a-half. Parker and his men chased the Apaches into the canyon where they stopped and made a stand. The troopers dismounted and opened fire on the Apaches who were only one hundred yards away. Acting first sergeant with the unit was Sgt. Thomas Shaw with Sergeant Jordon commanding the right flank. Sergeant Shaw took the front of the command to blunt any attacks from that position. Shaw was known as a sharpshooter. Jordon on the right flank was responsible for keeping the command from being encircled. In the fight, two troopers were killed, Pvts. Guy Temple and Charles Perry; three others were wounded; and nine army horses killed. The Apaches lost five warriors and an unknown number of wounded. For his bravery in this battle Sergeant Jordon won the Certificate of Merit; he had earlier won the Medal of Honor for his actions at the Battle of Tularosa. Sergeant Shaw received the Medal of Honor for his actions at the Battle of Carrizo Canyon. They didn't receive their citations officially until December 1890.

On August 16 Troop I, 9th Cavalry, under the command of Civil War veteran 1st Lt. Gustavus Valois of Prussian ancestry, was camped at Canada Alamosa, New Mexico Territory. With Valois was 2nd Lt. George R. Burnett, fresh out of West Point. The troop was resting up after just getting back from a long patrol. About 10:00 a.m. a Mexican rancher came riding frantically into town screaming that the Apaches had murdered his wife and three children. This heaved the town into a total panic

Standing left to right are Sergeant James Wilson, First Sergeant David Badie, Sergeant Thomas Shaw and Sergeant Nathan Fletcher. Seated left to right are Chief Trumpeter Stephen Taylor, Sergeant Edward McKenzie, Sergeant Robert Burley and Sergeant Zekiel Sykes. Noncommissioned officers, 9th Cavalry, Fort Robinson, Nebraska, 1889.

(Courtesy Old Courthouse, St. Louis, National Historic Site) with people praying for God to save them from imminent doom and destruction.

When Lieutenant Valois gave the order to saddle up, it was done in an incredibly brief time. The troopers rode out to the ranch and found the wife and children mutilated. Lieutenant Burnett took a detachment in the direction of the trail left by Nana and his warriors. Accompanying Burnett was 1st Sgt. Moses Williams of Lake Providence, Louisiana. Williams was an eleven year veteran of the Indian Wars. The trail led to the Cuchillo Negro Mountains. Naturally the Apaches had taken up strong defensive positions in the mountains. Lieutenant Burnett had been joined at the Mexican ranch by some Mexican vaqueros. This contingent brought his strength up to about fifty men. The Apaches numbered between eighty and one hundred men. Many of the Apaches wore sombreros and carried blankets on their shoulders like Mexicans as a subterfuge, but the troopers were able to identify the hostiles.

On locating the Apaches, Lieutenant Burnett created a right flank under Sergeant Williams, a left flank under one of the Mexicans, and he took the center. It was a running fight until Burnett ordered his command to dismount due to the heavy gunfire in the canyon. They tried to outflank the Apaches, but were not successful. The Apaches were fighting hard because their plundered livestock and supplies were in the canyon. They fought for several hours when Burnett sent a courier to get relief from Valois, who was in the vicinity. Valois received the message and was able to reinforce Burnett, but the Apaches held firm. Valois' command during the firefight had dismounted and become trapped on a small hill. Burnett had to redeploy and charge to save Valois' command. The mounted charge was carried out in perfect military fashion, but four of Valois' troopers were cut off and out in the open.

Lieutenant Burnett sized up the situation and asked for volunteers to go to the rescue. Only two men, 1st Sgt. Moses Williams and Pvt. Augustus Walley, responded to the call. Lieutenant Burnett with the two troopers began the rescue operation by advancing on the Apache position under concealment, but firing all the while. The marksmanship caused the Apaches to pause. This delay allowed two of the trapped soldiers to run to safety. The third man was wounded; Walley went back to his horse, mounted up, rode rapidly to where the wounded man was lying, got down off the horse, put the wounded man in the saddle, mounted up behind him, and galloped to safety at the rear. All the while Apaches rained gunshots upon them. The fourth soldier appeared to be disoriented and was walking toward the Apache positions. Lieutenant Burnett, realizing the Indians were trying to isolate this trooper, ran back to his horse, mounted him, rode toward the trooper, placed himself between the soldier and the Apaches, and guided the trooper to the rear to safety. Burnett was firing his pistol constantly and miraculously was not hit, but his horse was shot twice. They fought until nightfall at which time Nana got away, although he did have to leave his stolen stock and plunder behind. Burnett, Williams, and Walley all received the Medal of Honor for their actions during this engagement.

The last incident where a 9th Cavalry trooper received a Medal of Honor in the Apache Campaign was also in action against Nana's band in New Mexico Territory.

On August 19, 1881, a fight took place in Gavilan Canyon, New Mexico Territory. What happened during the battle was later deemed by many members of the 9th Cavalry as the greatest example of courage accomplished by any of its troopers during the Indian Wars.

Lt. George W. Smith of Troop B, with twenty soldiers, left Fort Cummings on August 17 and headed north. The mission was to intercept Nana who was heading south trying to cross over into Mexico. Smith was later joined by rancher George Daly and twenty heavily armed cowboys on the Goodwin Trail between Lake Valley and Georgetown. They followed Nana's trail into Gavilan Canyon near the Mimbres River. The cowboys had the point, the troopers pulled up the rear. Smith was very cautious about riding into the canyon without first sending in scouts. The cowboys threw caution to the wind and galloped into the canyon. Smith followed, but with trepidation. The cowboys rode smack into an Apache ambush, and the warriors had the vantage point of being fortified in the canyon walls. Lieutenant Smith and Daly were killed by the oncoming Apache gunfire; more than a few cowboys were wounded. The cowboys fled the canyon pell-mell.

With their officer dead the black troopers were left to defend against the Apaches. They also lost civilian saddler James Brown and Pvts. Thomas Golding and Monroe Overstreet early in the surprise ambush. Ten of their horses were also killed.

Sizing up the situation, Sgt. Brent Woods took over the command. Under Woods' leadership the troopers fought the Apaches to an impasse. Sergeant Anderson and a detachment from Troop H came to their assistance after being in the vicinity and hearing gunfire. With reinforcements Woods ordered a charge against the Apache positions. Nana was caught off guard by the frontal attack. The black troopers fought until they reached the high ground, driving the Indians away in confusion. Nana was able to gather his dead and wounded and make an escape in the surrounding mountains. One of the white cowboys later said, "That Sergeant Woods is a son of a bitch to fight, if it had not been for him, none of us could have come out of that canyon." Lieutenant Smith's widow, years later, remarked about the black troopers in her husband's command, "a braver set of men never lived."

For some reason the proper paperwork was not done to recognize Woods' actions in Gavilan Canyon. The incident, however, was talked about so glowingly over the years that affidavits were taken from soldiers who witnessed the action. Thirteen years later, the commanding general of the army, Maj. Gen. John M. Schofield approved the Medal of Honor for Woods. He received the medal on July 12, 1894. Woods retired from the army in 1902 and moved back to his native state of Kentucky with his wife, Pearly. He died at the age of fifty-four in 1906.

After fourteen years of service on the frontiers of Texas, New Mexico, and Arizona, the headquarters of the 9th Cavalry Regiment was transferred to Fort Riley, Kansas with Troops assigned to Fort Supply, Fort Reno, and Fort Sill in the Indian Territory. For the next four years, the 9th was mainly committed to evicting white settlers and squatters known as "Boomers," who were attempting to homestead illegally in the Oklahoman Indian Territory.

In the Creek Nation of the Indian Territory there was political friction between full-blood and mixed-blood Creek Indians. The mixed-blood Creeks had political control of the

Troop H, 9th Cavalry, Fort Wingate, New Mexico Territory, 1899
(Courtesy Museum of New Mexico)

Creek Nation and were led by Chief Sam Checote. The full-bloods were led by Isparhecher (Spi-e-che). Lighthorsemen (Indian police in the Creek Nation) attempted to arrest one of Isparhecher's men near Okmulgee, Creek Nation for carrying a weapon. An argument ensued and more full-bloods got involved. Before it was over, two Creek Lighthorsemen, Sam Scott and Joe Barnett, lay dead from gunshot wounds.

After this incident many of the followers of Isparhecher, who was a candidate for chief, moved into the Sac and Fox Indian Nation, which was just west of the Creek Nation. This was done to get away from reprisals and revenge raids led by Chief Checote's men. One of Isparhecher's most ardent followers was the Black Creek freedman Dick Glass. In the Creek Nation most of the black freedmen sided with the full-bloods on political issues. The Creek mixed-blood leadership during the Civil War fought with the Confederacy, while most of the full-bloods and blacks had fought with Union forces. Glass, when not fighting in political causes, was known to be one of the most notorious out-laws in the Indian Territory. His exploits are detailed in my first book, *Black, Red, and Deadly*.

After a large contingent of armed full-bloods was seen gathering in Muskogee, the principal town of the Creek Nation, Indian Agent Tufts asked for U.S. Army soldiers to be sent from Fort Gibson. Immediately, fifteen men from the 20th Infantry Regiment (a white regiment) were sent to Muskogee. The next day, December 25, Company K, 20th Infantry was sent to Okmulgee.

In February of 1883, Creek Chief-to-be Pleasant Porter, a Creek mixed-blood leader of African-Indian-European ancestry and a former Confederate soldier, led a command of 550 men against the followers of Isparhecher in the Sac and Fox nation. The Sac and Fox Indian Agent Jacob V. Carter talked Porter out of attacking the full-bloods and freedmen. Porter's army returned to Okmulgee where it was disbanded.

Indian Inspector Pollock came from Washington, D.C. to Muskogee to investigate and report on the situation in the Creek Nation. One of the full-blood leaders, Sleeping Rabbit, with a party of forty Creeks, came over from Greenleaf Creek in the Cherokee Nation to confer with Pollock about their situation.

On February 23 Porter, who had been made a general by Checote, arrested Sleeping Rabbit and twenty-five of his followers. They were herded into the Patterson Mercantile Company's yard in downtown Muskogee. Sleeping Rabbit was taken to the Creek Council House in Okmulgee where he was killed under the pretense he was trying to escape.

Isparhecher decided to negotiate with the reservation Indians in the western portion of the Indian Territory, and he spoke with the Comanche, Kiowa, Arapaho, and Cheyenne. He thought he might be able to get some allies to fight Checote. While Isparhecher was visiting Asahabit and the Comanche leaders at the Wichita Indian Agency, an army detachment led by Lieutenant Lowe from Fort Gibson located him. Accompanying Isparhecher were 500 men, women, and children in a caravan of forty-two wagons; their horses for the most part were worn out.

On March 20 presidential orders were given to arrest Isparhecher and his band. The lead officer was Maj. J. C. Bates of the 20th Infantry of Fort Gibson. Bates found Isparhecher and his band camped six to fifteen miles west of Anadarko.

The Creek leader agreed to go back to the Creek Nation under military escort. But the Creeks later balked at going back, even after being given a delay by the General of the Army. Major Bates asked for assistance from the commanding officers at Fort Reno and Fort Sill. Both commanders sent two troops of cavalry. Capt. Henry Carroll was in charge of four troops of the 9th Cavalry Regiment who rode to the Wichita Agency to assist Major Bates.

On April 21, 1883, the ten day delay for the Creeks expired. Captain Carroll and his four troops of 9th Cavalry broke camp to locate Isparhecher and his band. Carroll located the camps on April 23 early before daybreak, but found no men. After daylight Carroll located the Creek men about a mile and-a-half beyond, drawn up in battle formation. Major Bates asked for their surrender which they refused.

The Creeks, about 200 in number, were on a high ridge on the other side of a small stream from the troopers' position. Two of the troops remained in front of the Indians, while two troops gained the ridge about 800 yards higher up at a better crossing and more gradual ascent. As they advanced along the ridge, the remaining black troops dismounted and moved across and up on the ridge. Major Bates ordered no firing until the Creeks fired a shot; no shot was fired. As they got within one hundred yards of the insurgents, an order was given to charge. The Creeks broke and ran except for a few who were captured. The black troopers immediately mounted up and went after the Creeks. After a ten mile chase, Isparhecher and sixty of his men were captured and taken prisoner.

The infantry had taken control of the Creek camps. Major Bates spent the next several days collecting the scattered Creeks in the area using soldiers from the 20th Infantry and 9th Cavalry Regiments under his command.

On April 28 Major Bates started back to the Creek Nation with Isparhecher and his band in tow. The black troopers from Fort Sill and Fort Reno were sent back except a detachment of twenty-five troopers from the 9th under the command of Lieutenant Taylor, who accompanied Major Bates and his infantrymen to Fort Gibson. They marched into Fort Gibson with 484 Creek prisoners: men, women, and children. Checote's men taunted them at a distance as they moved through Muskogee on to nearby Fort Gibson.

Gen. Philip Sheridan, from his headquarters in Chicago, sent General Forsyth to Muskogee to make an investigation on the civil unrest in the Creek Nation. General Forsyth, after several days, reported that he and his staff were convinced Isparhecher had been badly treated by Chief Checote and his government. They felt that the full-blood Creeks should be allowed to return to their homes so they could sow their crops. Because of threatened reprisals by Checote, however, they would require protection to insure their safety.

As part of the protection for the full-blood Creeks, a troop of black cavalry was sent from Fort Sill during the summer of 1883. The Checote government complained about black soldiers being stationed in the Creek Nation. Shortly thereafter, things cooled down, and eventually the black troopers were sent back to Fort Sill. This incident, known as the Green Peach War because the peaches were green in the Creek Nation when the insurgency began, was one of many incidents where black soldiers were used to quell civil unrest on the frontier.

In June of 1885 the 9th Cavalry Regiment was sent to the Department of the Platte, on the northern Great Plains. They were stationed at Fort Niobrara and Fort Robinson in Nebraska and Fort Du Chesne in Utah. Now the 9th spent much of their time protecting railroad work crews from outlaws and hostile Indians.

The 9th in 1890 were called on to assist with subduing the Lakota Sioux at the Pine Ridge Reservation in the Dakotas. The Indian agent at the reservation, Dr. D. F. Royer, became nervous and scared when the Lakota began the "Ghost Dance" to return their powers and buffalo. In November at least one-half of the U.S. Army was concentrated on or near the reservations. The 9th was involved in several actions, but did not participate in the massacre at Wounded Knee where 146 men, women, and children were slaughtered on December 29.

In 1891 Troop K of the 9th Cavalry was sent to Fort Myer, Virginia, to be posted to Washington, D.C., as a reward for their service in the West. These black troopers took part in burials, escorts, and presidential parades. While in Washington, D.C., the 9th Cavalry detachment became known for their fine horsemanship. They returned to Fort Robinson in 1894.

The 9th Cavalry was called to fight in Cuba in 1898, in what was known as the Spanish-American War. The regiment, *en masse*, traveled by train from Fort Robinson, Nebraska, to Tampa, Florida. They embarked on June 8, 1898, for Siboney and Daiquri, Cuba. The 9th, like all the cavalry regiments sent to Cuba, fought as dismounted infantry. The black troopers of the 9th served alongside the white westerners known as the Rough Riders, who were commanded by Lt. Col. Teddy Roosevelt. They were there in the thick of the battles at Santiago and San Juan Hill.

At the end of the Spanish-American War, the 9th Cavalry Regiment was sent to the Philippines, a former colony of Spain. The people of the Philippines didn't feel they should be a colony of the United States after being a colony of Spain. They wanted their freedom. But it would have to wait. The 9th was successful in several military campaigns against the Moros.

During the Philippine Insurrection several troops of the 9th Cavalry Regiment were stationed at the military fort in San

9th Cavalry Band, marching in the Memorial Day Parade, Santa Fe, New Mexico Territory, 1880
(Courtesy U.S. Army Military History Institute)

9th Cavalry, Fort DuChesne, Utah, 1896
(Courtesy U. S. Army Military History Institute)

Francisco, California, known as The Presidio. The black troopers had a lengthy stay at this important military base. The Presidio was a strategic spot because it guarded San Francisco Harbor and was a major shipping facility for the U.S. on the West Coast.

All four black military regiments passed through the gates of the Presidio during the turn of the century. Some were sent to the Philippines or other western posts or forts. The 9th Cavalry was the first black unit assigned to the Presidio and was regularly given duty assignments at this important post. There are 455 African American soldiers buried at the San Francisco National Cemetery, located in the heart of the Presidio.

At the turn of the century the 9th's service was over on the western frontier, but they maintained a presence in the west, guarding the borders of the U.S. In addition, the following duties were performed:

1903   9th escorted President Theodore Roosevelt as his Honor Guard on an official visit to the Presidio in San Francisco. It was the first time any regular black troops had been named the Honor Guard for a U.S. president.

1903   9th assigned to patrol the national parks in California, which included Sequoia, General Grant, and Yosemite. Capt. Charles Young, the third black West Point Military Academy graduate stationed at the Presidio with the 9th, named Acting Superintendent of Sequoia National Park during the summer of 1903. The U.S. Army patrolled the national parks until 1918 when the National Park Service was created.

1907   Black troopers of the 9th were assigned to the Military Academy at West Point to teach cadets riding, mounted drill methods, and concepts. This instruction took place on an area now known as Buffalo Soldier Field.

1916   9th Regiment units were sent to the Philippines for

another five-year tour of duty. During that year some troops of the regiment were involved in the Punitive Expedition in Mexico led by General John J. Pershing. This was an attempt to locate the Mexican revolutionary Pancho Villa. The expedition was not militarily successful. The 9th took part in the last "cavalry charge"—along with the 7th Cavalry Regiment—of what was known as the "modern era." After this period the 9th Cavalry was assigned to patrolling the Mexican border.

The era of the "Wild West" was over, and the 9th had done as much as any U.S. military unit in taming that part of our country.

9th Cavalry troopers after returning from Cuba, Camp Wikoff, Montauk Point, Long Island, New York, September 1898
(Courtesy U.S. Army Military History Institute)

Troop E, 9th Cavalry at the Presidio, San Francisco, California, en route to the Philippines, 1900
(Courtesy U.S. Army Military History Institute)

CHAPTER TWENTY-THREE

10th U.S. Cavalry

General of the Army John J. Pershing made the following comments concerning the 10th U.S. Cavalry Regiment:

> The record of the phenomenal growth and expansion of our country is resplendent with the contributory and glorious achievements of its Army. From the pioneer days when our forefathers carved their way into the wilds and dangers of the west to the present, the Army has played a most important part in shaping the destiny of this country. It has been an honor, which I am proud to claim, to have been at one time a member of that intrepid organization of the Army which has always added glory to the military history of America—The 10th Cavalry.
>
> Several years of my early military life were spent with that organization, and as I look back I can but feel that the associations with the splendid officers and men of the 10th Cavalry were of the greatest value to me ...

General Pershing was nicknamed "Black Jack" for his fondness of the troopers of the 10th.

The Tenth U.S. Cavalry initially saw service in Kansas. The 1st Troop and the 2nd Troop were detailed to the Kansas Pacific Railroad in 1867. The black troopers did guard duty of railroad property and protected the work crews. On August 6, 1867, the 10th's regimental headquarters were moved to Fort Riley, Kansas from Fort Leavenworth. Detachments of the 10th were posted also at Fort Hays, Fort Harker, Fort Larned, and smaller posts along Smokey Hill River in Kansas.

Troopers of the 10th first came under attack by hostile Indians on August 2, 1867, about forty miles northeast of Fort Hays, near the Saline River. Three hundred Cheyennes attacked Troop F, which was patrolling the Kansas Pacific Railroad. The strength of the troop was two officers and thirty-four horse soldiers. The engagement lasted six long hours. Troop F was forced to retreat, but inflicted heavy casualties on the Indian warriors. For the 10th, troop leader Capt. G. A. Armes was wounded and Sgt. William Christy was killed.

Christy was the first combat casualty for the 10th in the Indian Wars. This engagement came about because Troop F had trailed the Cheyennes who had killed seven railroad workers at Campbell's Camp, Kansas, on August 1. During the summer of 1867 three troops of the 10th U.S. Cavalry were assigned to the Indian Territory. These were Troops D, E, and L; they were located at Fort Gibson and Fort Arbuckle.

Nineteen days after his wounding, Captain Armes with Troop F was back in pursuit of hostile Cheyennes. They were accompanied by two companies of the 18th Kansas Cavalry, a volunteer unit, under the command of Capt. George Jenness. The volunteers numbered about ninety men. Troop F, 10th Cavalry was about forty men. Captain Armes was in charge of the two commands. They left Fort Hays and traveled in the direction of the Solomon River where the Cheyenne were reported to be located. After scouting the Solomon River during the night with no results, the soldiers encamped for the evening. The next day they set out for Beaver Creek. Armes and his troopers were a short distance ahead of Jenness and his volunteers. Both groups were attacked by surprise via a large war party of Cheyenne Indians. The units were forced to take up defensive positions and by the next day were able to link up forces, but were incessantly besieged by the much larger Indian war party. The Cheyenne commanded the hills and nearby ridges and taunted the soldiers to come out and fight.

Captain Armes decided to do just that. Troop F charged the Cheyenne warriors and drove them back, but they continued to fight. When the sun went down, the Cheyenne departed. Captain Armes took his command back to Fort Hays. Troop F had one man killed in action and thirteen wounded. Captain Jenness had two dead and sixteen wounded. Captain Armes reported that fifty Cheyenne had been killed and 150 wounded. The Cheyenne war party was estimated to be 1,000 warriors strong. The black troopers had represented themselves well in battle.

At this time, according to regimental returns, the black troopers were not called "Buffalo Soldiers" but "Wild Buffaloes," by the Cheyenne. Later, such writers as Frederic Remington changed it to "Buffalo Soldiers," the popular term used today for black troops of the western frontier.

On September 15, 1867, a railroad camp west of Fort Hays was attacked by seventy Cheyenne warriors. Two railroad men and a trooper, Pvt. John Randall, were near camp, hunting game, when they were attacked by the large war party. Both of the railroad workers were killed, and Randall was severely wounded. Before the Cheyenne could attack the camp, Sergeant Ed Davis and his small detachment of nine soldiers of Troop G, 10th Regiment, led a rifle assault on foot against the Indians. The detachment had been assigned to protect the railroad camp.

The Cheyenne were shook by the deadly carbine fire and broke off their attack. Sergeant Davis ordered his men to mount up and look for the three hunters. Before they located them, the Cheyenne attacked again, and the black troopers killed or wounded thirteen of the Indians. With such loss of life, the Cheyenne retreated for the day. The troopers located the dead hunters. Randall was found badly wounded in a depression near the railroad tracks; they were able to locate him by his cries for help.

During the summer of 1867, Troops D, E, and L were assigned to Fort Arbuckle in the Indian Territory. Their main goal was to rebuild Fort Arbuckle and keep an eye out for boot-leggers, livestock, thieves, and bandits. Many mail carriers had been murdered trying to deliver the mail between Fort Arbuckle and Fort Gibson; white men refused the job. Armed Indian scout detachments were used to ferry the mail, then the Buffalo Soldiers took up the task. In November 1867 Capt. Henry Alford and Troop M, 10th Cavalry set up residence at Fort Gibson, Indian Territory. Near Fort Arbuckle there had been serious problems with Kiowa and Comanche raiding the horse and cattle herds of the Chickasaw and Choctaw, two members of the Five Civilized Tribes, as they were called in the Indian Territory. During 1867 and 1868 the 10th spent much of its time in Kansas and Indian Territory scouting, guarding mail, and protecting wagon trains.

In the summer of 1868 the Cheyenne Dog Soldiers were causing big problems with white settlers in west Kansas and southern Colorado. In September Capt. G. W. Graham and thir-ty-six soldiers of Troop I, 10th Cavalry picked up the trail of a large party of hostile Indians on the Denver Road. They located the Cheyenne Dog Soldiers at Big Sandy Creek, numbering more than one hundred. An intense battle took place and was hard fought. At sundown the fighting ceased. The Cheyenne Dog Soldiers' losses were eleven killed and fourteen wounded. The Buffalo Soldiers had one wounded and eighteen horses killed or missing. The 10th was beginning to make a name for itself on the Plains as a first-rate military unit.

In October 1868 Capt. L. H. Carpenter and Troops H and I, 10th Cavalry rode 230 miles in nine days on a mission out of Fort Wallace. They killed ten Cheyenne in battle and wounded many more. The Buffalo Soldiers suffered three men wounded. Gen. Phillip Sheridan recommended Captain Carpenter for the Medal of Honor and personally commended Troops H and I of the 10th. During the march to escort Maj. Gen. Eugene A. Carr to the 5th Cavalry stationed at Fort Harker, Kansas, the black troopers had to fight off 500 Cheyenne warriors at Beaver Creek. Carpenter deployed his wagons in a horse-shoe forma-tion and used them as parapets to good advantage.

In January 1869 Captain Byrne, in command of twenty-five men of Troop C, 10th Cavalry left Fort Dodge, Kansas, in pursuit of Indian horse raiders. On January 29 they located the Pawnees with the stolen horses. A battle ensued, and the Pawnee suffered seven killed and one wounded. The black troopers had two men wounded in the battle. The stolen horses were recovered.

Fort Cobb in the Indian Territory was set up by the government as a sanctuary for Cheyenne, and Arapahos who wanted peace. Troops D, L, and M of the 10th were sent there to protect them.

The headquarters of the 10th Cavalry was transferred in April of 1869 from Fort Riley, Kansas, to Camp Wichita in the Indian Territory. While stationed in Colorado, one of the scouts who served with the 10th at Fort Lyon was the famous gunman "Wild Bill" Hickock.

Camp Wichita would soon be renamed Fort Sill for one of General Sheridan's fellow officers who had been killed in action during the Civil War. Fort Sill was located near the junction of Medicine Bluff Creek, Cache Creek, and close by the Wichita Mountains.

The black cavalry troopers built the fort from the ground up. An old sawmill was secured from Fort Arbuckle which was used for cutting lumber from trees taken from the Wichita Mountains. The black soldiers not only had to cut wood, they burned lime, laid stone, squared logs with broadaxes, and dressed lumber. The fort was built to hold ten troops of cavalry and included barracks, stables, storehouses, and officers' quarters. Much of the original fort is used today as a museum for the present-day post near Lawton, Oklahoma. Fort Arbuckle was closed after Fort Sill became operational.

All of the troops of the 10th Cavalry consolidated at Fort Sill. This included the three troops that had been stationed at Fort Arbuckle and the one troop at Fort Gibson, Indian Territory.

While at Fort Sill Colonel Grierson put a lot of attention into the regimental band. A big inspiration for the 10th was that Colonel Grierson was an accomplished musician. The 10th's band was not organized from musicians, but soldiers who could read and write and were then taught to play music. Grierson found a band leader in Chief Trumpeter James H. Thomas who performed with the band for thirty years. The other black regiments—the 9th Cavalry, 24th Infantry, and 25th Infantry—also had good regimental bands. Sometimes these African-American military bands were the main source of entertainment for isolated posts and towns on the western frontier. The 9th's band built a reputation performing for ceremonial functions in the territorial capital of Santa Fe, New Mexico Territory, during the 1870s. In 1880 they performed for U.S. President Rutherford B. Hayes, the man who ended Reconstruction, on his visit to Santa Fe.

Towana Spivey, the present-day post historian at Fort Sill, Oklahoma, told me that the old fort had a long and glorious history with all four black frontier regiments. He believes that Fort Sill today should be considered the historical home of the Buffalo Soldier. The first African-American graduate of the U.S. Military Academy at West Point, Henry Flipper served his first assignment on the frontier at Fort Sill with the 10th Cavalry. When he arrived at the post there was a severe problem with malaria caused by mosquitos. The problem stemmed from a swampy area in the fort that wouldn't drain. Flipper, also a student of engineering, designed a drainage system where the water ran uphill! The ditch was made from stones acquired from the surrounding hills. Today, Flipper's Ditch is one of the tourist attractions at Fort Sill.

In June 1872 Colonel Grierson moved the command headquarters to Fort Gibson, Indian Territory, until January 5, 1873. Grierson had been given a temporary duty assignment in the East. Lt. Col. John Davidson took over command at Fort Gibson from February 24, 1873, to April 20, 1873. Davidson moved the command headquarters back to Fort Sill. Detachments of the 10th at this time were stationed at Fort Dodge in Kansas, Forts Gibson and Arbuckle, Camp Supply, and the Cheyenne Agency in the Indian Territory.

In August of 1874 there were problems at the Wichita Agency at Anadarko, Indian Territory. On August 21 Col. John "Black Jack" Davidson was sitting on his veranda at Fort Sill, enjoying a cool drink in the shade on a warm day. An orderly rode up on a lathered, tired horse stumbling from a hard ride. He brought a dispatch from Capt. Gaines Lawson, 25th Infantry, commander of a company stationed on guard duty at the Wichita Agency. Lawson wrote in the message that a hostile band of Noconi Comanche had come in and were camped at the agency

Lieutenant Henry O. Flipper, 10th U.S. Cavalry, first African-American graduate of West Point, United States Army Military Academy
(Courtesy Fort Davis National Historic Site)

Company A, 25th Infantry, Fort Snelling, Minnesota, 1883
(Courtesy Fort Davis National Historic Site)

under the leadership of Chief Red Food. Lawson indicated that there was going to be trouble. The next day, Saturday, August 22, would be ration day at the Wichita Agency for the Indians. The Penateka Comanche, Wichitas, Caddoes, and Delawares were camped at the agency for their rations.

Besides Red Food's Noconis, there were Kiowa under the leadership of Lone Wolf who were not supposed to be at the agency. They were there looking to take rations from the more peaceful Indians. Colonel Davidson left Fort Sill at 10:00 p.m. with four troops of the 10th Cavalry headed for Anadarko, thirty-seven miles north of the fort. The military units in the command included Troops C, E, H, and L under Capts. Charles Viele, George T. Robinson, Louis H. Carpenter, and Little respectively.

When Colonel Davidson arrived at the Anadarko Agency near noon on Saturday he had Chief Red Food summoned. Davidson informed Red Food he must give up his weapons and surrender his followers as prisoners of war. Red Food resisted. A skirmish soon ensued between the Buffalo Soldiers and the Kiowas and Comanches sympathetic to Red Food's plight.

The infantry under Lawson cleared the field of battle in about ten minutes, but there was continued sniping from the surrounding hills. Hostile Indians were intermingled with friendly Indians in the various camps. The infantry moved toward the agency sawmill to try to prevent hostiles from escaping down the bank of the Washita River.

Davidson had his command of cavalry dismount as they were being attacked from the rear. Indians were now firing at them from the commissary and corral. But Captain Little, with Troop L, drove the Kiowas out of the commissary and corral. The hostile Indians next headed for the nearby farm of the Delaware Chief Black Beaver. Captain Carpenter had Troop H mounted in pursuit of this group, but couldn't prevent the deaths of four white civilians who had been cutting hay and did not hear the shooting. Two other white civilian workers were killed near Black Beaver's farm. Before any more damage could be done, Carpenter and Troop H routed this group of Kiowa. The hostile Indians looted the agency store owned by a man named Shirley. Davidson regrouped his command to secure the agency perimeters, although they still received sniper fire. Captain Viele and Troop C, riding hard, cleared the hills and bluffs overlooking the agency as the sun began to set behind the hills.

That night Davidson solidified his position by posting guards at Shirley's store, the commissary, and the agency cornfield. Six of the black troopers were detailed to burn Red Food's camp; this amounted to burning several tons of needed supplies, food, and weapons.

The next morning about 300 hostile Indians had amassed to retake the bluffs. On their charge up the hills, they were met by Troops E, H, and L led by Captain Carpenter who turned them around and held the bluffs.

The Comanche tried to start a grass fire in hopes of burning the agency down. The Buffalo Soldiers started counterfires that saved all the agency buildings. Now completely thwarted, the Comanches retreated. This incident became known as the "Battle of Anadarko." The Noconi Comanche lost all their property and were now scattered over the Plains. Davidson, in his official report, stated that fourteen Comanches had been shot off their horses while the army command only had four troopers and six horses wounded. This battle was part of the larger campaign known as the "Red River War."

The "Red River War" was considered a major military success. Total U.S. army troop strength was 3,000 soldiers in five columns, including the 10th Cavalry under Colonel Davidson's command. A large number of Plains Indians voluntarily surrendered to the reservation agencies. The U.S. army captured more than 400 Indian hostiles and 3,000 of their livestock and ponies.

The 10th Cavalry moved their regimental headquarters to Fort Concho, Texas, in March of 1875. Troops B and E were posted at Fort Griffin, Texas; Troops C and K at Fort McKavett, Texas; Troop H at Fort Davis, Texas; Troop M at Fort Stockton, Texas; and Troops A, D, F, G, I, and L at Fort Concho. They were spread out over the expanse of West Texas. The army brass felt the situation was quiet enough in Indian Territory for the crack 10th to move to where things were a little more unsettled on the southwest frontier. The main assignment for the 10th was to guard the Chisholm Trail in Texas which was continuously harassed by outlaws and hostile Indians. Davidson's plan was to keep two troops of cavalry in the saddle, busily guarding the cattle trail, north and south, for 300 miles.

Colonel Grierson resumed command of the 10th on April 30, 1875. The 10th was headquartered at Fort Concho for seven long years. They fought hostile Indians, Mexican bandits, and white outlaws. They made numerous forays into Mexico against Lipan and Kickapoo raiders.

In the spring of 1876 U.S. troops had been given permission to cross the Mexican border to pursue thieves and bandits. A large amount of cattle and horses had been stolen in Texas by the Kickapoo and Lipan, then transported south into Mexico.

Col. William R. Shafter was instructed by Gen. E.O.C. Ord to take a strike force deep into Mexico to attack a hostile Indian camp near Zaragoza, Mexico in July of 1876. Shafter's force included Troops B, E, and K, 10th Cavalry. Lieutenant Bullis led a contingent of Seminole Negro Scouts and detachments of the 24th and 25th mounted Infantry on this mission.

The Mexican government didn't approve of this incursion into their country. Shafter was concerned that the Mexican army would block his exit back across the Rio Grande. Shafter's main group of black soldiers encamped and took up defensive positions in case the Mexican army attacked them. Shafter sent Lt. George Evans, 10th Cavalry with twenty handpicked troopers to assist Lieutenant Bullis and his Seminole Negro Scouts in locating the hostile camp.

Evans and Bullis in twenty-five straight hours had traveled 110 miles and located the hostile village of twenty-three lodges, five miles from Zaragoza. As the sun rose on July 30, 1876, the troopers from the 10th charged the village. The fighting was intense: at close quarters, hand to hand, and carbines were used as clubs. The black troopers killed fourteen of the warriors and put the rest to flight. They captured ninety stolen horses. The cavalry suffered only three wounded. They quickly burned down the village and went back to Shafter's position due to movement of Mexican troops in the vicinity. After rejoining Shafter, the total command moved north and crossed the Rio Grande into the safety of U.S. soil. The only casualty was Joseph Titus of Troop B, who drowned in the river crossing.

On August 4, Capt. T. C. Lebo with Troops B, E, and K, 10th

Cavalry, crossed the Rio Grande riding for the Santa Rosa Mountains. After eight days Lebo found a Kickapoo village on August 12, 1876. The Buffalo Soldiers destroyed the hamlet of ten lodges and captured sixty stolen horses.

For the remainder of the year, Grierson and the 10th Cavalry were all over West Texas, constantly seeking and hunting renegades and desperadoes. The regiment didn't get a rest until December. In 1877 during the time the 10th Cavalry was stationed in West Texas they had only eighteen desertions—the white 4th Cavalry had 184.

For the remainder of the 1870s, it would be Grierson's policy to keep as many men as possible in the field at all times. This was done because West Texas was such a huge expanse of land, and soldiers had to patrol the entire area. It was truly a thankless job, but well appreciated by the white settlers in that part of the Texas frontier.

The next dangerous adversary for the 10th Cavalry was the famous Apache Chief Victorio, second only to Geronimo in notoriety on the southwest frontier. At the heart of the matter was the fact that Victorio was upset about a treaty broken by white hunters going into the Fort Stanton Reservation in New Mexico Territory. Plus, the U.S. government wanted Victorio to take his people to the hated San Carlos Reservation in Arizona Territory.

Grierson protested to top commander Gen. Phil Sheridan that the 10th Cavalry should not be moved into the New Mexico Territory from Texas. Grierson understood that Victorio and his band would try to find a safe haven in West Texas from the Mexican troops and U.S. forces in New Mexico Territory.

Indian scouts picked up a trail sign that Victorio was doing just what Grierson had forewarned. Therefore, Sheridan allowed him to keep his command in West Texas. The 10th would be involved in some of the fiercest clashes between the cavalry and Victorio and his warriors.

Grierson, a top military strategist and a hero of the Civil War, devised a plan to counter the guerrilla hit-and-run tactics of the Warm Springs Apaches. Grierson noticed the troopers were being worn down by trying to pursue the elusive Apaches. He decided to post his soldiers at key mountain passes and water holes.

In July of 1880 Victorio was being pushed northward out of Mexico into Texas by the Mexican army. Where and when Victorio would cross the border was a big concern for Grierson. The initial thought on July 29, was that Victorio would cross at Eagle Springs, Texas. Later Grierson found out from his scouts that the Apaches would come through Tinaja de las Palmas, fifteen miles west of Eagle Springs—the only watering hole in the immediate area. The colonel with his son, Robert, and seven black troopers made a camp at Tinaja de las Palmas and dug in on a ridge near the road. A stagecoach came by, and Grierson sent a message for reinforcements to come quickly from Eagle Springs. Around midnight, military messengers informed Grierson that Victorio was camped about ten miles away. Grierson became concerned about his small command confronting a larger contingent of Apaches. He sent couriers to Fort Quitman to have Troop A under Captain Nolan come immediately; time was of the essence.

Early the following morning, Lt. Leighton Finley arrived with ten men from Troop G, 10th Cavalry. They thought they were going to escort Colonel Grierson to Eagle Springs, but were ordered to take defensive positions on the ridge. Grierson sent a fast rider back to Eagle Springs to bring back every available trooper to Tinaja de las Palmas.

Victorio and his warriors rode toward the troopers at nine o'clock in the morning. Spotting the soldiers, they veered eastward to avoid conflict. They didn't know how many soldiers they faced. Grierson ordered Lt. Finley to take ten troopers and attack the Apaches in the hope of containing them until reinforcements arrived. Finley accomplished his task until ten o'clock when Captain Viele and Troop C arrived. The Apaches fought tenaciously while being pushed backward. With the arrival of Nolan's command, the Apaches broke and rode for the Rio Grande.

The fight lasted for four hours, and Pvt. Martin Davis of Troop C was killed in action. The 10th also had an officer wounded and lost ten horses in the action. Victorio had seven warriors killed in battle. The Apaches were forced back into Mexico, but Grierson felt they would make yet another attempt to enter West Texas.

On August 5, 1880, Colonel Grierson accompanied a contingent of the 10th who were trying to cut Victorio off before he could reach Rattlesnake Springs after reentering West Texas. Grierson pushed his horse soldiers from Eagle Springs to Rattlesnake Springs, a distance of sixty-five rugged miles, in twenty-one hours.

By August 6 Grierson had positioned Troops C and G in Rattlesnake Canyon to surprise Victorio on his arrival at the watering hole. Victorio and his band arrived early in the afternoon, and as they came into rifle range, the Buffalo Soldiers opened up on them. Victorio, caught off guard, pulled his warriors back immediately, out of harm's way.

Later that afternoon Grierson's supply wagons guarded by Company H, 24th Infantry, and a detachment of 10th Cavalry troopers were nearing the springs when they were attacked by Apaches. The soldiers repulsed them successfully. In the twilight Captain Carpenter and his black troopers beat back one final attempt by Victorio to gain access to the water hole. This would turn out to be Victorio's worst defeat on U.S. soil.

On August 11 a contingent of the 10th Cavalry forced Victorio and his band across the Rio Grande into Mexico for the last time. Mexican troops would shortly strike a decisive blow against the Apaches. On October 14 the Mexican army attacked Victorio, killing him and sixty of his warriors.

On the U.S. side of the border, Colonel Grierson and the 10th Cavalry killed and wounded at least thirty of Victorio's warriors and destroyed more than seventy-five of their ponies. Grierson's strategy in suppressing the Apaches had been militarily brilliant. The Buffalo Soldiers had performed admirably in their duties against the Apache.

During the summer of 1881 Troops D, E, I, and M of the 10th Cavalry were sent to the Indian Territory (Oklahoma) to assist with the expulsion of white intruders (Boomers) who were illegally living on Indian lands.

Things became a little quieter on the New Mexico-Texas border after Victorio's demise. In July 1882 the 10th headquarters was transferred from Fort Concho to Fort Davis, twenty miles north of Marfa, Texas, until 1885. With the arrival of spring in 1885, the 10th Cavalry was transferred to the Department of

Arizona. Moving west, the black troopers rode alongside the tracks of the Southern Pacific Railroad. At this time the regiment consisted of thirty-eight officers and 696 troopers. There were twelve troops of cavalry and the regimental band.

On April 11 at Bowie Station, Arizona Territory, the total regiment gathered for the first time in its history. Shortly thereafter, the soldiers were deployed to various forts and posts in Arizona Territory.

Headquarters, along with Troop B, were stationed at Whipple Barracks near Prescott; Lt. Col. James Wade with Troop A was assigned to Fort Apache; Maj. Anson Mills with Troops C, F, and G was assigned to Fort Thomas; Maj. C. B. McClellan with Troops I and M was assigned to Fort Verde; and Maj. Van Vliet had Troops D, E, H, K, and L at Fort Grant. The Department of Arizona was commanded by Gen. George Crook.

The major problem in Arizona Territory for the United States military at this time was the Chiricahua Apaches. These Apaches did not agree with the U.S. reservation policy. Life at the San Carlos and Fort Apache Reservations was unfavorable and unpleasant. Some of the Apaches relented, but many would fight to the death trying to maintain their freedom and traditions.

On May 17, 1885, medicine man Geronimo and Nachez (Naiche), son of Cochise, along with 124 Apaches left the San Carlos Reservation and headed south for Mexico. It is estimated that at least three-fourths of the Chiricahua Apaches on the reservation refused to join Geronimo.

During the military action which became known as the "Geronimo Campaign of 1885–1886," the Apache hostiles would kill thirty-nine white people in New Mexico Territory and thirty-four white people in Arizona Territory. Geronimo became known for attacking isolated ranches and mines. On some occasions, Geronimo would attack Apaches who were friendly to whites.

After the Apache breakout from the reservation, the 10th Cavalry assigned the task of looking for Geronimo in the Black Range, Mogollons, and the Chiricahua Mountains. Other military units located Geronimo in June and chased him into Mexico. General Crook stationed detachments of the 10th and other units at every watering hole along the border, and along

Troop A, 10th Cavalry, Fort Apache, Arizona Territory, 1887
(Courtesy Fort Davis National Historic Site)

John T. Glass, Chief of Scouts, Fort Apache, Arizona Territory. Formerly Trumpeter of Troop A, 10th Cavalry, 1876. Served twelve years with the 10th Cavalry then became Chief of Scouts, White Mountain Apaches, 1888. After retiring from government service, Glass and his Mexican wife made their home in Santa Fe, New Mexico. (Courtesy Arizona Historical Society)

the tracks of the Southern Pacific Railroad, to try to prevent Geronimo from re-entering the United States.

It didn't work. Geronimo slipped across the border in October 1885 and raided a large horse herd at a ranch in White Tail Canyon. Captain Viele with Troops C and G, 10th Cavalry gave pursuit. They followed the trail all the way to Ascension in Chihuahua, Mexico, where the troopers' horses gave out, and they had to give up the chase.

On April 27, 1886, Geronimo crossed the border and raided the Santa Cruz Valley. The Apaches captured the Peck Ranch. Mrs. Petra Peck and her baby were killed, and Mr. Arthur Peck and his twelve-year-old niece were captured. Mr. Peck, suffering from temporary insanity, was released by the Apaches, but they kept the girl.

Captain Lebo and Troop K, 10th Cavalry, were in the vicinity and picked up Geronimo and his band's trail. Lebo chased the Apaches for 200 miles into Mexico. On May 3, thirty miles south of the border, the Buffalo Soldiers located Geronimo and his raiders in the Pinto Mountains in Sonora. A fierce gunfight ensued with the Apaches well-concealed and shooting down on the troopers. The horse soldiers dismounted and attempted a frontal attack. Private Hollis was killed, and Corporal Scott received a bad gunshot wound. Scott was rescued by the heroic action of Lt. Powhatan H. Clarke who ran through a barrage of bullets, picked Scott up, and carried him to safety. Clarke won the Medal of Honor for his bravery.

After forcing the troopers to take a defensive position by their superior positioning, Geronimo and his band pulled out and went on the run again. Lebo and his men chased after them for four more days until they were relieved in the field by a troop from the 4th Cavalry Regiment. Nevertheless, Geronimo escaped into the mountains of Mexico.

Geronimo later surrendered to General Miles on September 3, 1886, after he was contacted by Lt. Charles B. Gatewood, 6th Cavalry and a small detachment of Apache Indian Scouts in Mexico. Gen. Nelson A. Miles had replaced General Crook in the spring of 1886, when Crook, frustrated with U.S. Army policy, asked to be relieved.

General Miles asked Washington if he could remove all the

Chiricahua Apaches, hostile and non-hostile, from the Arizona Territory to Fort Marion, Florida. The answer was in the affirmative.

Lt. Col. James Wade, 10th Cavalry, commander at Fort Apache was given the task of gathering and transporting all the Apaches to Holbrook, Arizona Territory, for their departure to the East. It would take half of the 10th Cavalry Regiment to complete the task of moving more than 400 men, women, and children to the railroad station at Holbrook.

The last Chiricahuas on the warpath in Arizona Territory were a small group under the leadership of Mangus. This renegade band included two male warriors, and eight women and children. On September 18, 1886, Capt. Charles Cooper and a detachment of Troop H, 10th Cavalry, located their trail in the White Mountains. After a fifty-five mile chase with the last fifteen miles being a running gunfight, Mangus surrendered to the Buffalo Soldiers.

Headquarters for the 10th Cavalry had moved to Fort Grant, Arizona Territory, in July 1886, then to Santa Fe, New Mexico Territory in November 1886.

The 10th spent much of 1887 chasing a former Apache army scout who became an outlaw renegade known as the "Apache Kid." The Kid was never located after committing several depredations in the territory.

Colonel Grierson was promoted in December of 1888; he relieved Gen. Nelson A. Miles as commander of the Department of Arizona. In Grierson's official farewell to his beloved 10th, he made the following remarks:

HEADQUARTERS TENTH CAVALRY
Santa Fe, New Mexico, December 1, 1888

Orders No. 51:

In pursuance of General Orders No. 97, current series, Headquarters of the Army, announcing his assignment to the command of the Department of Arizona, the undersigned relinquishes command of the Tenth U.S. Cavalry.

In doing so he desires to express his deep regret at being thus separated from the regiment he organized and has so long commanded, but he is gratified to be able, at this time to refer, even briefly, to it's splendid record of nearly twenty-two years service to the Government, while under his command; rendered, as it has been, in the field and at the most isolated posts on the frontier; always in the vanguard of civilization and in contact with the most warlike and savage Indians of the plains.

The officers and enlisted men have cheerfully endured many hardships and privations, and in the midst of great dangers steadfastly maintained a most gallant and zealous devotion to duty, and they may well be proud of the record made, and rest assured that the hard work undergone in the accomplishment of such important and valuable service to their country, is well understood and appreciated, and that it cannot fail, sooner or later, to meet with due recognition and reward.

That the high standard of excellence gained by the regiment for discipline and efficiency in the past will be fully sustained in the future; that the most signal success will ever attend the officers and soldiers of the Tenth Cavalry in all their noble efforts and undertakings, official or otherwise, is the heartfelt wish of their old commander.

> (signed) Benjamin H. Grierson
> Colonel Tenth U.S. Cavalry
> Brevet Major-General

Grierson was promoted to brigadier general in April 1890 and retired July 8, 1890. Lt. Col. George C. Hunt became acting commander of the 10th and in August 1890 Col. J. K. Mizner became the commander of the 10th Cavalry, joining the regiment at Fort Apache.

The only enlisted man in the 10th Cavalry to win the Medal of Honor during the Indian Wars was Sgt. William McBryar.

McBryar, originally from North Carolina, had three years of college and spoke Spanish and Latin. He joined the 10th Cavalry in early 1887 in New York City. In March 1887 McBryar became a member of Troop K under the leadership of Capt. Thomas C. Lebo.

McBryar would be involved in the last army action against renegade Apaches in the southwest. He was stationed at Fort Thomas when word came in on March 2, 1890, that a small band of Apaches had ambushed and killed the passengers of a wagon freighter just west of the San Carlos Indian Reservation. General Grierson gave an order to "capture or destroy the murderers." Immediately, Lt. Powhatan Clarke took ten men of Troop K, including McBryar, out on the search. They linked up with Lt. James Watson, 10th Cavalry, leading a detachment of Apache scouts and 4th Cavalry troopers.

The Apache scouts determined they were trailing five men. After a long march, the troopers were re-supplied by Sgt. Alexander Cheatham of Troop I, 10th Cavalry. He met them with a wagon and several mules loaded with supplies. Cheatham was an original enlistee of the 10th and a veteran of the Civil War.

After an exhausting 200 mile chase, the troopers caught up with the renegades on March 7 in the gorge of the Salt River, near Globe, Arizona Territory. They trapped the Apaches in a shallow cave that couldn't be directly fired into. Sergeant McBryar, an excellent rifle shot, fired shots off the rocks so that they ricochetted directly into the cave. After this outstanding display of rifle fire, the Apaches surrendered.

McBryar won the Medal of Honor for his actions in this engagement. In his letter of recommendation, 1st Lt. J. W. Watson said, "Sergeant McBryar demonstrated coolness, bravery, and good marksmanship under circumstances very different from those on the target range." Two of the hostile Apaches were killed. The troopers had ridden more than 290 miles in nine days.

After a request for "change of station" by commander Col. J. K. Mizner in the summer of 1891, the 10th Cavalry moved to the Department of Dakota in the spring of 1892.

The headquarters and the band were stationed at Fort Custer, Montana, along with Troops A, B, E, G, and K; Troops C and F, Fort Assinniboine, Montana; Troop D, Fort Keogh, Montana; Troop H, Fort Buford, North Dakota, and Troop I, Fort Leavenworth, Kansas. Troops L and M were skeletonized and assigned to headquarters. Tenth Cavalry headquarters moved to Fort Assinniboine on November 20, 1894.

Troops B, E, G, and K, 10th Cavalry were involved in protecting the Northern Pacific Railroad and its property in the summer of 1894 from striking workers. They suppressed a

group of disenchanted railroad workers called "Coxey's Commonwealers" earlier during the spring.

During the summer of 1896, the 10th was totally committed
to rounding up Cree Indians who had revolted and left their
reservation in Canada. Six hundred Cree were apprehended
and turned over to Canadian authorities. In regards to this duty,
Lt. John J. "Black Jack" Pershing, commander Troop D, 10th
Cavalry covered more than 600 miles that summer locating
Crees on American soil. Pershing had joined Troop D in October 1895 at Fort Assiniboine

Colonel Mizner was promoted to Brigadier General in June
1897, thereby relinquishing command of the 10th Cavalry.

Col. Guy V. Henry took command of the 10th on October 29, 1897. Henry was a veteran of the Civil War and had
served with the black troopers of the 9th Cavalry as a major from
June, 1881 to January, 1892 at which time he had been appointed a lieutenant colonel in the 7th Cavalry.

The 10th left Montana in April due to the oncoming
Spanish-American War. The 10th Cavalry served with distinction
in Cuba and the Philippines between 1898 and 1902. Five troop-
ers of the 10th won the Medal of Honor in Cuba: Sgt. Maj.
Edward L. Baker Jr.; Pvt. Dennis Bell, Troop H; Pvt. Fitz Lee,
Troop M; Cpl. William H. Thompkins, Troop A; and Pvt.
George H. Wanton, Troop M.

Col. Theodore Roosevelt stated in a letter shortly after the
war had ended:

> The Ninth and Tenth Cavalry Regiments fought one on either
> side of mine at Santiago, and I wish no better men beside me
> in battle than these colored troops showed themselves to be.
> Later on, when I come to write of the campaign, I shall have
> much to say about them.

Roosevelt would go on to become President of the United
States, but would say very little about the black soldiers who
fought with him at San Juan Hill. Roosevelt was commander
during the Spanish-American War of the volunteer cavalry regiment known as the "Rough Riders."

Although black soldiers performed heroically on the western frontier, they did so in obscurity. The Spanish-American War

gave prominence and attention to four African American regular U.S. army regiments that served in Cuba. They became heroes to the oppressed black community. The famous Howard University historian Rayford Logan wrote:

> Negroes had little, at the turn of the century, to help sustain our faith in ourselves except the pride that we took in the Ninth and Tenth Cavalry, the Twenty-fourth and Twenty-fifth Infantry. Many Negro homes had prints of the famous charge of the colored troops up San Juan Hill. They were our Ralph Bunche, Marion Anderson, Joe Louis and Jackie Robinson.

Lt. John "Black Jack" Pershing was the Regimental Quartermaster for the 10th Cavalry during the war in Cuba. Pershing later became the commanding general of the United States Army during World War I.

After the Spanish-American War and peacekeeping duties in Cuba and the Philippines, the headquarters for the 10th Cavalry in May 1902 was Fort Robinson, Nebraska. The 10th would be headquartered at this post until 1907. Things were very quiet except for an incident in 1906 when they had to go to Montana to put down a Ute Indian insurrection.

During this era the 10th's athletic teams distinguished themselves in competition. These sports included rifle and pistol target matches, baseball, football, and equestrian polo.

In 1907 the 10th Cavalry was sent to the Philippine Islands again for occupation duties. In 1909 the 10th was moved to Fort Ethan Allen, Vermont. In October 1913 the 10th was ordered back to the southwest border in Arizona, which was unstable due to the political turmoil in Mexico. The headquarters for the regiment was located at Fort Huachuca, Arizona, during this period.

The last major military action the 10th Cavalry was involved in on the southwest border was the Punitive Expedition of 1916. On March 8, 1916, the Mexican revolutionary Doroteo Arango, better known as Pancho Villa, with his army raided and sacked the town of Columbus, New Mexico. The War Department decided to punish Villa for his attack of a U.S. town.

General Pershing was put in command of the Punitive Expedition in Mexico. There were 10, 000 U.S. soldiers under Pershing's leadership trying to find Pancho Villa and his army.

The U.S. military units involved in the expedition included the 5th, 6th, 7th, 10th (black), 11th, and 13th Cavalry Regiments; 6th, 16th, 17th, 20th, and 24th (black) Infantry Regiments; Battery A, 4th Field Artillery, Batteries B and C, 6th Field Artillery; First Aero Squadron (eight airplanes); Signal Corps; Company E, G, and H, 2nd Battalion, Engineers; Field Hospital No. 7; Ambulance Wagon Companies No. 1 and No. 2; 1st New Mexico Infantry, National Guard; and 2nd Massachusetts Infantry, National Guard. The National Guard units never entered Mexico.

All of the 10th Cavalry Regiment was sent to Mexico except Troops L and M and the regimental band, which remained behind at Fort Huachuca. The American Expeditionary Force, as it was called, assembled in Mexico at Colonia Dublan, which was a small Mormon town in the state of Chichuahua. This meeting took place after March 16, when the 10th left Columbus, New Mexico, and headed south into Mexico. This marked the first time the 10th had gone into Mexico since they pursued hostile Apache warriors.

A new weapon had become part of the 10th Cavalry arsenal. The light machine gun that was to prove so effective in the trenches of World War I was introduced to the U.S. military with the 10th Cavalry Regiment. The regiment's Machine Gun Platoon originated and developed overhead and indirect machine gun fire, which they demonstrated at a 1908 training session in the Philippines. Military journals from all over the world discussed these innovations. The 10th's Machine Gun Platoon was organized at Fort Robinson, Nebraska, in 1906; 1st Lt. Albert E. Phillips was the commander. The platoon consisted of twenty-one troopers. The 10th's platoon was the first and the best in the U.S. Army and proved it again and again in competition. The 10th's Machine Gun Platoon did see its first action as part of the American Expeditionary Force in Mexico.

On April 1, 1916, the Second Squadron, 10th Cavalry, left San Diego del Monte riding toward the west. The First Squadron, 10th Cavalry, stayed in camp to patrol the roads in the area.

At about a distance of twelve miles from camp, at a location known as Agua Caliente, Troop E, 10th Cavalry, was attacked by

150 Mexican insurgents led by the infamous Beltran, one of Pancho Villa's allies.

Maj. Charles Young, third black graduate of West Point, class of 1889, was in command of Troops F and H, 10th Cavalry. Young was given an order to have his troops attack an enemy position behind a stone wall. Major Young ordered a charge with drawn automatic pistols. In support of the charge, Capt. Albert E. Phillips with his Machine Gun Troop used overhead machine gun fire. The Mexican bandits broke and ran leaving behind three dead. Overhead machine gun shots fired from behind, over the heads of the advancing soldiers into the enemy's position, were very effective.

The most famous—or infamous incident—the 10th Cavalry was involved in during the expedition was the "Charge at Carrizal." General Pershing received news in June 1916 that Mexican President Venustiano Carranza was amassing 10,000 Mexican soldiers near Villa Ahumada on the Mexican Central Railroad line. The Mexican government, although engaged in hostilities with Pancho Villa and other revolutionaries, didn't want uninvited U.S. troops in their country. Pershing was worried the Mexican army might try to cut off his supply line to the States and attack his soldiers deep in Mexico.

The American Expeditionary Force had been successful in breaking up Villa's army, but they had not captured him as they had hoped. With Villa out of the way, Carranza consolidated his hold on Mexico and turned his attention to Pershing's command.

Pershing directed Capt. Charles T. Boyd, commander Troop C, 10th Cavalry, to take his troop and reconnoiter in the direction of Ahumada. This would be for the purpose of gathering as much information as possible on the Mexican army in that vicinity. Boyd was instructed to avoid a fight if at all possible, and Pershing further instructed him to "stay out of any place garrisoned by federal troops."

Boyd, on the morning of June 18, led Troop C out of Colonia Dublan headed eastward toward Ahumada. Boyd had sixty-four black troopers with him. Capt. Lewis S. Morey, Troop E, 10th Cavalry, left his camp at Ojo Federico with forty-eight black troopers with orders to join Boyd on the scouting expedition toward Ahumada. After two days in the saddle, Morey sent back his supply transport after loading his men with as much as they could carry on their mounts. He was left with thirty-six troopers as the others took the supplies back to camp.

Each of Morey's men carried twenty pounds of grain, six pounds of rations, and 150 rounds of .30-06 ammunition for their 1903 Springfield rifles, which at that time was the main weapon for the U.S. Cavalry.

On June 20 Morey met up with Boyd's command at Santo Domingo Ranch, which was pretty much an oasis in the Mexican desert. That evening Boyd had a conference with Morey, Lt. Henry R. Adair, Troop K's second in command, Lemuel Spilsbury, a white American Mormon guide, and W. P. McCabe, the white American foreman of the Santo Domingo Ranch.

Boyd told the men that Mexican Gen. Jacinto B. Trevino, commander of Carranza's federal forces in Chihuahua City, had sent a telegram to Pershing not to allow American forces to move in any direction but north to the United States border. Trevino warned that his troops would attack if necessary.

McCabe informed the group that more than 400 Mexican cavalrymen led by Gen. Felix U. Gomez had recently stayed at the Santo Domingo Ranch before moving on to the small eastern village called Carrizal on the road to Ahumada. He also informed them that the Mexican Force had two machine guns.

McCabe felt that Carrizal was a trap for the United States troopers. Captain Boyd asked Spilsbury, the guide for Troop C, his opinion. Spilsbury stated they were a hundred miles from the United States base and the Carranzistas were within three hours of getting reinforcements from Ahumada. Captain Morey believed that, in his judgment, the Mexican troop strength at Carrizal was too strong for the U.S. army troopers to force their way through the village.

But Captain Boyd, the ranking officer, stated he was going through the village of Carrizal. Some writers have given the opinion that Boyd had unwritten orders from Pershing to force a fight with the Mexican soldiers. This, however, is conjecture since no corroborating evidence exists. Boyd could have been arrogant, cocky, or foolishly brave. All that is known today is that he decided to lead his 10th Cavalry troopers against a

10th Cavalry troopers who were captured by the Mexican army after the battle at Carrizal, Mexico, June 21, 1916
(Courtesy El Paso Public Library)

much larger Mexican army contingent in a small Mexican desert village.

On the morning of June 21, 1916, the Buffalo Soldiers were up at 3:00 A.M. and broke camp by 4:00 A.M. after eating a hot breakfast of bacon, beans, and bread. Each trooper had a rifle, a .45 automatic pistol, a filled cartridge belt, and an extra bandolier of ninety rounds of ammunition worn over the shoulder.

At five miles from the village, but within sight, the United States troops rested. Captain Boyd and Lem Spilsbury went into Carrizal to request permission to pass through. There was a road that passed around the village, but Boyd wouldn't hear of it. The Mexican General Gomez got out of his bed to talk to Captain Boyd and Spilsbury. Boyd didn't speak Spanish, so Spilsbury had to interpret for him. Gomez told them politely he had been ordered to stop any United States troops, but if they would wait until he could receive permission from General Trevino at Chihuahua City, he would let them pass through town. Otherwise, he would have to prevent them from going through. Captain Boyd was told what Gomez said and responded by saying, "Tell the son-of-a-bitch that I'm going through."

Boyd went back to his troop's position near the village and prepared the black troopers for battle. Every fourth trooper on line became a horseholder and this procedure moved the horses to the rear. The dismounted cavalry troopers, about sixty in number, prepared to charge a Mexican army position with 300 to 400 soldiers, including two machine guns.

Captain Boyd, still mounted, gave the orders for the bugler to blow the command for "charge." The black troopers moved forward, the Mexican soldiers opened up with rifle and machine gun fire, and hell was now in Carrizal.

One of the first casualties was the Mexican commanding officer, General Gomez. He was hit by three rifle bullets in the chest, and death was instantaneous. The Mexican machine gunners found the range on the 10th's horseholders. The black troopers lost control of the horses, and those that weren't hit ran off into the desert.

The Mexicans were firing on the United States soldiers from an irrigation ditch just outside the village. Troop C, 10th Cavalry, managed with bayonets on rifles, to reach the ditch. It was hand to hand, bayonet against machete. The black troopers even managed to capture the two Mexican machine guns. Then the Mexican reserve cavalry charged from a nearby tree line. From that point, the outlook went from bad to worse for the Buffalo Soldiers.

Captain Boyd, fighting at the ditch, was shot out of the saddle and was dead by the time he hit the ground. Captain Morey was wounded in the arm and shoulder. Lieutenant Adair, shot in the heart by Mexican rifle fire, was also dead. The black troopers held their ground against superior numbers for more than an hour. The sergeants ordered a retreat with most of the non-commissioned officers wounded.

The retreat of the 10th Cavalry troopers was not a rout. Four troopers helped Morey reach an abandoned adobe hut about a mile from the battlefield. Eighteen soldiers of Troop C and K and the white guide, Spilsbury, were captured. Most of the captured were wounded. Two officers and ten troopers of the 10th were killed. The Mexican army took such heavy casualties they didn't try to press the retreating Americans. The Mexicans lost their commander, General Gomez, and seventy-four men killed with scores wounded.

The retreating troopers found some provisions that Captain Morey had left in the desert along the route. Morey and the survivors, after a hundred mile walk, were found by patrols of the 11th U.S. Cavalry sent out to find them.

The black troopers taken prisoner at Carrizal were sent to Juarez after ten days, then released to United States authorities at El Paso. This was accomplished after demands were made on the Mexican government by the U.S. State Department. Most of the dead soldiers were also sent to El Paso.

Thus ended the most tragic episode of the 10th U.S. Cavalry in its regimental history. Pershing called for an all-out assault on the Mexican army, but the United States government downplayed the event. Mexican troops, after this battle, never threatened to attack U.S. military forces again. The Punitive Expedition in Mexico was the United States Army's last major use of equestrian cavalry against a hostile enemy. During the expedition, Pancho Villa sustained 273 of his men killed, 108 wounded, and nineteen captured. The revolt was over by June 30, 1916.

The 10th U.S. Cavalry Regiment was the last regular American military unit to be engaged in a fight with hostile Indians. The event occurred on January 9, 1918, while World War I was still being fought. The last time U.S. troops had fought Indians prior to this was against the Chippewa in Minnesota during 1898.

The 1918 engagement took place in Arizona. During 1917, the Yaquis were regularly buying and securing guns in Arizona and taking them to Mexico. The Yaquis were in a protracted war with the Mexican government, which they hated. Many of the Yaquis would sneak north of the border to work the mines and citrus and cotton farms for wages to buy firearms around Tucson and Phoenix.

The Yaquis never attacked any United States citizens, but would sometime kill a steer or two for food. The ranchers and miners reported seeing armed bands of Yaquis crossing the border. The Mexican government asked that the gun purchases be stopped. The United States government agreed to step up cavalry patrols on the border near the mining towns of Ruby, Oro Blanco, and eastward to Lochial, Arizona. The 10th Cavalry stationed at Fort Huachuca, Arizona, assigned units to patrol the trails in these areas to look for Yaquis. It is important to note that none of the four black regular U.S. army regiments were sent to Europe during World War I. Their primary task was to guard the United States' borders.

In January, Phil Clarke, a rancher and Ruby, Arizona, storeowner, visited the cavalry camp on the Oro Blanco trail which was located on the border. He reported that a neighbor had noticed signs of Indians in the nearby mountains to the north. Capt. Blondy Ryder, commander of Troop E, 10th Cavalry, on the very next day, January 9, sent 1st Lt. William Scott, along with a few more soldiers, to strengthen the observation post on the Oro Blanco trail.

Lieutenant Scott was the first of the post detachment to see movement. He signaled "attention" and then communicated "enemy in sight," to the troopers. Their quarry was only a quarter of a mile distant. 1st Sgt. Samuel H. Alexander got the detachment mounted in a hurry; their horses were already saddled. By the time they left the horse corral the Yaquis were not

A sergeant of the 10th Cavalry at Fort Bayard, New Mexico Territory, ca. 1890
(Courtesy U.S. Army Military History Institute)

to be seen. Lieutenant Scott, however, motioned to the south, toward the border.

In a very short ride the Buffalo Soldiers noticed the Yaquis had discarded supplies, decided they were nearby, and dismounted in the canyon. As they advanced in a southeasterly direction, they came under rifle fire. Captain Ryder ordered the troopers to return fire and a full-fledged gunfight ensued. One of the Indians was hit and after thirty minutes the Yaquis signaled they wanted to surrender. Captain Ryder ordered the troopers to "cease fire" with his whistle.

Ten Yaquis had surrendered, but the troopers noticed a larger group had escaped across the border into Mexico. One of the Indians was an eleven-year-old boy who fought bravely and fired a rifle that was nearly as long as he was tall.

The Indian who was wounded was the leader and later died. The nine surviving Yaquis were tried in the Federal District Court at Tucson. They were indicted with charges of illegal exportation of firearms to Mexico. The charges against the eleven-year-old were dismissed. The Yaquis told the black troopers the reason they fired on them was because they thought they were Mexican troops on the United States side of the border.

The Mexican consul wanted the Yaquis to be deported to Mexico to stand trial and possibly death before a firing squad. On April 8, 1918, Federal Judge William H. Sawtelle sentenced the eight defendants to thirty days in the Pima County Jail in Arizona. Deportation was nixed.

The 10th U.S. Cavalry was headquartered at Fort Huachuca, where they patrolled the Mexican border until October 11, 1931. The headquarters for the regiment was moved to Fort Leavenworth, Kansas, which also became the base for the regiment's First Squadron. A detachment of the 10th Cavalry was sent to the War College in Washington, D.C. to train cadets in equestrian skills. A troop of the 10th Cavalry was also sent to Fort Meyer near Washington D.C. for ceremonial duties for the War Department.

On February 1, 1941, the 10th U.S. Cavalry assembled at Fort Leavenworth under the new command of Col. Paul R. Davison. The following year the regiment was transferred to the U.S. Army Cavalry Training Center at Camp Lockett, California.

On March 10, 1944, while en route to Africa on transport ships, the 10th U.S. Cavalry officially disbanded. The achievements of the 10th United States Cavalry Regiment will live forever in the annals of United States military history. They were among the best horse soldiers our country ever produced. Their legacy will not be forgotten.

CHAPTER TWENTY FOUR

Buffalo Soldiers to the Rescue

Frequently on television or Hollywood westerns, the cavalry shows up at the last minute to save the day. Examining the research of the "real" history of the western frontier, on many occasions it was the Buffalo Soldiers riding to the rescue of white settlers, friendly Indians, or fellow soldiers. It isn't possible to include all of the rescues; I have, however, written about some of the most famous occurrences.

One of the earliest and most well-known rescues by Buffalo Soldiers occurred at Beecher Island, Colorado, in September of 1868. Before the Beecher Island incident took place, Troop I, 10th Cavalry, led by Capt. G. W. Graham, was patrolling the Leavenworth-to-Denver road. The captain and his thirty-six black troopers were attacked by more than a hundred Cheyenne Dog Soldiers, who were some of the finest warrior horsemen of the Great Plains. In the battle that ensued, the Cheyenne casualties were eleven dead and fourteen wounded. The Buffalo Soldiers only had one trooper wounded.

On September 21, 1868, Capt. Louis H. Carpenter left Fort Wallace, Kansas, with Troop H (Company), to continue to patrol the same route and road as Captain Graham had earlier. Carpenter didn't encounter any hostile Indians, but did remain near the vicinity at a location known as Cheyenne Wells, Colorado.

Earlier, Maj. George A. Forsyth had been given authority by Gen. Philip H. Sheridan to assemble a group of fifty volunteer frontier scouts in west Kansas to fight the Indians. This was because the regular army troop strength was weak and strung out over a wide area. In addition, the hostile Indians were raiding numerous locations. Many of the scouts were rugged buffalo hunters or experienced plainsmen who were good with a gun. Forsyth was able to recruit his volunteers at Forts Hays and Harker where they were given new revolvers and Spencer repeating rifles. Forsyth was assisted by Lt. Frederick Beecher and Dr. J. H. Mooers, the medic for the unit.

One of Forsyth's scouts was an African American named Samuel Garland who was originally from Mississippi and later settled in the black town of Nicodemus, Kansas. Garland's father was an African and his mother a Cherokee.

The scouts, armed and ready, struck out from Fort Wallace on September 9, in search of Indians who had attacked a wagon train near Sheridan. Forsyth and his scouts followed the trail of the raiders to a small valley beside the Arikaree Fork of the Republican River, about seventeen miles south of the present town of Wray, Colorado. It was at this location that they set up camp for the night. The next day before they saddled up and hit the trail, they would face their worst nightmare.

Forsyth and his small command were attacked at the Arikaree Fork by over 1,000 Arapaho, Lakota, and Cheyenne warriors under the leadership of the Cheyenne Chief, Roman Nose.

The scouts used their horses as shields and dug rifle pits in a sandbar on the Republican River. They were able to use their seven-shot Spencer rifles to great effect; they beat back numerous attacks on their precarious position. In the fighting, Chief

Roman Nose was shot and killed along with many of his warriors. Of Forsyth's scouts six were killed, including the second in
command, Lieutenant Beecher, and many were wounded. The
sandbar was later renamed Beecher's Island in memory of the
slain officer.

The surviving scouts were under siege on the sandbar for
nine long days. The only food they had was the rotting flesh of
their dead horses. They hoped and prayed that someone would
rescue them before they all perished.

On September 22, 1868, near noon, five days after the attack
on Beecher's Island, two troopers of the 10th Cavalry were riding
westward from Fort Wallace with dispatches for Captain
Carpenter, who was forty-five miles from Fort Wallace on Sandy
Creek. Two of Forsyth's scouts had been able to slip through the
Indians' lines and go for help the night before. These scouts,
Jack Stilwell and Pierre Trudeau, came across the two black
troopers on the prairie. They told of the dire predicaments of
Forsyth's command: no rations, no medical supplies, and with
many wounded, they were on the verge of annihilation.

Trudeau and Stilwell continued on their way to Fort Wallace
for help. The two troopers found and alerted Captain Carpenter, who was closer to Forsyth's location, about the crisis at
the Arikeree Fork.

Moving at a swift pace, Carpenter and Troop H covered
thirty-five miles before sunset on September 23. Carpenter met
another of Forsyth's scouts who had escaped on the trail, Jack
Donovan. He had made it to Fort Wallace and was returning
with four other riders to help search for Forsyth. Donovan found
that most of the soldiers had already left the fort looking for
Forsyth's command.

Carpenter decided to take thirty of his best troopers, along
with a supply wagon, and move out in the direction of the
Arikaree at a gallop. The remaining troopers would follow as
fast as possible.

Noticing the approach of the Buffalo Soldiers, the Indians
broke the siege of the island and left the area. Some reports have
the Indians losing seventy dead in the siege. Others, as the following report states, say the numbers were much higher.

Ruben Waller, one of the veterans of Troop H, 10th Cavalry,

gave this account of the rescue on Beecher Island many years later:

... Colonel L. H. Carpenter with his Company H, Tenth U.S. Cavalry was at Cheyenne Wells, Colorado, one hundred miles from Beecher Island. Jack Stilwell brought us word of the fix that Beecher was in and we entered the race for the island, and in twenty-six hours Colonel Carpenter and myself, as his hostler, rode into the rifle pits. And what a sight we saw—thirty wounded and dead men right in the midst of fifty dead horses, that had laid in the hot sun for days.

And these men had eaten the putrid flesh of those dead horses for eight days. The men were in a dying condition when Carpenter and myself dismounted and began to rescue them.

By this time all the (black) soldiers were all in the pits and we began to feed the men from our haversacks. If the doctor had not arrived in time we would have killed them all by feeding them to death. The men were eating all we gave them, and it was a plenty. Sure, we never gave a thought that it would hurt them. You can imagine a man in starvation, and plenty food suddenly set before him. He can't think of the results until too late. That is the condition that Company H, Tenth Cavalry, fixed for the Beecher Island men. We were not aiming to hurt the boys. It was done through eagerness and excitement.

God bless the Beecher Island men. They were a noble set of men....

After Roman Nose had killed all the horses he was sure he had the fifty men at his mercy and so he fixed up for a grande charge that he thought would be fatal to the white men, but he had better not have made the charge. It was the greatest mistake that Roman Nose ever made.

I had several rounds with him (Roman Nose), and he was always careful about mistakes when he met regular soldiers. He was too smart for us. We most always had "heap too many" (black troopers) and I suppose he thought fifty whites "heap little," but (that) also (was) his fatal mistake.

... Let me say here, that I had many fights with the Indians for ten years after the Beecher fight, and I never saw anything to equal it. I say it was the greatest fight that was ever fought by any soldiers of the regular army at any-time, not excepting the Custer fight or the massacre at Fort Phil Kearney, and I say further that in all the fights we had with the Indians, I mean the regular army, we never killed as many

Indians. I saw Lone Wolf, who was in the Beecher fight and he told us that they lost 400 killed and fatally wounded....

... hundreds of lives of settlers of Kansas and Colorado were saved from massacre and destruction by the brave stand of fifty brave men....

... After the fight and rescue we stayed at the island three days. We buried the five men who were killed.

... We used the funeral flag of Company H to bury the dead, which flag I now have in my possession.

... We arrived at Fort Wallace and the scouts were disbanded, and were reorganized under the leadership of Lieutenant Pappoon....

After we had been at Fort Wallace about two weeks, and the scouts had gotten rested a lot of us soldiers took French leave one night and went to Pond Creek, three miles west of Wallace. Well, when we got there we met the Beecher scouts, as they had been paid off. They sure treated us black soldiers right for what we had done for them.

Of course, we all lost respect for prohibition, and of course all got on a very wet drunk. The scouts would have us drink, and we did not resent their courtesy, and everyone in town was on a drunk, and we had everything going our way....

Ruben Waller mustered out of the 10th Cavalry at Fort Sill, Oklahoma Territory. He settled down in El Dorado, Kansas, where he raised six children and outlived four wives. For thirty years Waller served as superintendent of the Sunday School at the Colored Methodist Church in town. He died on August 20, 1945.

On the day following the Beecher Island fight, September 26, 1868, soldiers from Fort Wallace arrived on the scene. Capt. G. W. Graham with Troop I, 10th Cavalry along with Captain H. C. Bankhead, 5th Infantry, with a detachment of 5th and 38th Infantry joined Carpenter. Among the six dead with the scouts was the medical doctor, J. H. Mooers. Forsyth was wounded in both legs, and fifteen other scouts received wounds from the fight.

Captain Carpenter later received the Medal of Honor for his actions in rescuing Forsyth and his scouts and military actions in western Kansas and eastern Colorado as commander of Troop H, 10th Cavalry.

Louis Henry Carpenter enlisted in the army as a private in

the Civil War out of Philadelphia from an upper-class family. He first served with the 6th U.S. Cavalry, Army of the Potomac. Two months after enlisting in 1862, Carpenter was made a sergeant; in the spring of 1863 he was made a second lieutenant.

Carpenter won citations for bravery at Gettysburg and Winchester and was brevetted to rank of captain. In the spring of 1864 Carpenter was made an aide-de-camp to Maj. Gen. Philip H. Sheridan, commander of U.S. Cavalry forces. Later he served as troubleshooter at Cavalry Corps headquarters. In 1864 Carpenter was elevated to first lieutenant. In the autumn of 1864 Carpenter was offered the position of lieutenant colonel of the 5th United States Colored Cavalry. He accepted, even though he was aware that white officers were discriminated against by superiors, and if caught by Confederate forces, executed. The commanding officer of the 5th U.S.C.C. was on detached duty so for all practical purposes, Carpenter became the commander of the regiment of 937 black horse soldiers.

Carpenter and the 5th U.S.C.C. distinguished themselves in a number of battles during the war. By the end of the rebellion, Carpenter, at the age of twenty-six, was made a colonel.

At the end of the Civil War, due to the downsizing of the army, officers were given lower ranks. Carpenter was made a first lieutenant in the 6th U.S. Cavalry. On November 7, 1866, Carpenter accepted a promotion to captain of Troop H (Company), 10th Cavalry. Once again, he would serve with African Americans whom he had learned to respect and trust.

Of the Beecher Island rescue Carpenter said:

> We instantly rushed forward, and on nearing the place were received by the whole party and loud cheer. I threw up my cap and shouted, and never felt more excited in my life. These men, in this out-of-the-way place, seemed to me like a party on a wide ocean, for they certainly were as helpless ... Forsyth took me by the hand and seemed quite affected. He told me that it seemed fatal that we should meet in places out of the way an [sic] far apart....

Carpenter served with the 10th Cavalry until 1883, when he was promoted to major and transferred to the 5th U.S. Cavalry. He later made the rank of brigadier general, led a full infantry division during the Spanish American War, and was made a military governor in Cuba after the war.

In September, 1883, Carpenter was interviewed by the *Omaha Bee*:

> What sort of soldiers do the colored men make Colonel?
>
> "A great deal better than many suppose. The records show that there have been less desertions in the Tenth Cavalry than in any other regiment in the service. We had fewer court martials, fewer offenses against regulations, and as good general discipline as can be found anywhere in the army. The men are unusually cleanly [sic] and tidy, and spend more on their dress than the white soldiers; they drill well and are obedient to their superiors."
>
> How are they in action? Can they stand fire?
>
> "My experience has been that they are as reliable as white soldiers in action. I have seen them in a number of Indian fights, and they behaved unusually well. You know their record during the war (Civil War), and since then the troops in the colored regiments have maintained their reputation. I certainly have no fault to find. In '68 the two companies that I commanded did excellent service and deserved all the compliments that they got...."

In December of 1877 the 9th Cavalry came to the rescue of some Texas Rangers who were embroiled in the famous Salt War that took place near El Paso, Texas. For years Mexicans and Anglos had freely gathered salt from deposits near El Paso. After the Civil War the small Rio Grande villages south of El Paso, Ysleta, Socorro, and San Elizario became the centers of salt production. A white district judge named Charles Howard decided there was a profit to be made on the salt deposits. He had them surveyed, put up signs, and charged a fee. The larger Mexican population was furious because the salt was always gratis before. Luis Cardis, a Mexican political leader, mounted opposition with other Latinos against the fees on the saltworks. Judge Howard, on October 10, 1877, went to El Paso with a double barrel shotgun looking for Cardis. The judge located Cardis in the Schultz & Brothers Store and shot Cardis with both barrels of the shotgun. He died instantly.

Judge Howard believed his action was going to end political opposition over the saltworks. The Mexican community, however, was outraged over the killing and roamed the streets of Ysleta, Socorro, and San Elizario in armed bands talking about reprisals. Governor Hubbard of Texas, after receiving pleas from the white minority in El Paso, sent Maj. John B. Jones of the Texas Rangers to investigate.

Jones organized a company of twenty Texas Rangers and placed them under the command of Lt. John B. Tays. Jones felt the rangers could get the job done; keep the peace and protect the saltworks. He went back to resume his regular duties at Austin.

In early December Judge Howard learned that the Mexicans were going to try to take over the saltworks near San Elizario. He left for the mines with Ranger Tays and other escorts. He had intentions of arresting and prosecuting the Mexicans as trespassers. When the Mexican community found out Howard was on his way to San Elizario, a mob formed to meet him there. On the evening of December 12, Howard and Tays were forced to take up defensive positions in the rangers' office at San Elizario. A white store owner in the town, Charles Ellis, tried to talk to the mob; he was promptly killed, shot, and mutilated.

Tays was able to get word to Fort Bliss for help. Capt. Thomas Blair, 15th Infantry, with a detachment of nineteen soldiers, was turned back by the Mexicans once he reached San Elizario. Thomas returned to Fort Bliss after determining he didn't want to fight the Mexicans.

On Thursday, December 13, the Mexicans attacked the rangers' office at San Elizario. After almost a week of fighting there were three dead rangers and two seriously wounded. Tays' food and supplies were running very low. He decided to parley with the Mexicans under a white flag. Tays was told by the mob everyone would be free to leave; they just wanted Howard. Tays, however, refused. Later, after Howard demanded, he and Tays went out together to talk to the Mexican mob. They were promptly seized and disarmed. The other Texas Rangers in the building surrendered. A firing squad of Mexicans shot Howard and threw his body into a nearby well. Two other white merchants who were also in the building were promptly killed. The Mexican mob then started looting homes and businesses owned by whites in San Elizario.

Governor Hubbard had requested military assistance when the fighting became known to him in Austin. Colonel Edward Hatch, 9th Cavalry, was ordered to El Paso on the double quick. Hatch reached El Paso on December 19 with nine troops of cavalry, which quickly took command of the town. The colonel went on to San Elizario with fifty-four black troopers and two cannons. Once he arrived at the town, Hatch found 500 Mexicans ready for a fight. The rest of the command of the 9th soon arrived in town and were ready to oblige the rioters if they wanted to skirmish. The Mexicans realized they were facing battle-hardened black troopers who would give as good as they got. The mob quickly retreated from the town without a fight. During the previous week, at least eleven people had been killed. The Texas Rangers were freed when the troopers entered the town. The rangers retrieved their weapons and promptly killed two Mexicans who they said were trying to escape. Hatch made an investigation and found the two bodies had been bound when shot. The colonel made an official proclamation that there would be law and order at the saltworks at all cost, and anyone caught disobeying this order would be punished. This ended the Salt War at El Paso, Texas, with the Buffalo Soldiers once again, riding to the rescue.

On occasions Buffalo Soldiers had to protect Indians on the western frontier. In 1879 Maj. John B. Jones, commander of the Texas Ranger Frontier Battalion, had given orders to G. W. Arrington, captain of Company C, Texas Rangers, to kill any armed Indians found on the North Texas frontier. The rangers located some armed Kiowa on January 15, along the Pease River. The rangers attacked the Indians and killed one of them. The small band of Indians fled to a nearby Kiowa village of fourteen tepees. Arrington's company was preparing to kill and scalp as many Indian men, women, and children as they could. As they were on the verge of charging the village, Capt. Nicholas Nolan and Troop A, 10th Cavalry, rode up and stopped them. Nolan informed Arrington that this group of Kiowa had permission to leave the reservation in Indian Territory for purposes of hunting and were under U.S. Army protection.

One of Frederic Remington's most famous paintings is *Captain Dodge's Colored Troopers to the Rescue*. The action that inspired this painting took place from September 29th to October 5th in 1879, on the banks of Milk Creek in the northwestern corner of Colorado.

The Native Americans that were native to this area of Colorado were the Ute. Their hostility to white men started in 1859 when they began to be pushed off their traditional hunting ground. Hostilities were kept to a minimum due to the diplomacy of a Ute chief named Ouray, who brokered treaties with the U.S. government in 1863, 1868, and 1873. Each treaty was a loss of land for the Ute. The U.S. policy with the Ute was two-pronged: military coercion and pacification through annuities that arrived late or never at all.

Nathan C. Meeker was appointed the agent to the Northern Utes in early 1878. Meeker had been an agricultural editor for Horace Greeley's *New York Tribune*, and founder of the Union Colony at Greely, Colorado. The Ute agency was called the White River Agency, about 185 miles south of Rawlins, Wyoming. Meeker thought he could turn the nomadic Utes into farmers, thereby not making any trouble for white people coming into the territory.

Things went from bad to worse when Meeker ploughed up the Utes favorite race horse track on their reservation. Meeker requested military protection for himself, family, and employees of the White River Agency. On Tuesday, September 16, at Fort Frederick Steele in Wyoming (east of Rawlins), Maj. Thomas T. Thornburgh was ordered to take a contingent of soldiers to the White River Ute Agency, Colorado, to assist Agent Meeker. Thornburgh's command included three troops of the 5th Cavalry, one company of the 4th Infantry, and a supply train of twenty-five wagons.

The Utes were led by Chief Colorow. Aware of the troop movement, they broke camp at the agency to move twelve miles further and prepare for battle. Meeker continued to send out messages for help.

Thornburgh had reached Milk Creek on September 29, 1879. As the soldiers watered their horses in the creek, Ute warriors ambushed them from the bluffs and ridges above with rifle fire. There were more than 300 Indians in the attacking party. Major Thornburgh ordered his men to fall back to the wagons that had been corralled in a circle. Almost immediately

Thornburgh and twelve other soldiers were shot dead as they retreated to the wagons. Capt. J. Scott Payne took over the command, and he promptly received two gunshot wounds.

Meanwhile at the agency, Ute warriors attacked the headquarters, dragged Meeker from it, stripped him naked, and shot the sixty-one-year-old agent in the head. They then tied a logging chain around his neck and shoved an iron bar down his throat. Eleven white male employees at the agency were also killed. All the white women and children were taken captive by the Utes.

Captain Payne ordered his men to dig in as best as possible. The Utes shot and killed almost all the soldiers' horses and mules except for four. Payne sent a courier to Rawlins where he was received by Col. Wesley Merritt, commander of the 5th U.S. Cavalry. Another courier, John Gordon, located Captain Dodge on October 1.

Capt. Francis S. Dodge, commander of D Troop, 9th Cavalry, stationed at Fort Garland, Colorado, en route to the agency, was camped on the Grand River after receiving Meeker's plea for help. On the night of October 1, under the cover of darkness, Dodge and Troop D headed for Milk Creek, where Thornburgh had set up camp earlier to parley with the Utes.

Dodge had two white officers, thirty-five black troopers, and four white citizens in his command. They rode seventy miles in twenty hours to reach Milk Creek the next day.

As they reached the battle scene the Utes did not fire on them. A huge cheer went up from the encircled cavalrymen. But when Dodge and his troopers arrived in the trenches, the Ute warriors opened fire. All of Dodge's horses were shot except four. Now Dodge and his troopers were also trapped. They did, however, offer inspiration and fresh guns to the besieged command.

During this engagement Sgt. Henry Johnson, Troop D, 9th Cavalry, distinguished himself in battle. Johnson was responsible for the outpost on the perimeter as sergeant of the guard. He had to make the rounds to check his troopers; in doing so he exposed himself to hostile gunfire on a regular basis. Johnson was able to inspire his men by his actions, without getting shot. On October 4 Johnson led a group of soldiers to the creek to get water for the wounded. Johnson had to fight his way to the creek and back at night. Sergeant Johnson received the Medal of Honor for his actions at Milk Creek.

On October 5, 1879, early in the morning, Colonel Merritt arrived at Milk Creek with five troops of the 5th U.S. Cavalry to relieve the trapped troopers. The Utes did not put up any fight and retreated. In the siege, the Utes suffered casualties of thirty-seven warriors killed while the U.S. Army casualties were fourteen dead and forty-three wounded. Most of the army horses and mules were also killed.

The white women and children who were captured by the Utes were soon released. The Ute Indians were forced out of Colorado, their ancestral home, to reservations in barren Utah.

Although Sergeant Johnson distinguished himself in combat at Milk Creek and won the Medal of Honor, he didn't receive the actual medal until September 22, 1890, eleven years after the battle. He had to petition the authorities in Washington D.C., to receive the medal he courageously won in the military conflict. Captain Dodge also received the Medal of Honor for his actions during the engagement.

Some historians consider the greatest extrication the Buffalo Soldiers were involved in during the frontier era was the rescue of Custer's former regiment, the 7th Cavalry, from annihilation in the Dakotas in 1890.

A Pauite named Wovoka started a new religion with the Plains Indians called the Ghost Dance. The religion spread the word that a messiah was to come and return the Indians' land and buffalo by the turn of the century. The Lakota on the Pine Ridge, Rosebud, Cheyenne River, and Standing Rock Reservations embraced the religion due to the despotic conditions they lived under; hunger, poverty, and inhumane treatment by the United States government.

The Ghost Dance disturbed the white Indian agents at the aforementioned agencies. They requested military assistance because the Indians had weaponry which they were allowed to keep so they could hunt game.

The agents, however, felt the mixture of guns and religion was going to spell trouble on the reservations. Dr. D. F. Royer, agent at Pine Ridge, sent a message to T. J. Morgan, Commissioner of Indian Affairs in Washington, D.C. General Miles, commanding the Division of the Missouri, ordered Brig. Gen. John R. Brooke, commanding the Department of the Platte, to make a strong military statement at Pine Ridge Reservation with a show of force.

The first soldiers to reach Pine Ridge were the black troopers of the 9th Cavalry from posts in Nebraska and Wyoming.

Two troops of the 9th went to the Rosebud Reservation. Three troops from Fort Robinson, Nebraska and one troop from Fort McKinney, Wyoming went to Pine Ridge Reservation. These troops formed a battalion under the command of Maj. Guy V. Henry, a Civil War Medal of Honor recipient. By the end of November 1890 there would be over 5,000 U.S. soldiers in the vicinity of the Lakota reservations.

The Indians were naturally alarmed by the strong show of force by the U.S. military and felt they might be massacred. The military maintained that their mission was only to serve as peacekeepers. Matters took a turn for the worse when Chief Sitting Bull was killed by Indian police at the Standing Rock Agency on December 15, 1890. Sitting Bull had been seen as a troublemaker by Agent McLaughlin at Standing Rock. The agent had sent forty Indian agency police and two troops of 8th U.S. Cavalry to arrest Sitting Bull.

The chief's death exacerbated the suspicions of the Lakota that the U.S. government had ominous plans for them. Gen. Nelson Miles decided that all the Lakota should be placed within the Pine Ridge Reservation until things cooled down.

A large number of Sitting Bull's followers under the leadership of Big Foot couldn't be found. Major Henry with Troops D, F, I, and K, 9th Cavalry left Pine Ridge on December 24 to locate Big Foot and his band. After scouring the Badlands for four days, the troopers could not pick up any sign of Big Foot. After Henry was unable to find the Indians, General Brooke ordered Maj. S. M. Whitside with four troops of the cavalry and a platoon of Battery E, 1st U.S. Artillery, with two Hotchkiss guns, to search for the Indians. Whitside located Big Foot as the chief and his followers were coming peacefully into the Pine Ridge Agency. The soldiers and Indians encamped on the night of December 27, 1890, on Wounded Knee Creek.

Big Foot had offered no resistance when he was told he must surrender, but on the morning of December 29, the army attempted to disarm the Lakota braves. Among the Lakota were 320 Miniconjous and thirty-eight Hunkpapas, and of these there were 120 warriors with Colt revolvers and Winchester rifles. The United States troop strength on Wounded Knee Creek consisted of 500 soldiers.

At first the Indians gave up some weapons, but not enough to satisfy the army soldiers. A detachment of troopers was given orders to search the Lakota lodges. At this point some of the Indian warriors pulled rifles out from under blankets and fired pointblank into the soldiers. Now all hell broke out.

The troopers returned fire with their Springfield carbines as they retreated. As the soldiers moved away, the artillery unit opened up indiscriminately on the Indians with the two Hotchkiss guns. (These guns could fire a shell a second with an experienced crew. The shells could be primed to explode overhead of target to great effect.) In just minutes 150 Lakota men, women, and children were dead and at least fifty were wounded. Twenty-six of the Cavalry troopers were killed and thirty-nine were wounded in the short, but intense battle. Afterwards the Lakota would always refer to this battle as the Wounded Knee Massacre.

The massacre created bedlam at the Pine Ridge Agency where 6,000 Lakota could hear the gunshots in the distance. As Forsyth returned with his command from Wounded Knee they were attacked by small Indian war parties continuously. General Brooke sent a messenger for Major Henry and the Buffalo Soldiers to return to Pine Ridge Agency as soon as possible. The 9th Cavalry Battalion had just finished a fifty-mile scout of the Badlands when they got the message on the evening of December 29.

Instead of bedding down and giving their horses a needed rest, the black troopers ate and hit the saddle again. The weather was bitter cold and freezing. Troops F, I, and K led out first, while their supply wagons were escorted by Troop D. The first three troops of the 9th arrived at the Pine Ridge Agency at 5:30 A.M.; in twenty-four hours they rode over eighty miles in the cold. Troop D and the supply wagons following behind were

attacked an hour later by fifty Lakota warriors, two miles from the agency. One of the troopers on point, Pvt. Charles Haywood, was killed by an Indian brave dressed as a soldier.

The supply wagons were circled in a defensive position. Captain Loud, in charge of the supply wagon train, tried to get his Indian scouts to ride to the agency for help, but they replied their horses had no run left in them. Cpl. William Wilson, Troop D, volunteered to take the message. Wilson was one of the best marksmen in the 9th. He was also flamboyant; he wore a black leather coat, wide-brimmed white hat, and large cowboy spurs on his boots. As Wilson spurred his horse out of the wagon circle, the other troopers gave him a covering rifle fire for protection. Wilson must have ridden the fastest horse available because he easily outdistanced the warriors who tried to catch him. Once at Pine Ridge, Wilson informed Major Henry what was happening; immediately the black troopers rode back and rescued the supply wagons.

As soon as the 9th Cavalry troopers returned from saving the supply wagons, word came into the agency that eight troops of the Cavalry were trapped by Lakota warriors under the leadership of Two Strike, about five miles away in a valley near Drexel Mission. The Lakota had earlier set fire to a cabin near the mission to draw the soldiers into a trap. As the Cavalry rode into the narrow valley pursuing a small group of Indians, they dismounted to pursue them up the slopes. They were instantly surprised by a war party of over 1,000 Lakota warriors in superior positions among the higher ledges of the valley. The Lakota felt this would be a winnable battle with the hated Cavalry, whom they had once defeated before.

Col. James Forsyth, commander of the Cavalry, sent a messenger back to Pine Ridge for immediate help. Major Henry of the 9th received the message at the agency around noon on December 30, 1890. Henry ordered the bugler to call for boots and saddles, and within minutes the battalion was in motion to rescue their fellow soldiers.

After moving his exhausted horses at a trot, Major Henry and his black battalion reached the valley near Drexel Mission at 1:30 P.M. Henry immediately ordered Troops I and K to take the high ground and charge the east slope, supported by a Hotchkiss gun. Troops D and F dismounted and charged up the west slope. The Lakota warriors were attacked from the rear, pushed back, and driven off. The new troops had relieved the cornered cavalrymen. The white soldiers who had been pinned down rushed to embrace their black rescuers.

The 9th Cavalry battalion in thirty hours had spent twenty-two hours in the saddle, ridden 100 miles in bitter cold weather, and fought two tough battles with Lakota warriors. Cpl. William O. Wilson won the Medal of Honor for his deeds. The forced march of the 9th U.S. Cavalry in extreme weather conditions was one of the most outstanding actions of any cavalry regiment during the Indian Wars.

This photo is possibly Corporal William O. Wilson, Medal of Honor recipient, at Pine Ridge Agency, 1891
(Courtesy Denver Public Library, Western History Department)

CHAPTER TWENTY-FIVE

Buffalo Soldiers Fighting Outlaws

Black troopers on the western frontier had many clashes and conflicts with outlaws in the "era of the Wild West." This chapter will highlight a few of the most celebrated cases.

The most famous outlaw the Buffalo Soldiers went against was William Bonney, better known as "Billy the Kid," during the Lincoln County War in New Mexico Territory. During the territorial era of New Mexico in the 1870s, Lincoln County covered all of the southeastern portion of the territory with the county seat being the town of Lincoln. Nine miles west of the town of Lincoln was Fort Stanton where the black troopers of the 9th U.S. Cavalry were stationed.

Being a true frontier town, Lincoln was a hangout for outlaws, rustlers, and desperadoes during the 1870s. In 1877 a white outlaw from Alabama named Frank Freeman shot and wounded a black soldier in a restaurant in Lincoln just because he didn't like black people. Freeman was arrested, but escaped from the military authorities on his way to Fort Stanton. Freeman joined up with a band of outlaws headquartered on the Ruidoso River. Lt. George W. Smith, with a detachment of fifteen black troopers from the 9th, along with a sheriff and posse located and cornered the gang in December of 1877. The outlaws surrendered except for Freeman who was killed while trying to escape.

In the 1870s Lincoln County was politically and economically controlled by Lawrence G. Murphy and James J. Dolan. They were business partners with Thomas B. Catron, president of the First National Bank of Santa Fe, U.S. district attorney, powerful rancher, and land baron. Murphy and Dolan owned a general store in Lincoln named L. G. Murphy & Company. The store supplied food to Fort Stanton and held the contract to supply the Mescalero Apache Indian Agency with food. Most of the time they delivered less to the Apaches than contracted for and made a nice profit for themselves.

Problems arose for Murphy and Dolan when Texas cattleman John S. Chisum moved into southeast New Mexico Territory on the Pecos River. Chisum won the bid to supply the Mescalero Agency with beef. He also formed a partnership with Lincoln attorney Alexander A. McSween, the nemesis of Murphy and Dolan. In 1877 a young man from England named John H. Tunstall opened a store in Lincoln and aligned himself with Chisum and McSween. In 1878 Troops F, H, and M of the 9th U.S. Cavalry were stationed at Fort Stanton along with Company H of the 15th U.S. Infantry. In February 1878 there were clashes between the two competitors in Lincoln County that turned ugly. Deputy U.S. Marshal Robert Widenmann requested military support from Fort Stanton. A detachment of black troopers assisted Widenmann in serving arrest warrants on a few of the Murphy-Dolan men for civil disturbance.

A few days later Widenmann (again with black troops), confronted Lincoln County Sheriff William Brady and his posse in Tunstall's store. Widenmann arrested some of Brady's possemen, confiscated property that was in Brady's possession and sent them home.

Lincoln County Sheriff Brady, with a posse, killed Tunstall while he was riding with some friends. The friends included

Billy the Kid and others who were participating in a hunt for wild game, some distance from Tunstall. Billy the Kid and his buddies heard the shooting of Tunstall and made good their escape.

The killing of Tunstall turned the county upside down. Governor Samuel B. Axtell, fearing large scale civil unrest, visited Lincoln. Axtell sent a telegram to Col. Edward Hatch, commander of the 9th Cavalry at regimental headquarters in Santa Fe, requesting troops from Fort Stanton be sent to Lincoln for maintenance of law and order. Axtell laid all the blame for the unrest on McSween.

Hatch sent Capt. George A. Purington with twenty-five soldiers of Troop H, 9th Cavalry, to Lincoln. A few days later a lieutenant and a detachment of white infantry joined the small command in Lincoln. Captain Purington found the situation in Lincoln to be confusing and unstable. McSween had organized a group of thirty gunmen, some of whom had been deputized by Justice of the Peace John B. Wilson, to arrest members of Sheriff Brady's posse. At the same time, Brady was demanding assistance from the military to arrest McSween's men. Hatch ordered Purington to assist the Sheriff since he was the official authority in the county.

The gunmen for McSween, empowered by arrest warrants from Justice of the Peace Wilson, called themselves regulators. They arrested two of Tunstall's killers, Frank Baker and William Moore. While taking the two prisoners back to Lincoln, the regulators decided Brady would turn them loose so they executed them on the road to town. Shortly afterwards in March 1878 Sheriff Brady and Lieutenant Smith, with a detachment of Troop H, 9th Cavalry, went to Chisum's ranch to arrest McSween. They didn't arrest McSween, but his wife informed them that he was going to turn himself in on April 1 in Lincoln.

In Lincoln on April 1, Sheriff Brady and two of his deputies, Jacob B. Mathews and George Hindman, were ambushed on Main Street. Brady and Hindman were mortally wounded. Of the men accused of the murders, Billy the Kid was identified.

Captain Purington and Lieutenant Smith with Troop H, 9th Cavalry, rode back to Lincoln along with George Peppin, a member of the Murphy-Dolan faction. They made quite a few arrests of suspects without a warrant and searched the McSween home. The military was more sympathetic toward the Murphy-Dolan faction at this time.

On April 5, a bounty hunter hired by Murphy-Dolan, Andrew "Buckshot" Roberts, went manhunting. On the Mescalero Apache Reservation at a location known as Blazer's Mill, Roberts was killed in a shootout with Billy the Kid and his associates. On the same date, Lt. Col. N.A.M. Dudley took over as commander at Fort Stanton.

The next county sheriff was a McSween sympathizer named John Copeland. Eventually Dudley assigned Cpl. Thomas Dale and three privates from Troop H, 9th Cavalry, to assist Sheriff Copeland in Lincoln.

The Buffalo Soldiers were again summoned to Lincoln when a large scale gunfight broke out between the McSween and the Murphy-Dolan gangs. Lieutenant Smith and twenty black troopers rode into town and hostilities ended without a shot being fired. Sheriff Copeland was soon replaced by George Peppin, an ally of Murphy-Dolan, as county sheriff.

Peppin requested assistance from the military command at Fort Stanton several times during the month of June. On one occasion Lt. Millard F. Goodwin refused to assist Sheriff Peppin because he (Peppin) had a group of notorious gunmen with him making arrests in the county.

Colonel Hatch became increasingly disillusioned with the politics of Lincoln County and wrote headquarters at Fort Leavenworth for clarification of military policy in civil matters. The Secretary of War informed all concerned that the army as a posse comitatus was not authorized; this was written as General Orders No. 49. Headquarters informed Hatch, who then told Dudley at Fort Stanton that regular army soldiers couldn't be used in Lincoln County politics. History shows that Dudley totally disregarded Hatch's orders.

On July 15, 1878, a major battle between the opposing factions in Lincoln County took place. Almost sixty heavily armed McSween men rode into Lincoln and took up defensive positions in Jose Montano's store, Isaac Ellis' store, and the McSween home. Later that day Sheriff Peppin, Dolan, and a posse of more than forty gunmen rode into Lincoln and took up offensive positions where they could watch and fire on the McSween men. Peppin sent his deputy to serve an arrest warrant at the McSween house. He was promptly fired on as he approached the structure. The battle for Lincoln County was on, and it would last for five days.

Peppin requested a cannon from Fort Stanton. Commander Dudley sent black Pvt. Berry Robinson with a message to Peppin that a cannon or soldiers were not possible at this time due to military constraints. But he also let it be known he would gladly do anything he could to assist Peppin.

While riding into Lincoln, Private Robinson was accosted by four men painted up like Indian warriors. They pulled their pistols and tried to stop Robinson. The private told them he was on government business, threw a shell into his rifle, and kept going. As he entered town, Robinson was fired on by the McSween men. He was, however, able to reach Peppin safely and give him Dudley's message.

A Mexican delegation of citizens who lived near Lincoln requested intervention by the military stationed at Fort Stanton. Most of Commander Dudley's black troopers were out searching for hostile Apaches in the Sacramento and Guadalupe Mountains. Dudley decided that with the plea from the citizens, and what had occurred to Private Robinson, he would intervene in Lincoln. He ordered his troopers to wear their full dress uniforms including swords. Every available man at Fort Stanton rode with Commander Dudley into Lincoln. This included five officers, eleven black horse soldiers, twenty-four white infantrymen, one Gatling gun, one twelve-pound brass cannon, 2000 rounds of ammunition, and rations for three days.

Upon arrival, Dudley stated he was in Lincoln primarily to protect women and children. He also quickly obtained arrest warrants for McSween, Billy the Kid, and a few other members of the faction under siege. Dudley pointed his cannon toward the buildings occupied by the McSween gang.

The night of July 19 Sheriff Peppin, bolstered by the military presence, ordered McSween and company out of the house where all his men had congregated after abandoning the stores. When no one came out, Peppin set fire to the house. Billy the Kid and a few others escaped out of the rear of the house as it burned. At daybreak the house was still burning and McSween, with three of his men, tried to escape. They were shot down and killed by the posse; one deputy sheriff was also killed in the gun battle. McSween's body was later retrieved by the Buffalo Soldiers on July 21 after it had laid in the street for quite a while. Tunstall's store was ransacked by the Murphy-Dolan men. Commander Dudley didn't try to intercede, and his small command returned to Fort Stanton.

From regimental headquarters in Santa Fe, Colonel Hatch sent Lieutenant Colonel Dudley a telegram informing him his actions at Lincoln were illegal and were to cease at once. Violence continued in Lincoln County for the remainder of the summer.

On September 30, 1878, Gen. Lew Wallace was made Territorial Governor of New Mexico, replacing Axtell who had been partisan to the Murphy-Dolan faction. On October 8 there was a presidential proclamation issued for "those responsible for the lawlessness in Lincoln County to disperse peaceably to their homes before noon on October 13 or military action would be meted out to transgressors." This amnesty proclamation was taken to Lincoln by a black trooper of the 9th Cavalry. By the end of the month there was a general amnesty for everyone except military officers at Fort Stanton.

On December 7 Governor Wallace requested Colonel Hatch to remove Dudley as commanding officer at Fort Stanton. The governor stated Dudley had "excited the animosity of parties in Lincoln County to such a degree as to embarrass the administration of affairs in that locality."

Mrs. McSween's lawyer, Houston Chapman, a friend of the governor, was killed in front of the Lincoln County courthouse on February 18, 1879, by Murphy-Dolan gunmen. The new sheriff George Kimball was at Fort Stanton at the time. He returned to Lincoln with Lt. Byron Dawson and a detachment of black soldiers from Troops F, H, and M, 9th Cavalry. The soldiers retrieved the lawyer's body. It had laid in the street for a long time; reportedly the citizens were scared to touch it.

Governor Wallace traveled to Lincoln with a guard of black troopers. Dudley was removed from command at Fort Stanton and sent to Fort Union until further orders. Commander Dudley was replaced by Capt. Henry Carroll.

In April Dudley was indicted for arson in the burning of the McSween home. He was acquitted of those charges because he didn't participate in the act, although he didn't try to stop it either. Dudley was later given the military command of Fort Cummings.

The 9th Cavalry continued to battle outlaws and renegades in Lincoln and Dona Ana Counties. They were involved in two unsuccessful manhunts of Billy the Kid, who had broken out of jail earlier in the year.

An interesting side note in regards to the Lincoln County War was the participation of two black ex-soldiers. George Washington, an employee of McSween, was a gunman for his boss and a former cavalry trooper. Sebrian Bates worked in the McSween home and had earlier been a trooper of the 9th Cavalry from 1866 to January 1877, when he was discharged from Fort Stanton. Bates had been sent by McSween to talk to the soldiers during the battle in Lincoln. Sheriff Peppin arrested Bates and forced him to help bury McSween and others. Bates remained in the employ of Mrs. McSween after the battle. Bates and Washington gave critical courtroom testimony about the battle and against Commander Dudley.

The other well-known conflict that black soldiers were involved in was the famous Johnson County Range War that took place in Wyoming in 1892. The powerful ranchers in northern Wyoming had formed a Stockgrowers Association to run out or kill rustlers in their county. For this purpose twenty-five gunmen were recruited from Texas.

On April 15, 1892, an army of gunmen numbering forty-nine men under the auspices of the Stockgrowers Association left Cheyenne, Wyoming, by train, led by Frank Wolcott. At Casper, Wyoming, they detrained, mounted up, and rode to the nearby KC Ranch, where they thought they were going to find fourteen rustlers. They did kill two of the cowboys they found on the ranch, at which time they were told an even larger posse of local citizens were on their way to the KC Ranch to do battle with the hired thugs. Knowing they were outgunned, the stockgrower's men headed to the TA Ranch located thirteen miles south of Buffalo. At this ranch they were met by a contingent of U.S. cavalry from Fort McKinney who had been requested by

Acting Governor Amos Barber. The cavalry gave Wolcott and his men an escort to Fort D. A. Russell, near Cheyenne, where they were all imprisoned pending trial for murder of the two cowboys.

On June 1 six prominent members of the Stockgrowers Association sent a telegram to Wyoming U.S. Senator Joseph M. Carey that stated:

> ... Order Major Fechet and the two companies of the Sixth Cavalry from McKinney to Niobrara, anywhere else out of that country. He and his men have relations with the sheriff and his gang that make the whole command very undesirable for us. Send six companies of Ninth Cavalry from Robinson to McKinney. The colored troops will have no sympathy for Texas thieves and are the troops we want. . . .

Senator Carey made a request to Secretary of War Stephen B. Elkins for troops to be concentrated in northern Wyoming. Two weeks later units of the 9th Cavalry were packed up and moving to Wyoming. Maj. Charles S. Ilsley led a command of six troops, comprised of 310 officers and soldiers to the Powder River where they established Camp Bettens in Sheridan County, Wyoming, on June 13.

The Buffalo Soldiers remained in Wyoming throughout the summer on peacekeeping duties. The biggest problems they encountered were the racist sentiments and actions of the white citizens of Suggs, Wyoming, located near Camp Bettens.

Four troops of the 9th left Wyoming on September 26 for Fort Robinson, the last two in a month's time. Although they didn't have to fight, their presence brought about peace and stability, except when they ventured into the nearby town on leave. Most of the interaction the Buffalo Soldiers had with outlaws was generally in the Indian Territory (Oklahoma) or Texas.

In the book, *Carbine and Lance: The Story of Old Fort Sill*, Col. W. S. Nye called Lt. William R. Harmon, 10th Cavalry, "one of the most energetic and successful thief catchers the frontier produced."

According to the Fort Smith, Arkansas, federal criminal records, in April of 1870 Lieutenant Harmon arrested a stock thief named Frank O'Brien near Gainesville, Texas. O'Brien and a man named Mangin had been selling illegal whiskey and stealing livestock in the Indian Territory. Harmon had been tipped about O'Brien stealing three U.S. army mules and selling them in Shreveport, Louisiana. O'Brien made a full confession to Harmon after he was arrested including the fact that the mules were branded "U.S." when they were stolen. Additionally, he stated that the mules were stolen at a location in the Indian Territory known as Stinking Creek in January of 1870. O'Brien tried to sell the mules in Texas, but couldn't find a buyer so he then took them to Louisiana.

Harmon took O'Brien and some other prisoners he arrested to Fort Arbuckle, Indian Territory, on April 15, 1870. Major Yard at Arbuckle took command of the prisoners that morning. By the evening nine prisoners were turned over to a black sergeant and a detachment of 10th Cavalry troopers for transport to Fort Sill. Harmon watched the detail as it left Fort Arbuckle. About three quarters of a mile from the fort shooting was heard coming from the direction of the detail. Harmon rode out to see what was going on. As he neared the detail he heard the sergeant say, "My orders are to take you to Fort Sill, just take the road and march, if any of you attempt to get away I'll ... you along." The prisoners had somehow gotten loose from their ties except O'Brien and another prisoner he was tied to. Most of the prisoners were trying to run into the thickets except four who had been shot dead. The prisoners were all rounded up and taken on to Fort Sill except O'Brien who was placed in the Fort Arbuckle hospital with an arm wound. His arm was later amputated. O'Brien was tried for larceny in the Van Buren, Arkansas, Federal Court in July of 1870 and found guilty.

That same year on May 6, a white outlaw band stole 139 mules from a government wagon train at Bluff Creek, Indian Territory. The outlaws with the stolen livestock headed south across the Red River into Texas.

Lieutenant Harmon, with five black soldiers from Troop M, 10th Cavalry, picked up their trail and pursued them doggedly. They caught up with the thieves in Montague County, Texas, two days later. There were five outlaws in the band as they chased them across the prairie. Near Clear Creek in Cook County, the outlaws let one hundred of the mules go. Lieutenant Harmon and the troopers cornered the outlaws after an eighteen mile chase in a forested ravine. A brief gunfight ensued, one of the Texas outlaws was killed, and the four others surrendered. They told Harmon that they were to meet up with three other outlaws. The lieutenant waited for the three to show up. When they did, he promptly arrested them also. Harmon and his five black troopers took seven prisoners, two wagons, three horses, and 127 government mules back to Fort Arbuckle in the Indian Territory. It was a good haul. Three men were eventually tried for larceny at federal court at Van Buren, Arkansas. The men were Samuel W. Cady, Jacob Black, and William Whelock. They were tried and convicted on November 14, 1870.

At Fort Richardson, Texas, on April 22, 1873, Cpl. John Wright, Troop L, 10th Cavalry, along with two privates assisted a deputy sheriff in transporting an escaped convict to Weatherford, Texas.

From September to December of 1873, units of the 10th Cavalry recovered almost 100 head of stolen livestock, killed four white outlaws, and arrested seventeen more in Texas.

In September of 1879, the Indian Territory was plagued by a large confederacy of white and mixed-blood Cherokee outlaws. The army command at Fort Sill decided to act on this menace. U.S. Army General Order #188 authorized an expedition to be launched against the outlaws' base, located at a ranch on the Cimarron River.

Capt. Wirt Davis, 4th U.S. Cavalry was assigned as commander of the expedition. His orders were to break up and capture a band of outlaws existing to the northeast of Fort Sill, Indian Territory.

Others in Captain Davis' command included 2nd Lt. T. W. Jones, 10th Cavalry, 2nd Lt. A. M. Patch, 4th Cavalry, and Assistant Army Surgeon A. T. Fitch. The command strength included all of the members of Troop F, 4th Cavalry and Troop G, 10th Cavalry and two Indian scouts as guides. The expedition left Fort Sill on September 9, 1879, and would not return to post for more than a month. The troopers would travel more than 200 miles in their search for the outlaws.

After a long ride through the territory, the military command located the ranch that the desperadoes used as a headquarters on September 25. This location today is probably close to where Langston University is situated, near the Cimarron River.

The blue clad troopers encircled the ranch house. Somehow Lieutenant Patch fractured his right leg as the soldiers moved in on the outlaws. There is no record of a battle or resistance by the renegades, but the outlaws may have put up a brief struggle before surrendering. No one was injured in the command except the lieutenant. The outlaws were placed in restraints. They included James Arsenia, an escaped convict and well-known stock thief, Clay Collins, Lindsey Collins, Andrew W. Wofford, and John W. Wilson. The latter four were all members of the Cochran gang of Cherokee outlaws. Clay Collins, also known as Clay Charles, was wanted for selling illegal whiskey in the Indian Territory. Also arrested were Eck Ross, wanted for an attempted murder charge near Tahlequah, Cherokee Nation; Newton Scriemscher, an escaped convict, and Henry Taylor, wanted for questioning in the murder of a man named Johnson at Wanderer's Creek, Texas; James Riley, also known as James Rider, and Milton H. Lukens, also known as Milt Lukum, arrested for guilt by association.

Lieutenant Patch was taken to the Pawnee Indian Agency where Surgeon Fitch examined his injured leg. The doctor said it was a compound fracture, and he shortly thereafter amputated the leg below the knee.

The command, with prisoners, meanwhile was in transit to Fort Sill, where they arrived on October 29. In completing the expedition, black and white troopers rode 494 miles round-trip across the Oklahoma prairie.

Two of the prisoners later escaped from the Fort Sill post guard house with a third confederate who was lodged in jail with them on a different charge. The eight other prisoners were taken to the Fort Smith, Arkansas, federal jail by Deputy U.S. Marshal James H. Mershon of Judge Isaac C. Parker's court.

While the 10th U.S. Cavalry was stationed at Fort Davis, Texas, in the summer of 1882, one of the organizational returns read as:

Troop M—Pina Colorado, Texas. Saddler Ross mortally wounded. Sergeant Winfield Scott and Private Augustus Dover wounded in line of duty while attempting to arrest desperado on military reservation. The desperado W. A. Alexander was killed resisting arrest. [Pina Colorado is located in the Big Bend country of West Texas near Alpine.]

At Camp Cantonment, Indian Territory, in the fall of 1882, detachments of the 24th Infantry Regiment and the 9th Cavalry Regiment were stationed there to protect the Indians and guard the cattle trails. Camp Cantonment was located on the North Canadian River where the Caldwell Cattle Trail crossed. On many occasions a trail herd of cattle was held up to allow it to rest before crossing the river. A good supply of legal whiskey was available at the post trader's store. Cowboys generally would quench their thirst here given an opportunity.

A cattleman named Johnson had 1,000 head of cattle moving from Fort Cobb, Indian Territory, to Hunnewell, Kansas, for shipment to Kansas City. During the drive the herd was stopped across the river from Camp Cantonment.

The herd foreman and one of the cowhands made a visit to the post, bought some whiskey, and proceeded to get intoxicated. The two cowboys mounted their ponies and rode through the U.S. Army Indian scouts' camp firing their pistols into the tepees. They killed the dog of one of the scouts and shot up the post trader's store.

Capt. Charles C. Hood, 24th Infantry, was the commander of the post at that time. Previously Hood had been stationed in Texas on the dangerous Rio Grande for twenty years. He attempted to use mounted infantry to catch the cowboys, but they got away. Captain Hood then decided to order twenty-five experienced Buffalo Soldiers from Troop K, 9th Cavalry, who were stationed at Camp Cantonment to take up the hunt. The horse soldiers with Indian scouts picked up the cowboys' trail and located them. They encircled the cowpunchers' position on the prairie and gave them an ultimatum to surrender, which they did promptly. They knew the black troopers meant business.

The white Texas cowboys were belligerent when they were brought into the post. While being questioned by Major Hood, they bragged about their shootouts and fights in Texas. One said that he had built the courthouse in the county where he was born with the fines he had paid due to his many escapades. Major Hood replied that he was a pretty bad man himself; he was going to send them before the "hangin' judge," Isaac C. Parker at Fort Smith, Arkansas—a location the outlaws in the Indian Territory called "hell on the border." Fort Smith was the federal court for the entire Indian Territory during the 1880s.

When the army ambulance, which also served as a prisoner's wagon and escort, arrived at the post adjutant's office to transport the prisoners to Fort Smith, the outlaws had changed their demeanor.

The outlaws began to plead and beg for mercy. The foreman said the cattle were left in his charge by the owner and were worth $75.00; if he was sent to Fort Smith to stand trial the cattleman would incur a great loss.

Major Hood personally knew the owner of the cattle and didn't want him to take a monetary loss. He told the two cowboys if they would pay the Indians for the damages he would drop the charges and release them. The much relieved cowboys paid twenty dollars for the dog they killed and gave the Indian scouts five head of cattle.

CHAPTER TWENTY-SIX

A Soldier's Soldier

It would probably be impossible to find a soldier who would be considered the best Buffalo Soldier. But after researching the records of the African American troopers, my favorite is Horace W. Bivins.

Bivins was born a free black man in Pungoteague, Accomack County, Virginia, May 8, 1862. He grew up on his father's farm. When he was fifteen, Bivins was put in charge of an eight-horse farm one mile from Keller Station, Virginia.

Horace W. Bivins entered Hampton Normal and Agricultural Institute on June 13, 1885, at which time he received his first military training. He also attended Wayland Seminary. Bivins had a great desire for adventure and wanted to see the western frontier of the country. He enlisted in the United States Army on November 7, 1887, at Washington, D.C. After ten days, Bivins was sent to Jefferson Barracks in St. Louis, Missouri where he took lessons in mounted and dismounted drill. Bivins was assigned to Troop E, 10th Cavalry, and joined it on June 18, 1888, at Fort Grant, Arizona Territory. Just days after arriving at Fort Grant, Bivins' troop was ordered out due to reports that Apaches had left the San Carlos Reservation and were headed for Mexico.

Troop E scouted along the Saint Pedro River, east and west, but found no Apaches. On February 22, 1889, Troop E was sent to San Carlos, Arizona Territory. The soldiers camp was set up on the north side of the Gila River. At San Carlos at this time there were Troops E and F, 10th Cavalry; Troop G, 4th Cavalry; and Companies C and G of the 24th Infantry which were assigned to the agency. Young Bivins was given duty as a lineman, riding between San Carlos and the town of Globe, about thirty miles, keeping the telegraph line in repair. The route took Bivins close by the camp of a band of renegade Apaches led by Churchana. The Indians never attempted to impede or molest Bivins while he was doing his job.

Churchana, an Apache chief, had set up camp near the village known as Benson's Camp and dared the army to arrest him. A detachment of twelve troopers and one officer were assigned to guard Benson's Camp located about two miles from Churchana's band.

On April 9, 1889, Lieutenants Watson, Dade, and Littlebrant, all of the 10th Cavalry, with three troops and sixty Apache scouts, surrounded the camp of Churchana and demanded surrender with conditions. If the Apache chief was to identify and surrender all murderers to the army and government, then he wouldn't be prosecuted for previous crimes.

When the followers of Churchana found out the chief was going to surrender, they mutinied. In the fight that took place, four hostiles were killed, and Churchana suffered numerous knife stab wounds. He was taken to the army hospital, after being saved by the black troopers. The next day Lieutenant Watson positioned two Hotchkiss guns approximately six hundred yards east of the Apaches' fortified positions. With the deadly guns aimed at their positions, the Apaches surrendered.

Bivins' troop was ordered to change posts with Troop I, 10th Cavalry. Troop E arrived at Fort Apache, Arizona Territory on October 17, 1889, after a seven day ride over rough terrain.

Bivins was given the position of clerk in the regimental adjutant's office until June 15, 1890, when he made the rank of corporal.

Corporal Bivins began target practice with his troop while they were at San Carlos. From the beginning it was recognized that Bivins had superior skills shooting both rifle and pistol. The very first time he engaged in sharpshooting, he finished second in his troop of sixty men. Bivins was given the medal as sharp-shooter in 1889 and led his troop for the duration of his tenure in the regiment as top marksman.

In 1892 the 10th Cavalry was transferred to Montana, arriving at Custer Junction after passing through Billings on May 4. After coming from the scorching southwest, the regiment de-trained in a snow blizzard. There was almost a foot of snow, and they marched to Fort Custer the following day.

Bivins and the 10th Cavalry stayed six years in Montana. Things were fairly quiet for the regiment during those years. On one occasion they were called out when a sheepherder was mur-dered by a small group of renegade Cheyenne. Responding to the Canadian government, they helped locate and transport Crees who had crossed the border illegally. Additionally, Bivins was involved in guard duty along the Northern Pacific Railroad in 1894 during the rail strike and the labor dispute known as "Coxey's army" disturbance.

Corporal Bivins, during these years, was making a reputa-tion as a crack shot with the carbine and revolver pistol. After winning medals in competition with soldiers at Fort Keogh and Fort Assiniboine in 1892 and 1893, he won first place in cavalry competition for the Department of Colorado and Dakota. In 1894 Bivins won first place in the carbine team for the entire United States Army and had the highest combined score for car-bine and pistol. That same year Bivins won five different gold medals for his marksmanship.

In 1896 the famous national showman Col. William F. "Buffalo Bill" Cody made an offer to Bivins to give a shooting exhibition in his wild west show. Cody sought to obtain a fur-lough for Bivins and pay him $100 a month and expenses. Cody wanted Bivins to shoot competitively against the famous Annie Oakley. One hundred dollars a month (before the turn of the century) was a lot of money for an African American. Yet Bivins

Expert marksman, Sergeant Horace W. Bivins, 10th Cavalry and his dog Booth. Taken from Under Fire with the Tenth U.S. Cavalry, *published in 1899.*   (Author's collection)

turned it down because he was committed to the army, and his officers had promised him the rank of ordnance sergeant. If Bivins had taken Cody up on his offer, it is interesting to speculate how that would have impacted the image of African Americans on the western frontier, because Cody never had any black stars in his wild west show. Cody's show, highly romanticized, helped shape the mythology of the American west.

In 1897 Bivins again attended Hampton Institute, this time on an army furlough. He took a special course in military tactics under orders from the War Department.

When Bivins rejoined Troop G, 10th Cavalry, they were on patrol on the Blackfeet Reservation in Montana. The United States government had announced that some Blackfeet lands would be opened to white settlement on April 10, 1898. The regiment was ordered to Chickamauga, Tennessee, on April 14, 1898, due to the political actions in Cuba. The regiment would be one of the regular army units to serve in the Spanish-American War besides many volunteer units.

The 10th Cavalry left Fort Assiniboine, Montana on April 19, 1898. Once they had arrived in Tennessee, they were ordered to Florida, where, like all the other cavalry regiments, they found out they would have to leave their horses on the mainland. Therefore they would fight as dismounted cavalry during their stay in Cuba.

Troop G, 10th Cavalry had a Hotchkiss Gun Detachment as part of the 2nd Cavalry Brigade, 5th Army Corps on the island of Cuba. Sergeant Bivins served with this Hotchkiss Gun Detachment. The 10th Cavalry landed on the Caribbean island on June 22, 1898.

While in Cuba, Sergeant Bivins fought at Santiago and at San Juan Hill. During the attack on San Juan Hill, Bivins helped in shooting down the Spanish observation balloon which had directed enemy gunfire on United States military positions. Bivins' Hotchkiss gun detachment, under Lt. James B. Hughes, crossed San Juan Creek, opened fire on the Spanish army blockhouse on Kettle Hill, and forced the Spaniards to leave the hill. Later on they took a position on the crest of a hill occupied by the 1st U.S. Volunteer Cavalry Regiment and did effective work against another blockhouse in front of that regiment.

The gun detachment had four Hotchkiss guns which were pulled by mules. Seven men were assigned to each gun. During the Battle at San Juan Hill, many of the men in the detachment, including two officers, were wounded or overcome with heat. Sergeant Bivins had to operate his Hotchkiss gun by himself. After each shot the gun would bounce back six to eight feet. He then had to pull the gun back into position, reload, set the range, and fire. Sergeant Bivins repeated this procedure seventy-five times during the Battle of San Juan Hill.

When Bivins' Hotchkiss gun ran out of ammunition, he picked up his carbine and joined the famed "Rough Riders" (1st Volunteer Cavalry Regiment) 300 yards to his right and opened fire on the Spanish positions 600 yards below. When an officer nearby asked him who he was, Sergeant Bivins replied, "This is no time to ask such foolish questions," and continued firing his carbine.

Half an hour later the order to cease fire was given. Bivins turned around and asked the officer closest to him if he was the one who had spoken earlier. The officer affirmed his answer, identifying himself as Col. Theodore Roosevelt, commanding officer of the Rough Riders. After hearing Bivins' explanation, Roosevelt made no further objection to his fighting alongside his men. For his actions with the Hotchkiss gun on San Juan Hill, Sergeant Bivins received the Silver Star for meritorious conduct in battle.

In 1901 Sergeant Bivins was in the squadron of the 10th Cavalry that was sent to the Philippine Islands. They were stationed from April until August on the island of Samar. Troop G, commanded by Capt. Robert D. Read, was stationed at the town of Moa in the eastern part of the island, charged with the pacification of a large territory.

For three months Sergeant Bivins was in command of a reconnaissance party of sixteen men and two corporals on the northeastern point of the island. It was their duty to patrol roads, open up lines of communication through the jungles, break up any concentration of hostile natives, obtain the surrender of, and bring into headquarters any revolutionaries found in the territory.

The carabao, a small water buffalo, was used for all their transportation needs, although on many expeditions it was necessary for the soldiers to pack and carry their own supplies. The detachment, in addition to its regular weapons, was armed with bolo knives for clearing the way through the jungle. During this operation, 560 miles of trails were penetrated, and many prisoners were secured. At one point 500 men surrendered and were taken by Sergeant Bivins and his small unit to the troop headquarters at Moa.

In 1902 the squadron returned to the United States. In 1906, Bivins served as ordnance sergeant under George Patton (who became the famous World War II general) at Fort Missoula, Montana. After five years service in Wyoming and Nebraska, the 10th Cavalry put in another tour of duty in the Philippines, from 1907 to 1909. In all, Sergeant Bivins served four years, three months, and twenty-two days in Cuba and the Philippines.

During his second tour of duty in the Philippines, Sergeant Bivins spent much time making a collection of Philippine birds as well as shells, fossils, and many other curios. Some of these were later bought by the leading museums in the United States. Two monkey-eating eagles that Bivins shot were placed in east coast museums. At the time, only six of the species had ever been brought into the United States. Taxidermy became one of Sergeant Bivins' hobbies.

Before his discharge from active duty in 1913, Sergeant Bivins served under General Pershing as acting commissary and quartermaster sergeant at Camp Hamilton, Cuba and Fort Sam Houston, Texas.

While retired, Bivins was offered a position with the Liberian government in Africa. He was to supervise the drilling and training of an army of 115,000 men which was being raised to fight the Germans in West Africa, after the small African republic followed the United States into World War I.

Bivins declined the offer, preferring to serve with American troops. The position would have meant a substantial pay increase in addition to retirement pay from the United States Army.

Bivins was commissioned a captain of infantry of the officer's reserve corps on November 11, 1919, shortly after reverting to the retired list of the regular army. His Silver Star for gallantry at Santiago was issued by the War Department, January 8, 1925. He had been cited in general orders in 1900.

During the Spanish-American War in Cuba, Bivins had a pet dog named Booth. The dog was born in the west and spent his puppyhood around Fort Custer, where he swam the Little Bighorn River in pursuit of duck and geese dropped by the accurate rifle of Bivins. Booth was a full-blooded Irish water spaniel, a constant companion, and "soldier" of the 10th Cavalry.

Booth's ability and acceptance for duty as a messenger in the Spanish-American War was tested as the 10th Cavalry Regiment was preparing to embark for Cuba. Capt. Allyn Capron, who had charge of the transport on which the 10th was to sail, initially decided no dogs would be allowed on board the ship. Bivins told the captain that Booth could render valuable service.

"What can the dog do?" asked Captain Capron.

"He will act as messenger," answered Sergeant Bivins.

"All right. You take him uptown, about 500 yards away and have him bring me a letter."

When taken to the designated spot, Booth set off at a trot with the message and did not stop until he had reached Captain Capron.

At the Battle of Santiago, Booth guarded the remains of Pvt. William Slaughter, killed in the charge up San Juan Hill, until the body was found. The dog followed his master to the Philippines, but owing to the fear of contagion from some disease, Bivins was refused permission to bring him back to the states. Booth was left with some officers in Pensy, but shortly afterwards he disappeared and was never heard of again.

Horace W. Bivins made his retirement home in Billings, Montana. He became famous for his gardening activities, especially his outstanding sweet potatoes.

Bivins' wife, Claudia May Bivins, was born in Deadwood, South Dakota on June 26, 1881, the daughter of Mr. and Mrs. Walker Browning. Her family had moved to Billings in 1883. Sergeant Bivins married her on March 16, 1904, after which they resided in Missoula, Montana, for a short time. They had three children; two sons, Charles W. and Horace P., and a daughter, Ruth, who died in her teen years.

Mrs. Bivins was a notable person in her own right. She was an active member of the African Methodist Episcopal Church,

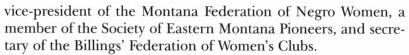

vice-president of the Montana Federation of Negro Women, a member of the Society of Eastern Montana Pioneers, and secretary of the Billings' Federation of Women's Clubs.

In 1899 Sergeant Bivins co-authored a book on the 10th Cavalry Regiment and its exploits during the Spanish-American War entitled, *Under Fire with the Tenth U.S. Cavalry*.

Bivins' collection of rare specimens of mammals, reptiles, and birds, as well as other curios from the Philippines, were donated to the Eastern Montana College of Education.

During his lifetime, Sergeant Bivins was the only man in the United States military to win three marksmanship gold medals in one year.

Mrs. Bivins died at the age of sixty-three in August of 1944. Horace W. Bivins remained in Billings, Montana until September of 1949, when at the age of eighty-three, he moved to Philadelphia, Pennsylvania, to live with his sons. Bivins spent his last years in the "City of Brotherly Love" and was a soldier to the end.

Buffalo Soldier Narratives

The following first-person accounts are reprinted verbatim from primary sources. Insertions or corrections have been made only where strictly necessary for clarity.

George Conrad, Troop G, 9th Cavalry
Indian Pioneer Papers
Oklahoma Historical Society

They sent us here [Oklahoma Territory] to keep the immigrants from settling up Oklahoma. I went to Fort Riley the 1st day of October, 1883, and stayed there for three weeks. Left Fort Riley and went to Fort Worth, Texas, and landed at Henryetta, Texas, on the 14th day of October 1883, then we had sixty-five miles to walk to Fort Sill. We walked there in three days. There, I was assigned to my company, Troop G, 9th Cavalry. We stayed and drilled at Fort Sill six months, then we were assigned to duty. We received orders to Stillwater, Oklahoma to move 500 immigrants under Captain Couch. We landed there on the 23rd of January, Saturday evening, and Sunday was the 24. We had general inspection Monday, January 25, 1885. We fell in line of battle, sixteen companies of soldiers to move 500 immigrants to the Arkansas [City], Kansas line.

We formed a line at 9:00 o'clock Monday morning, and Captain Couch ran up his white flag, and Colonel Hatch sent the orderly up to see what he meant by putting up the flag, so he sent word back, "If you don't fire on me, I'll leave tomorrow." Colonel Hatch turned around to the Major and told him to turn his troops back to camp, and detail three camps of soldiers of the 9th Cavalry to carry Captain Couch's troop of 500 immigrants to Arkansas City, Kansas. Troop L, Troop D, and Troop B took them back with forty-three wagons and put them over the line of Kansas. Then we were ordered back to our supply camp at Camp Alice, nine miles north of Guthrie in the Cimarron Horse Shoe bottom. We stayed there about three months, and Captain Couch and his colony came back into the Territory at Caldwell, Kansas, June 1885. I stayed there till August 8, then we changed regiments with the 5th Cavalry to go to Nebraska. There was a breakout with the Indians at Fort Reno the first of July, 1885. The Indian Agency tried to make the Indians wear citizens clothes. They had to call General Sheridan from Washington, D.C., to quiet the Indians. Now, we had to make a line in three divisions, fifteen miles apart, one non-commissioned officer of each squad and these men [were] to go to Caldwell, Kansas and bring him to Fort Reno that night, and he came that night so the next morning Colonel Brisbane reported to General Sheridan what the trouble was. General Sheridan called all the Indian chiefs together and asked them why they rebelled against the Agency; they told him that they weren't going to wear citizens clothes. General Sheridan called his corporals and sergeants together and told them to go behind the guards house and dig a grave for this Agency agent in order to fool the Indian chiefs. Then he sent a detachment of soldiers to order the Indian chiefs away from the guard house and to put this agent in the ambulance that brought him to Fort Reno, and take him back to Washington, D.C., to remain there till he returned. The next morning he called all the Indian chiefs to the guard house and pointed to the grave and said that "I have killed the Agent and buried him here." The Indians tore the feathers out of their hats rejoicing that they have killed the agent.

On the 12th day of that same July, we had general inspection with General Firesides from Washington, then we [were] ordered back to our supply camp to stay there until we got orders to our change. On August 8, we got orders to change to go to Nebraska to Fort Robinson, Fort Nibrary [sic], and Fort McKinney. We left on the 8th of August.

First Sergeant John F. Casey
Troop H, 10th U.S. Cavalry
U.S. Army Pension Files
Testimony recorded November 6, 1919

John F. Casey, late 1st Sgt., Troop H, 10th U.S. Cavalry enlisted at Kansas City, MO September 28, 1872, was assigned to Troop H, 10th Cavalry at Fort Gibson, I.T. [Indian Territory]. Served in several military campaigns at Parker, Kansas in pursuit of horse thieves and renegades. Troop transferred to Fort Sill, I.T., in 1873. Several Indian campaigns in 1873, Red River, 2nd Campaign, Washitaw [sic] Agency, in pursuit of Kiowa and Commanche [Comanche] Indians. In the spring of 1873 the Kiowa and Commanche Indians surrounded the Post of Fort Sill, which caused the command to keep their horses saddled and to arms for three consecutive days. The number of Indians were supposed to be between five and six thousand surrounding the Post, which were Kiowas and Commanches, whose chief was Lone Wolf. At that time the Indians were going on the war path so they called for volunteers, Col. B. H. Grayson [Grierson], commanding the Post, called for a volunteer to carry a dispatch to the Indian Agent who was about two and one-half or three miles east of the Post. Out of nine troops of Cavalry and three of Infantry and two U.S. Indian scouts none would volunteer, so the Sergeant Major, having known me personally before I entered the army, come to my troop and asked me would I volunteer to carry a dispatch for the Colonel to the Indian Agency. I told him I would, if they would permit me to ride my Captain's horse. He complied with my request and the orderly brought the horse to my barracks at once and I reported to the Adjutant for orders. He gave me a sealed envelope which contained the orders of the Commander to carry to the Indian Agent. I charged right through the Indians who lined the road and all the surrounding country, clear to the Indian commissary, got the dispatch Ok'd by the Indian Agent and returned safely without firing a shot, which would have been futile for me to do, as the Indians were in great numbers and had their bows and arrows pointing at me as I rode through, but they did not fire a shot. I returned safely, delivered the message to the Adjutant and in about two and one-half hours the Indians began moving away from the Post. This was not entered on my discharge, because at that time my captain had been promoted or was on leave and I was discharged by a young West Pointer, C. G. Ayres, who did not know my military career, therefore gave me no mark of distinction.

In a very short time, probably ten or twenty days, the regiment was moved out on a campaign in pursuit of Chief Lone Wolf and the Kiowas and Commanche Indians who had gone on the war path. This campaign lasted about one and one-half years, from 1873 to 1875. In this campaign the regiment was for ten days snowed in without rations but one hardtack a meal and very little coffee because our supply train was lost in the snow storm. For ten days they wandered across the plains and could not find our camp. In the meantime I was detailed under the Lieutenant with twenty men from my company to go to the rescue of a band of buffalo hunters who were surrounded by a band of Indians and had asked for reinforcement and we were sent to relieve them. During this trip each man was only allowed to carry one blanket and his poncho and we had to drive our picket pins between the pommel and canta [cantle] of the saddle. In this way we had to sleep with our heads upon our saddles and the horses kept us awake and uncovered most of the night. It was very cold and we nearly froze. After five days out we got orders to return to headquarters. On our return trip two days before we reached camp it rained and snowed and we had nothing to eat as we had no fuel for cooking. We had to burn buffalo chips and they were wet and would not burn and there were was no wood within twenty miles. When we returned to camp the command had moved, but they had left a wagon with hardtack, bacon and beans and coffee, which we came upon after being without food for two days and nearly froze. After we had eaten our meal and fed our horses we started to find headquarters, which was about twenty miles away.

It rained and snowed continually all day and night and we had no overcoats, only our ponchos. When we reached head-quarters, about 12 o'clock at night, the snow was six or eight inches deep. In this we had to lay down to sleep with our clothes and blankets wringing wet and the weather continued very cold during the entire time we were there, which was ten days or more. In the meantime we were on half rations or less. Our horses had no forage, as the train was lost in the snow storm and we could get nothing done [for] them or ourselves. We had to go one-half of a mile to cut down cottonwood trees and carry the limbs for the horses to eat. This was all the food they had dur-ing the whole ten days and we had to carry wood and build log heap fires in the rear of our horses, night and day, to keep them from freezing to death. We had no tents to sleep under only shelter tent halves. We lost between three and four hundred horses and mules for the three regiments, which were two of Cavalry and part of one Infantry in this camp. General Scofield [Schofield] was in command as near as I can remember. This ends this campaign of 1873, 74 and 75, which to the best of my knowledge ended along about February, 1875 at Fort Sill.

"When we arrived at Fort Sill there were orders waiting for our regiment to be transferred to Fort Davis, Texas. We arrived at Fort Davis, Texas, May 1, 1875, from which Post I was on con-tinuous scouting from ten days to thirty days, and from that to a year and a half at a period. At this post we were stationed ten years. From this Post we were continuously scouting either as a whole company or in detachments from ten to twenty men in each. In May, 1877, at 12 o'clock at night we were called to the rescue of a band of men who were besieged in Musker Canyon [?]. When we got to the canyon we had to file in and

charge the Indians in columns of fours, the canyon being so narrow we couldn't deploy. It was so dark we could not see one from
the other and there was danger of falling into a subterranean
lake. On this charge my horse [fell] into a partly filled up well or
spring and two horses fell on top of me, which knocked my left
shoulder out of place. In this condition I continued on the drive
for six days until I received relief and returned to the post.

In the year 1879 and 1880, I was on another campaign
which is know as the Victory [Victorio] Campaign, in pursuit of
Muschalary [Mescalero] Indians which came from New Mexico
to Texas, murdering and pillaging as they went, about four hundred strong. My company and several other troops in fact a
whole regiment or parts of regiments were sent in pursuit of
them. This campaign lasted about a year and four months.
During this campaign we tracked the Indians from Texas into
Old Mexico and the Mexicans drove them back into Texas crossing the Rio Grande near El Paso, Texas. We first intercepted
them at Eagle Springs, Texas, had a running fight about dark on
the following day, and drove them back toward Mexico and the
Copoka [?] Mountains and thence into the Crecey [?] Mountains
in the Salt Lake Valley [where] we engaged in battle and drove
them from the Salt Lake Valley into the mountains again, and
two companies of us kept them engaged all day until about three
o'clock in the afternoon when our ammunition ran out and we
were ... called to the Reserves and other troops took our place
in the firing line. Shortly after the Indians retreated going in the
direction of Old Mexico and between 4 and 5 o'clock in the
evening my company was ordered to flank them on the west and
keep them out of Old Mexico. While traveling over sage brush,
sand and alkali we became very thirsty and nearly perished from
a lack of water, as we had no fresh water, nothing but salty water
for two days. About seven o'clock that evening a cloud appeared
in the horizon and in about twenty minutes the rain commenced
pouring down in torrents which gave us fresh water for the first
time in twenty-four hours. We got water and watered our stock
and kept on the trail to Old Mexico. We arrived too late to keep
the Indians off. We followed the trail until we came to the Hot
Springs in the bed of the Rio Grande, where Indians had
crossed into Old Mexico. The Mexican soldiers, who were on the

opposite side, took up the trail and followed them into the Candleary [?] Mountains, Mexico, and there captured all of the band except eight, including Chief Victory [Victorio], who was the chief of the tribe. They beheaded him and carried his head to Mexico City. This ended this campaign.*

In 1885, April 1st, our regiment was ordered from Fort Davis, Texas to Fort Grant, Arizona, which was also headquarters at this time of the 1st U.S. Infantry. Sometime in July we were ordered on a campaign in pursuit of Geronomo [Geronimo], Chief of the Cherhuarhua [Chiricahua] Indians. This campaign lasted about one year and a half, which ended in the capture of Geronomo and his entire band of Indians in Skeleton [?] Canyon, Old Mexico. While on this campaign we had our supply camp in [?] Canyon, twenty miles south of Fort Bowie, Arizona. And from this camp which was our headquarters we continued scouting at various times from ten to twenty days at a time, down to the border of Old Mexico and as far as Silver City, New Mexico and into the Cherhuarhua Mountains. On this campaign in the fall of 1885 we encountered a very severe snow storm, rain, sleet and snow. While in this camp we were not able to build a fire on account of the rain, sleet and snow which continued for four days. Neither could we lay down on our blankets to sleep as our clothing was wringing wet and our blankets were frozen, and the earth was so wet that we couldn't lay down on the ground, so we had to cut down brush and ... logs. There were only two blankets to a man. On this campaign I contracted a cold which developed into catarrh, which caused the Captain to send for the doctor from Fort Bowie when we arrived in camp, and in the meantime a great many of our men developed symptoms of scurvy. The doctor gave us medicine, what it was I do not know, but it caused me and a great many of the men to suffer great pain and lose our teeth. This campaign ended in the capture of Geronomo and his entire band of Indians, in Skeleton [?] Canyon, Old Mexico, in 1886. During all of the campaigns I lost my health on account of my company being without water half of the time as we could not find water in the mountains and would have to make dry camp and travel all day in the hot sun and dust without any water to drink either for ourselves or horses. On account of the many campaigns I was on at the end of my term of service in 1888, I was completely broken down physically.... When I came off the campaign of 1886, I never was myself again, as I had to frequently have my teeth worked on and be excused from duty by my doctor or Captain, because I suffered with neuralgia of the head. In the winter of 1887 I contracted what the doctor called the catarrh. This confined me to my office for two weeks. Shortly after my time expired in March 1888, with no objections to re-enlistment. I then went to St. Joseph, Mo., and there took a back set of the same disease with which I suffered at Depcha [?], which the doctor in St. Joseph called the Grippe, which settled in my eyes, back and jaws, which caused me to lose my teeth and also my eyesight. I was almost totally [blind] for two months or more from which I only partly recovered by good medical treatment.

When I was in the service I had been a sharpshooter for several years and have been with three department rifle teams. From this you can see that at that time I have very good eyesight, but now my eyesight is very bad and I suffer with the neuralgia in my head so severely that I was compelled to quit working at my trade, which was a barber, and am now in the Military Soldiers Home at Leavenworth, Kansas, because I [am] no longer able to work and make a living for myself and family. I will further state that I never drank a drink of whiskey or beer in my life. My military career is [par excellence], with three fine discharges.

We were ordered back to our post at Fort Grant, and from there my company moved to Fort Apacha [Apache], Arizona. After we had been in Arizona but a short time, about October 17, 1886, our commanding officer received word that a band of Cherekow [Chiricahua] Indians which had been on the war path for about five years, and had been in and near the Candiery [?] Mountains in Old Mexico all this time, were on their way back to the United States and were committing depredations as they returned. Orders were received to send out detachments of one officer and twenty men each to intercept them as they tried to get back to the reservation. About six o'clock the evening of October 17th my detachment, consisting of Captain C. L. Cooper, twenty men, and two Indian scouts, sighted the Indians. We went into camp and put out a chain guard. Next morning we took the trail and followed it. In the meantime our two Indian scouts became sick and the Captain detailed me as trailer and scout and I selected Sergeant Cole to assist me in trailing. In this we followed the trail without difficulty, and about twelve o'clock we came in sight of them going down the mountain. We waited until they got to the foot of the mountain and we followed them. The mountain was so steep we had to hold the horses back to keep them from falling down. When we arrived at the foot of the mountain the Indians had not yet detected that we were following them and they were going up the opposite side, going west, making for the reservation, supposing that Geronomo was still on the reservation, not knowing that he had been captured. Chief Mangus was supposed to be Geronomo's half brother. Now we struck out on the trail and followed them to the side of the canyon and waited until they had all gotten to the top of the mountain. This way we had to walk and lead our horses, as the mountain was so steep we couldn't ride. Of course, me being the guide and trailer, had to go ahead with Sergeant Cole. While climbing this mountain there would be places two or three horses could pass each other on the trail. In this way six of us men got ahead of the command and the company followed on behind. The Captain being a very large man, had to stop and rest very often and of course we arrived at the top of the mountain one half hour ahead of the command. When we arrived at the top of the mountain we held a council of war of six men, Sergeant Cole and myself, Blacksmith Boyer, Corporal Foster, Privates Sparks and C. E. Miller, and we all swore to each other that we would follow the trail without the command because we knew if we would wait for the command they would get on the reservation and get mixed with the other Indians and we could never capture them, so we mounted our horses and followed the trail on walk, trot and gallop until we came to the rear of the renegades. We were then going down into a canyon which formed the letter "T," the canyon running due north and south. In this way they went in from the East and we hemmed them into the canyon. Two men went to the South, two to the North, Sergeant Cole and myself closing up the gap behind them. At a certain signal they commenced to firing, but not to hit them, but to intimidate them, and one of them returned about twenty shots, which was Mangus's young son, and they all surrendered to us six men, except the chief, his wife and his interpreter. When the Captain arrived we had them all captured and their ponies all carralled [corralled]. That night the Captain had to negotiate with Mangus' aged mother, and as I spoke Spanish, I induced her, by giving her something to eat and sending food to induce them to come in and surrender the next morning at eight o'clock, which they did. This capture occurred at about 4:30 P.M., October 18, 1886. For this service my Captain promoted me 1st Sergeant. I had held this rank off and on in the company for twelve or fourteen years, but had been reduced, then reinstated for this service. At this time I was Corporal, but I was promoted by my Captain to 1st Sergeant for distinguished service in the capture of Chief Mangus and his entire band of Cherekow Apaches and also was commended by General A. Miles, and given the honor of taking them to Florida under the command of a Lieutenant.

My time expired in this troop in the last military service March 6th, 1888, with character excellent on two of my discharges, and very good on one. Time of service 15 years.

I am drawing a pension of only $6.00 per month since 1905, for fracture of left shoulder and nasal catarrh.

Signed
J. F. Casey
Late 1st Sergeant,
Troop H, 10th U.S. Cavalry

Sergeant Casey died at the age of 73 on August 11, 1924

*Author Dan L. Thrapp in his book, *Victorio and the Mimbres Apaches*, writes that Chief Victorio was scalped by soldiers of the Mexican army along with seventy-seven of his followers. The army under the command of Colonel Terrazas marched triumphantly into the City of Chihuahua carrying the scalps four abreast on poles about ten feet long.

Military Engagements of the Buffalo Soldiers and Seminole Negro Indian Scouts in the Indian Wars

(other military units may have been involved)

1867

Aug. 2	Saline River, Kans	Troop F, 10 Cav
Aug. 21-22	Prairie Dog Creek, Kans	Troop F, 10 Cav
Sept. 16	Saline River, Kans	Detach G, 10 Cav
Oct. 1	Howard's Well, Tex	Detach D, 9 Cav
Dec. 5	Eagle Springs, Tex	Detach F, 9 Cav
Dec. 26	Near Ft. Lancaster, Tex	Detach K, 9 Cav

1868

Jan. ?	Ft. Quitman, Tex	Detach E, 9 Cav
Sept. 14	Horse Head Hills, Tex	Detachs C, F, and K, 9 Cav
Sept. 15	Big Sandy Creek, Colo	Troop I, 10 Cav
Oct. 18	Beaver Creek, Kans	Troops H and I, 10 Cav
Nov. 19	Near Ft. Dodge, Kans	Detach A, 10 Cav

1869

Jan. 29	Mulberry Creek, Kans	Detachs C, G, H, and K, 9 Cav

June 7	Johnson's River and Pecos River, Tex	Detachs G, L, and M, 9 Cav
Sept. 20-21	Brazos River, Tex	Detachs B and E, 9 Cav
Oct. 28-29	Headwaters of Brazos River	Detachs B, E, F, G, L, and M, 9 Cav Tex
Nov. 24	Headwaters of Llano River	Detachs F and M, 9 Cav Tex
Dec. 25	Johnson's Mail Station, Tex	Detach 9 Cav

1870

Jan. 3-Feb. 6	Scout on Rio Grande and Pecos Rivers, Tex	G and Detach L, 9 Cav and Detachs L and K, 24 Inf
Jan. 6-Feb. 10	Scouts in Guadalupe Mountains, Tex	Detachs H and I, 9 Cav
Jan. 16	Indian Village, Tex	Detach G, 10 Cav and Detach L, 9 Cav
Jan. 20	Delaware Creek, Guadalupe Mountains, Tex	Detachs C, D, I, and K, 9 Cav
April 3	San Martine Springs, Tex	Detach H, 9 Cav
April 6	Near Clear Creek, Tex	Detach M, 10 Cav
April 25	Crow Springs, Tex	Detachs C and K, 9 Cav
May 19-20	Kickapoo Springs, Tex	Detach F, 9 Cav
May 29	Bass Canyon	Troop K, 9 Cav
June 9	Near Camp Supply, Ind. T.	Troops A, F, H, I, and K, 10 Cav

1871

April 27	Ft. Sill, Ind. T.	Detach E, 10 Cav
May 12	Near Red River, Tex	Detach L, 10 Cav
May 17	Ft. Sill, Ind. T.	Troops B, D, E, and H, 10 Cav
May 21	Camp Melvin Station, Tex	Detach K, 25 Inf
June 30	Staked Plains, Tex	Detach I, 9 Cav
July 22	Headwaters of Concho River, Tex	Detach F (1 man), 9 Cav
July 31	Near Ft. McKavett, Tex	Detachs M, 9 Cav, and A, 24 Inf
Sept. 1	Near Ft. McKavett, Tex	Detachs M, 9 Cav, and E, 24 Inf
Sept. 19	Foster Springs, Ind. T.	Detach B, 10 Cav

1872

| May 20 | On La Pendencia, Tex | Detachs C, 9 Cav, and K, 24 Inf |

July 12	Deep River, Ind. T.	Troops A and L, 10 Cav
July 22	Otter Creek, Ind. T.	Troops A and L, 10 Cav
July 28	Central Station, Tex	Detach K, 25 Inf

1873

April 27	Eagle Springs, Tex	Detach B, 25 Inf
Aug. 31	Near Pease River, Tex	Troops E and I, 10 Cav
Oct. 1	Central Station, Tex	Detach K, 25 Inf
Dec. 5	Elm Creek, Tex	Detach D, 10 Cav

1874

Feb. 2	Home Creek, Tex	Detach A, 10 Cav
Feb. 5	Double Mountains, Tex	Troop G and Detach D, 10 Cav
May 2	Between Red River and Big Wichita River, Tex	Detach K, 10 Cav
May 18	Carrizo Mountains, Tex	Detach B, 25 Inf
Aug. 22-23	Wichita Agency, Ind. T.	Troops C, E, H, and L, 10 Cav, Company I, 25 Inf
Oct.4	Near Ft. Sill, Ind. T.	Troop K, 9 Cav
Dec. 20	Kingfisher Creek on North Fork of Canadian River, Ind. T	Troop D and Detach M, 10 Cav

1875

April 25	Eagle Nest, crossing of Pecos River, Tex	Seminole Negro Scouts
May 5	Battle Point, Tex	Detachs A, F, G, I and L, 10 Cav
Nov. 2	Near Pecos River, Tex	Troops G and L, 10 Cav

1876

Feb. 18	Carrizo Mountains, Tex	Detach B, 25 Inf
July 30	Near Saragossa, Mexico	Detach B, 10 Cav
Sept. 15	Florida Mountains, N Mex	Troop F, 9 Cav

1877

Jan. 23	Florida Mountains, N Mex	Detach C, 9 Cav
Jan. 28	Sierra Boca Grande, Mexico	Detach C, 9 Cav
April 1	Rio Grande, near Devils River, Tex	Seminole Negro Scouts
May 4	Lake Quenada, Tex	Troop G, 10 Cav

| Nov. 1 | Big Bend of Rio Grande, Tex | Seminole Negro Scouts |
| Nov. 29-30 | Sierra del Carmen, Mexico | Troop C, 10 Cav |

1878

| Aug. 5 | Dog Canyon, N. Mex | Troops F and H, 9 Cav |

1879

Jan. 15	Cormedos Mountains, N Mex	Troop A, 9 Cav
March 8	Ojo Caliente, N Mex	Troop I, 9 Cav
May 29	Black Range, Membres Mountains, N Mex	Detachs C and I, 9 Cav
July 25	Near Salt Lake or Sulphur, Tex	Detachs H, 10 Cav, and 25 Inf
Sept. 4	Ojo Caliente, N Mex	Detach E, 9 Cav
Sept. 16	Las Animas River, N Mex	Troops A, B, C, and G, 9 Cav
Sept. 28	Near Ojo Caliente, N Mex	Troop E, 9 Cav
Sept. 29	Cuchillo Negro River,	Detachs B, C, G, and L,
Oct. 1	Miembres Mountains, N. Mex	9 Cav
Sept. 30	Near Canada de Alamosa, N Mex	Detach E, 9 Cav
Oct. 2-4	Milk Creek, Colo	Troop D, 9 Cav
Oct. 5	Milk Creek, Colo	Troop D, 9 Cav
Oct. 10	White River, Colo	Troop D, 9 Cav
Oct. 27	San Guzman Mountains, near Corralitos, Mexico	Troops B, C, F, H, and M, 9 Cav

1880

Jan. 12	Rio Puerco, N Mex	Troops B, C, F, H, and M, 9 Cav
Jan. 17	San Mateo Mountains, N Mex	Troops B, C, F, H, and M, 9 Cav
Jan. 30	Cabello Mountains, N Mex	Detachs B and M, 9 Cav
Feb. 3	San Andreas Mountains, N Mex	Troops B, C, F, H, and M, 9 Cav
April 3	Near Pecos Fall, Tex	Troops F and L, 10 Cav
April 5	Miembrillo Canyon, San Andreas Mountains, N Mex	Troop A, 9 Cav
April 6-9	Miembrillo Canyon, San Andreas Mountains, N Mex	Troops A, D, F, and G, 9 Cav

April 6-9	Shake Hands Springs, Tex	Troop K, 10 Cav
April 16	Camp near South Fork, N Mex	Detach G, 9 Cav
April 16	Mescalero Agency, N Mex	Troops H and L, 9 Cav and D, E, F, K and L, 10 Cav
April 17	Near Dog Canyon, N Mex	Troops H and L, 9 Cav
April 20	Sacramento Mountains, N Mex	Detach L, 10 Cav
May 14	Old Ft. Tulerosa, N Mex	Detachs E, I, and K, 9 Cav
June 5	Cook's Canyon, N Mex	Troops A, D, K, and L, 9 Cav
July 30	Rock Bridge or Eagle Pass, Tex	Troops C and G, 10 Cav
Aug. 3	Alamo Springs, Tex	Detachs B, C, G, and H, 10 Cav
Aug. 4	Guadalupe Mountains, Tex	Detachs H, 10 Cav, and H, 24 Inf
Aug. 4	Near Rattlesnake Springs, Tex	Detachs H, 10 Cav, and H, 24 Inf
Aug. 4	Rattlesnake Canyon, Tex	Troops B, C, G, and H, 10 Cav
Sept. 1	Aqua Chiquita, Sacramento Mountains, N Mex	Detach G, 9 Cav
Oct. 28	Ojo Caliente, Tex	Detachs B and K, 10 Cav

1881

Feb. 5	Candelaria Mountains, Mexico	Detach K, 9 Cav
May 3	Sierra del Burro, Mexico	Seminole Negro Scouts
July 17	Alamo Canyon, N Mex	Detach L, 9 Cav
July 19	Arena Blanca, N Mex	Detach L, 9 Cav
July 25	White Sands, N Mex	Detach L, 9 Cav
July 26	San Andreas Mountains, N Mex	Detach L, 9 Cav
Aug. 3	Monica Springs, N Mex	Detach L, 9 Cav
Aug. 16	Rio Cuchillo, N Mex	Troop L, 9 Cav
Aug. 16	Near San Mateo Mountains, Black Range, N Mex	Detachs B and H, 9 Cav
Aug. 19	McEwer's ranch in Guerillo Canyon, N Mex	Detachs B and H, 9 Cav

1886

May 3	Near Penito Mountains, Sonora, Mexico	Troop K, 10 Cav

| Oct. 18 | Black River Mountains, Ariz | Troop H, 10 Cav |

1887

| June 11 | Rincon Mountains, Ariz | Detachs E and L, 10 Cav |

1889

| May 11 | Cedar Springs, Ariz | Detachs C and G, 10 Cav; Detachs B, C, E, and K, 24 Inf |

1890

March 7	Near mouth of Cherry Creek, Salt River, Ariz	Detach K, 10 Cav
Dec. 29	Wounded Knee Creek, S Dak	Troops D, E, I, and K, 9 Cav
Dec. 30	Near Pine Ridge Agency, S Dak	Troop D, 9 Cav
Dec. 30	Drexel or Catholic Mission, near White Clay Creek, S Dak	Troops D, E, I, and K, 9 Cav

1893

| Feb. 23 | Las Mulas ranch, Starr County, Tex (30 miles north of Ft. Ringgold) | Seminole Negro Scouts |

Muster Rolls of the Seminole Negro Indian Scouts

ORIGINAL MUSTER ROLL
Scouts were enlisted under Maj. Zenas Bliss

NAME	RANK	AGE	WHEN	WHERE
Kibbets, John	Sergeant	60	8/16/1870	Fort Duncan, TX
Dixie, Joe	Private	19	8/15/1870	Fort Duncan, TX
Factor, Dindie	Private	21	8/16/1870	Fort Duncan, TX
Factor, Hardie	Private	60	8/16/1870	Fort Duncan, TX
Factor, Pompey	Private	16	8/16/1870	Fort Duncan, TX
Fay, Adam	Private	18	8/16/1870	Fort Duncan, TX
Kibbetts, Robert	Private	20	8/16/1870	Fort Duncan, TX
Thompson, John	Private	18	8/16/1870	Fort Duncan, TX
Ward, John	Private	20	8/16/1870	Fort Duncan, TX
Washington, George	Private	21	8/16/1870	Fort Duncan, TX
Wood, John	Private	60	8/16/1870	Fort Duncan, TX

MUSTER ROLL OF 10/31/1898

Scouts were enlisted under 2nd Lt. E. H. Rubottom, 9th U.S. Cavalry

NAME	RANK	WHEN	WHERE
July, Ben	1st Sergeant	1/19/1898	Fort Ringgold, TX
July, John	Lance Corporal	1/20/1898	Fort Ringgold, TX
Clayton, Sie	Private	3/1/1898	Fort Ringgold, TX
Daniels, Charles	Private	2/17/1898	Fort Ringgold, TX
Fay, Sandy	Private	1/1/1898	Fort Ringgold, TX
July, Billy	Private	1/10/1898	Fort Ringgold, TX
July, Fay	Private	4/5/1898	Fort Ringgold, TX
McClain, Adam	Private	2/26/1898	Fort Clark, TX
Payne, Charles	Private	2/26/1898	Fort Clark, TX
Payne, Isaac	Private	1/22/1898	Fort Ringgold, TX
Shields, William	Private	2/17/1898	Fort Ringgold, TX
Washington, Sam	Private	1/16/1898	Fort Ringgold, TX
Williams, Bill	Private	1/17/1898	Fort Ringgold, TX

MUSTER ROLL OF 12/31/1910

July, Fay	1st Sergeant	4/5/1910	Fort Clark, TX
Remo, Joe	Sergeant	7/28/1908	Fort Clark, TX
Carlino, Warrior	Corporal	3/9/1910	Fort Clark, TX
Daniel, Caesar	Private	3/8/1910	Fort Clark, TX
Daniels, John	Private	6/29/1910	Fort Clark, TX
Jefferson, Curley*	Private	8/13/1908	Fort Clark, TX
Jefferson, John	Private	5/16/1908	Fort Clark, TX
July, Billy	Private	1/10/1910	Fort Clark, TX
July, Charles J.	Private	10/12/1908	Fort Clark, TX
Kibbetts, George	Private	6/25/1908	Fort Clark, TX
Perryman, Ignacio	Private	3/12/1910	Fort Clark, TX
Sanchez, Antonio	Private	4/1/1910	Fort Clark, TX
Shields, John	Private	2/26/1910	Fort Clark, TX
Washington, Lam	Private	1/17/1910	Fort Clark, TX
Wilson, Billy	Private	3/9/1910	Fort Clark, TX
Wilson, Isaac	Private	3/15/1910	Fort Clark, TX
Wilson, William	Private	3/9/1910	Fort Clark, TX

*Curley Jefferson was the last living Seminole Negro Indian Scout. He died in 1959.

Battles Fought
on the Western Frontier
by Black Civil War Soldiers

ARKANSAS BATTLES:

Arkansas River	January 18, 1865	54th U.S. Colored Infantry
Bayou Creek	December 13, 1864	3rd U.S. Cavalry
Big Creek	July 26, 1864	Battery E, 2nd Light Artillery
Boggs Mills	January 24, 1865	11th U.S. Colored Infantry
Camden	April 24, 1864	7th U.S. Colored Infantry
Steamer *Chippewa*	February 17, 1865	83rd U.S. Colored Infantry
Clarksville	January 18, 1865	79th U.S. Colored Infantry
Ft. Smith	August 24, 1864	11th U.S. Colored Infantry
Ft. Smith	December 24, 1864	83rd U.S. Colored Infantry
Helena	August 2, 1864	64th U.S. Colored Infantry
Horse Head Creek	February 17, 1864	79th U.S. Colored Infantry
Indian Bay	April 13, 1864	56th U.S. Colored Infantry
Jenkins Ferry	May 4, 1864	83rd U.S. Colored Infantry
Joy's Ford	January 8, 1865	79th U.S. Colored Infantry
Little Rock	April 29, 1864	57th U.S. Colored Infantry
Little Rock	May 8, 1864	57th U.S. Colored Infantry

Steamer *Lotus*	January 17, 1865	83rd U.S. Colored Infantry
Malfleton Lodge	June 29, 1864	56th U.S. Colored Infantry
Pine Bluff	July 2, 1864	64th U.S. Colored Infantry
Poison Springs	April 18, 1864	79th U.S. Colored Infantry
Prairie D'Ann	April 13, 1864	79th U.S. Colored Infantry
Rector's Farm	December 19, 1864	83rd U.S. Colored Infantry
Ross' Landing	February 14, 1864	51st U.S. Colored Infantry
Saline River	May 4, 1864	83rd U.S. Colored Infantry
Wallace Ferry	July 26, 1864	56th U.S. Colored Infantry
White River	October 22, 1864	53rd U.S. Colored Infantry

CHEROKEE NATION, INDIAN TERRITORY BATTLES:

Cabin Creek	July 1-2, 1863	1st Kansas Colored Infantry 1st Indian Home Guards
Cabin Creek	September 19, 1864	54th U.S. Colored Infantry
Ft. Gibson	September 16, 1864	1st Kansas Colored Infantry
Timber Hill	November 19, 1864	1st Kansas Colored Infantry

CREEK NATION, INDIAN TERRITORY BATTLES:

| Honey Springs | July 17, 1863 | 1st Kansas Colored Infantry 1st Indian Home Guards 2nd Indian Home Guards |

KANSAS BATTLES:

| Cow Creek | November 14 and 28, 1864 | 54th U.S. Colored Infantry |
| Lawrence | July 27, 1863 | 1st Kansas Colored Infantry |

MISSOURI BATTLES:

| Island Mound | October 27, 1862 | 1st Kansas Colored Infantry |
| Sherwood | May 18, 1863 | 1st Kansas Colored Infantry |

TEXAS BATTLES:

| Palmetto Ranch | May, 1865 | 62nd U.S. Colored Infantry |

Bibliography

BOOKS

Anderson, Martha E. *Black Pioneers of the Northwest, 1800-1918*. Privately published, 1980.

Bennett Jr., Lerone. *Before the Mayflower: A History of Black America*. Johnson Publishing Co. Chicago, 1982.

Bigelow, Jr., Lt. John. *On the Bloody Trail of Geronimo*. Westernlore Press. Tucson, Arizona, 1986.

Billington, Monroe Lee. *New Mexico's Buffalo Soldiers, 1866-1900*. University Press of Colorado. Niwot, Colorado, 1991.

Boyes, W. *Custer's Black White Man*. South Capital Press. Washington, D.C., 1972.

Britton, Wiley. *The Union Indian Brigade in the Civil War*. Kansas Heritage Press. Ottawa, Kansas, 1922.

Cantrell, M.L., and Harris, M., ed. *Kepis and Turkey Calls: An Anthology of the War Between the States in Indian Territory*. Western Heritage Books, Inc. Oklahoma City, 1982.

Carrol, John M., ed. *The Black Military Experience in the American West*. Liveright Publishing. New York, 1973.

Chase, Henry. *In Their Footsteps*. Henry Holt & Co. New York, 1994.

Connell, Evan S. *Son of the Morning Star; Custer and the Little Bighorn.* Harper Collins Publishers. New York, 1984.

Cottrell, Steve. *Civil War in the Indian Territory.* Pelican Publishing Co. Gretna, Louisiana, 1995.

Cottrell, Steve and Steele, Phillip W. *Civil War in the Ozarks.* Pelican Publishing Co. Gretna, Louisiana, 1995.

Cox, Clinton. *The Forgotten Heroes: The Story of the Buffalo Soldiers.* Scholastic Inc. New York, 1993.

De Barthe, Joe. *Life and Adventures of Frank Grouard.* Buffalo Bulletin. Buffalo, Wyoming. Reprint from self-published 1893 book.

De Barthe, Joe, ed. by Stewart, Edgar I. *Life and Adventures of Frank Grouard.* University of Oklahoma Press. Norman, Oklahoma, 1958.

Dolan, Sean. *James Beckworth; Frontiersman.* Chelsea House Publishers. New York and Philadelphia, 1992.

Epple, Jess C. *Honey Springs Depot: Elk Creek, Creek Nation, Indian Territory.* Privately published, 1964.

Foreman, Grant. *Muskogee: The Biography of An Oklahoma Town.* University of Oklahoma Press. Norman, Oklahoma, 1943.

Fowler, Arlen L. *The Black Infantry in the West, 1869-1891.* Greenwood Publishing Corp. Westport, Connecticut, 1971.

Gaines, W. Craig. *The Confederate Cherokees: John Drew's Regiment of Mounted Rifles.* Louisiana State University Press. Baton Rouge, Louisiana, 1989.

Gilbert, Hila. *"Big Bat" Pourier: Guide and Interpreter, Fort Laramie, 1870-1880.* Mills Company. Sheridan, Wyoming, 1968.

Gladstone, William A. *Men of Color.* Thomas Publications. Gettysburg, Pennsylvania, 1993.

Greene, Robert E. *Black Defenders of America.* Johnson Publishing Company, Inc. Chicago, 1974.

Greene, Jerome A., ed. *Battles and Skirmishes of the Great Sioux War.* University of Oklahoma Press. Norman, Oklahoma, 1993.

Hale, Donald R. *Quantrill: We Rode with Quantrill.* Np.

Hanson, Margaret Brock, ed. *Frank Grouard, Army Scout: True Adventures in the Early West.* Frontier Printing, Inc. Cheyenne, Wyoming, 1983.

Hauptman, Lawrence M. *Between Two Fires: American Indians in the Civil War.* The Free Press. New York, 1995.

Heard, J. Norman. *The Black Frontiersmen: Adventures of Negroes among American Indians, 1528-1918.* John Day Co. New York, 1969.

Heitman, Francis B. *Historical Register and Dictionary of the USA.* Volumes I and II. Government Printing Office, Washington, D.C., 1903.

Hollandsworth Jr., James G. *The Louisiana Native Guards: The Black Military Experience during the Civil War.* Louisiana State University Press. Baton Rouge, Louisiana, 1996.

Institute of Texan Cultures. *The Afro-American Texans.* University of Texas at San Antonio. 1975.

Report of the Adjutant General of the State of Kansas, 1861-1865. Kansas State Printing Co. Topeka, Kansas, 1896.

Lamar, Howard R., ed. *The Reader's Encyclopedia of the American West.* Harper & Row Pub. New York, 1977.

Leckie, William H. *The Buffalo Soldiers: A Narrative of the Negro Cavalry in the West.* University of Oklahoma Press. Norman, Oklahoma, 1967.

Littlefield, Daniel F. *Africans and Creeks: From the Colonial Period to the Civil War*. Greenwood Press. Westport, Connecticut, 1979.

Logan, Rayford W. *The Betrayal of the Negro, from Rutherford B. Hayes to Woodrow Wilson*. Collier Books. New York, 1965.

Main, Edwin M. *The Story of the Marches, Battles and Incidents of the Third United States Colored Cavalry*. Globe Printing Co. Louisville, Kentucky, 1908.

Muller, William G. *The Twenty Fourth Infantry, Past and Present*. The Old Army Press. Fort Collins, Colorado, 1972.

Mulroy, Kevin. *Freedom on the Border: The Seminole Maroons in Florida, the Indian Territory, Coahuila, and Texas*. Texas Tech University Press. Lubbock, Texas, 1993.

Nichols, Roger L. *General Henry Atkinson*. University of Oklahoma Press. Norman, Oklahoma, 1965.

Reedstrom, Ernest L. *Scrapbook of the American West*. The Caxton Printers, Ltd. Caldwell, Idaho, 1991.

Sandoz, Mari. *Crazy Horse: The Strange Man of the Oglalas*. University of Nebraska Press. Lincoln, Nebraska, 1942.

Schubert, Frank N. *Black Valor: Buffalo Soldiers and the Medal of Honor, 1870-1898*. Scholarly Resources. Wilmington, Delaware, 1997.

Schubert, Frank N. *On the Trail of the Buffalo Soldier*. Scholarly Resources. Wilmington, Delaware, 1995.

Swanson, Donald A. *Enlistment Record of Indian Scouts who served in one of the Scout Detachments at Fort Clark, Texas*. Ames-American Printing Co. Bronte, Texas.

Taylor, Quintard. *In Search of the Racial Frontier: African Americans in the American West, 1528- 1990*. W. W. Norton & Co. New York, 1998.

Thrapp, Dan L. *Encyclopedia of Frontier Biography*. Arthur H. Clark Co. Spokane, Washington, 1990.

Urwin, Gregory J. W. *The United States Cavalry: An Illustrated History*. Blandford Books, Ltd., Sterling Publishing Co., Inc. New York, 1984.

Wharfield, Colonel H.B. (Dave). *Tenth Cavalry and Border Fights*. Privately published. El Cajon, California, 1965.

Wilson, Elinor. *Jim Beckwourth: Black Mountain Man, War Chief of the Crows*. University of Oklahoma Press. Norman, Oklahoma, 1972.

Wilson, Joseph T. *The Black Phalanx: African American Soldiers in the War of Independence, the War of 1812, and the Civil War*. American Publishing Co. Hartford, Connecticut, 1890.

ARTICLES

Adams, Helen. "Captain Horace W. Bivins—Veteran of Three Wars," Unpublished article in the Helen Parmly Billings Library, Billings, Montana.

Ahlquist, Diron L. "Manhunt on the Cimarron." *Oklahombres Journal*. Vol. IX, Fall 1997.

Austerman, Wayne R. "The Black Scalp Hunters," *Real West*, June 1986.

Boudreau, Wm. H. "Ninth Cavalry Regiment—Early History" 1st Cavalry Division, 1996, Internet website: www.metronet.com/~harryb/1st team/ 9th rgmt.

Carle, Glenn L. "The First Kansas Colored" *American Heritage*, February-March 1992.

Carson III, Kit. "The Lives of Two Great Scouts," *1946 Brand Book*, The Westerners. Denver, Colorado, 1947.

Chatfield, Harry E. "Ed Rose, Negro Trail Blazer," *Real West*, September-October 1969.

Dearen, Patrick. "The Battle of Fort Lancaster," *True West*, January 1995.

Grote, Lieutenant Hutcheson. "The Ninth Regiment of Cavalry," *Journal of the Military Service Institution*, Vol. XVI, No.75, May 1895.

Holiding, Vera. "Cut Nose, Black Trail Blazer," *Pioneer West*, October 1970.

Irons, Angie. "Cantoment: Unnamed Army Post of the Plains," *True West*, October 1990.

Legg, John. "Shadowy Man of the Mountains," *Old West*, Fall 1988.

Longacre, E.G. "A Philadelphia Aristocrat with the Buffalo Soldiers," *Journal of the West*.

McConnell, Roland C. "Isaiah Dorman and the Custer Expedition," *Journal of Negro History*.

McRae Jr., Bennie J. "Civil War Heroism: Alfred Wood," *Lest We Forget*, Volume 1, No. 1, October 1993.

Mayhall, Mildred P. "Foster Child of the Kiowas," *Old West*, Spring 1968.

Meed, Douglas V. "Suicide Charge at Carrizal," *True West*, September 1993.

Porter, Kenneth Wiggins. "Negroes and Indians on the Texas Frontier, 1831–1876," *The Journal of Negro History*, Vol. XLI, July 1956.

———. "The Seminole Negro-Indian Scouts, 1870-1881," *Southwestern Historical Quarterly*, January 1952.

Robinson III, Charles M. "The Whirlwind and his Scouts," *Old West*, Summer 1991.

Rogers, W. Lane. "Bushwacked: The Wham Payroll Robbery," *True West*, July 1995.

Schubert, Frank N. "The Suggs Affray: The Black Cavalry in the Johnson County War," *The Western Historical Quarterly*, January 1973.

Spencer, G. "The Exploits of Edward Rose," *Real West*, October 1988.

Steed, Jack. "The Sibley Scout, Frank Grouard's greatest challenge," *Old West*, Fall 1988.

Thybony, Scott. "Against all odds, Black Seminoles won their freedom," *Smithsonian*, August 1991.

Wallace, Edward S. "General John Lapham Bullis, Thunderbolt of the Texas Frontier," *Southwestern Historical Quarterly*.

Zeller, Gary. "Occupying the Middle Ground: African Creeks in the First Indian Home Guard, 1862-1865," *The Chronicles of Oklahoma*, Spring 1998.

NEWSPAPER ARTICLES
(*Undated articles are from the archives of the Montana Historical Society.*)

Billings Gazette, Billings, Montana.
Billings Herald, September 29, 1949.
Coffeyville Daily Journal, August, 20, 1931.

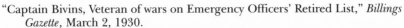
"Captain Bivins, Veteran of wars on Emergency Officers' Retired List," *Billings Gazette*, March 2, 1930.

"Death of Last of Kit Carson Scouts and Indian Fighters," *Pueblo Star Journal*, May 17, 1904.

"83-Year Old Retired Billings Army Officer Plans New Home in Philadelphia, Famed Scout Ended Trail of Murder," *Pueblo Chieftain*, April 23, 1967.

Helena Independent, Helena, Montana.

"Much-Decorated Billings Captain will revise history of Negro Cavalry," by Goodson, Ray. *Billings Gazette*, September 25, 1949.

"Rube Waller to the rescue," Empire Magazine, July 20, 1969, *Denver Post*, 2nd in series on Black Colorado.

"Sgt. Johnson, hero of Milk Creek," Empire Magazine, August 24, 1969, *Denver Post*, 5th in series on Black Colorado.

"Smokey Wilson, Negro Interpreter Who has Been an Adopted Member of the Crow Indian Tribe for 60 years and Who has lived Among its Members all That Time, Stands High with both White and Red Men; Friend of General Scott," *Montana Newspaper Association*, Inserts, September 8, 1930.

CORRESPONDENCE
(All correspondence is to the author.)

Darrell H. Jepson, Angleton, Texas.

Janet Michaelieu, Librarian, Arizona Historical Society.

Laura Holt, Librarian, Laboratory of Anthropology, Museum of Indian Arts and Culture, Museum of New Mexico.

Ann Nelson, Historian, Department of Commerce, State of Wyoming.

Jim Curry, Montana Room Librarian, Library, Billings, Montana.

Bob Clark, Reference Librarian, Montana Historical Society Library.

Mary L. Williams, Park Ranger, Fort Davis National Historic Site.

Bill Welgie, Head Archivist, Oklahoma Historical Society.

Bennie McRae Jr., Dayton, Ohio.

Diron L. Ahlquist, Oklahoma City.

Angela Walton-Raji, Baltimore, Maryland.

Archives, Montana Historical Society.

Arizona State History Museum.

Fort Scott National Historic Site.

Fort Davis National Historic Site.

Kansas State Historical Society.

Nebraska State Historical Society.

South Dakota State Historical Society.

Wyoming State Historical Society.

ARCHIVAL MATERIAL

Historical Sketch, Tenth United States Cavalry, 1866-1892, And Report of Operations, Spanish-American War, 1898, compiled from official records by Major John Bigelow, Jr. Roll 933. National Archives, Washington, D.C.

Indian Pioneer Papers, Archives and Manuscripts Division, Oklahoma Historical Society.

Military Service Records: A Select Catalog of National Archives Microfilm Publications. National Archives, Washington, D.C.

Negro in the Military Service of the United States, 1639-1886, The. M858. National Archives, Washington, D.C.

Returns from the Ninth Cavalry from 1866-1895, Rolls 87-90; Returns from the Tenth Cavalry from 1866-1896, Rolls 87-90. Located on *Returns from Regular Army Cavalry Regiments, 1833-1916*. M744. National Archives, Washington, D.C.

Returns from United States Military Posts, 1800-1916. M617. National Archives, Washington, D.C.

Ricker Papers, Archives Department, Nebraska Historical Society.

United States vs. Frank O'Brien, Fort Smith, Arkansas Criminal Files. National Archives, Southwest Branch, Fort Worth, Texas.

About the Artist

Bernard Williams is a native (b. 1964) of Chicago, Illinois. His paintings concern themselves with historical, cultural, and ethnographic issues. The artist has created a powerful series of paintings and portraits that celebrate Buffalo Soldiers and Black cowboys. Many of his recent paintings speak of the African American presence and contributions to western American history.

The artist says, "I consider myself a modern history painter. I have been very influenced by writers like Art Burton who have presented a revised American story. Through my personal readings, I have been moved to create paintings that visualize our incredible Black history which is thoroughly weaved into the broader American drama."

Bernard Williams holds a Master of Fine Arts Degree from Northwestern University in Evanston, Illinois. He has been teaching art at The School of the Art Institute of Chicago for over seven years. Williams has also been commissioned to create enormous outdoor murals around Chicago and is represented by the Jan Cicero Gallery in Chicago. The artist can be contacted at: P.O. Box 802784, Chicago, IL 60680; his phone is (312) 409-4304.

Index

abolitionists, 25
Absaroka, 6, 9
Absaroka Agency, 72
Absarokes, 6
Absentee Delaware, 28
Accomack County,
    Virginia, 239
Adair, Henry R., 202, 205
Addelman, ——, 38
Adobe Walls, 94
African Creeks, 113; *also*
    see Black Creeks
African-Seminoles, 87-102
Agua Caliente, 200-201
Alexander, Samuel H., 206
Alexander, W. A., 237
Alford, Henry, 180
Allen, Col., 109
Alma, 38
Amarillo, Texas, 95
American Expeditionary
    Force, 200, 201
American Fur Company,
    16, 46, 47
American Horse, 60-61
American Revolution, 27
American River, 18
Anadarko, Battle of, 185-186
Anadarko, Indian Terri-
    tory, 29, 182, 185-186
Anderson, Sgt., 165
Apache Kid, 195
Apache Wars, 79
Apaches, 78, 79-80, 90,
    100, 140, 142, 156-
    165, 188-190, 191,
    194-195, 196-197, 240
Appomattox, 131
Arango, Doroteo, *see* Villa,
    Pancho
Arapaho, 7, 19, 73, 85,
    168, 181

Arikaras, 9, 10-11, 13, 42-43
Arikaree Fork, 210-212
Arkansas River, 112
Armes, G. A., 178-179
Armstrong, Lt., 12
Army of the Frontier, 121
Arrington, G. W., 217
Arsenia, James, 236
Asa-Harvey, Chief, 23
Asahabit, 168
Ashley, William H., 10-12,
    16
Astor, John Jacob, 9
Atkinson, Gen. Henry, 11, 12
Autobees, Charles, 35
Axtell, Samuel B., 228, 231
Ayres, C. G., 251
Azimpi, 41
Bacon, Capt., 154
Badie, David, 162
Baker, Edward L., Jr., 198
Baker, Frank, 228
Bankhead, H. C., 213
Banks, Gen., 122
Barber, Amos, 233
Barnett, Joe, 167
Bates, J. C., 168-169
Bates, Sebrian, 232
Battery Wagner, 106
Battle of the Little Bighorn,
    see Little Bighorn
Baxter Springs, Kansas, 109
Beale Expedition, 36
Beale, Lt., 35
Bear Flag Rebellion, 17
Beaufort, Gen., 127
Beaver Creek, 54, 61, 178,
    180
Becker, John, 53
Beckwith, Jennings, 15
Beckwourth, James (Jim),
    12-13, 14, 15-20, 88

Beckwourth Pass, 18-19
Beckwourth Trail, 18
Beecher, Frederick, 210-211
Beecher Island, Colorado,
    209, 211, 212-213, 214
Beecher's Island, 211
Bell, Dennis, 198
Bell Rock, 75
Belle Fourche River, 65
Beltran, 201
Bennett, Lerone, 109
Benson's Camp, 240
Bent, William, 17
Bentzoni, Capt., 140
Bent's Fort, 17
Berthoud, E. G., 19
Beyer, Charles D., 157-
    158, 159
Big Foot, 221-222
Big Frame, Battle of, 81
Big Goose Creek, 58
Bighorn Expedition, 59
Bighorn Mountains, 52,
    57
Bighorn River, 6, 20
Big Sandy Creek, 180
Big Talk, 55
Big White, Chief, 8-9
Billings, Montana, 246, 247
Billy the Kid, 226-232
Biloxis, 89
Binckley, ——, 38
Bismarck, North Dakota,
    42, 47
Bivins, Charles W., 246
Bivins, Claudia May, 246-
    247
Bivins, Horace W., 239-247
Bivins, Ruth, 246
Black Beaver, 28, 185
Black Creek Seminoles, 102
Black Creeks, 89, 90, 167

Black Crows, 76
Black Hills, 65
Black Hills Stage, 64
Black, Jacob, 235
Black Kettle, Chief, 19
Black Lodge Pole, 46
Black Range, 191
Black Seminoles, 87-102
Blackfeet Indians, 16, 48, 243
Blair, Thomas, 216
Blazer's Mill, 229
Bliss, Maj. Zenas R., 90, 92, 102, 139, 140
Bloody Knife, 42
Bluff Creek, Indian Territory, 234
Blunt, Gen. James, 112, 113, 114-115, 116
Boehm, Peter, 96
Boggy Creek, 85
Bongas, 4
Bonito, 2
Bonner, Thomas D., 19
Bonney, William, see Billy the Kid
Boomers, 82-84, 165, 190
Booth, 242, 246
Bordeaux, Louie, 63
Bounden Barracks, St. Louis, Missouri, 126, 129
Bourke, John G., 62
Bowie Station, Arizona Territory, 191
Bowlegs, David, 100
Bowlegs, Jim, 90
Bowles, John, 115
Bowman, Sam, 79-80
Boyd, Charles T., 201-202, 204-205
Boyer, Blacksmith, 256
Boyne, Thomas, 158-159
Bozeman, Montana, 71
Bozeman Trail, 66
Brackettville, Texas, 91, 102
Brady, William, 227-228
Brazeau, John, 46, 47
Brazeau, Walter, 46, 62
"Brazo," 47
Brazos Island, Texas, 129
Brazos River, 22, 154
Breckenridge, Henry, 102
Bridger, Jim, 16, 20
Brisbane, Col., 249
Brooke, Gen. John R., 221, 222

Brooks, Col. W. S., 127
Brown, Benjamin, 143, 144, 145
Brown, James, 165
Brown, Simon, 113
Browning, Mr. and Mrs. Walker, 246
Brownsville, Texas, 95, 131, 148
Bruce, William, 36, 38
Bubb, John W., 59
Buckskin Jack, 49
Buffalo Soldiers (term), 179
Bullis, Lt. John Lapham, 92-94, 96-97, 99-101, 187
Bull's Bend, 65
Burbrige, Maj. Gen., 130
Burkburnett, Texas, 22
Burke, Maj., 55
Burley, Robert, 162
Burnett, George R., 161, 163-164
Butterfield Trail, 23
Byrne, Capt., 180-181
Cabell, Gen. William L., 110, 116, 119
Cabin Creek, 110-112
Cache Valley, 16
Caddoes, 185
Cady, Samuel W., 235
Cailloux, Andre, 107
Caldwell Cattle Trail, 237
Caldwell, Kansas, 249
California gold rush, 17
California Gulch, 39
Camden, Arkansas, 125
Camden Expedition, 119-120, 122
Camp Alice, 249
Camp Bettens, 233
Camp Cantonment, 237
Camp Hamilton, Cuba, 245
Camp Lockett, California, 208
Camp Ojo Caliente, New Mexico Territory, 156
Camp Supply, 182
Camp Wichita, Indian Territory, 181
Camp Wikoff, New York, 175
Campbell, Maggie, 145
Campbell's Camp, Kansas, 178
Canada Alamosa, New Mexico Territory, 161
Canadian River, 139

Cannonball River, 59
Cañon City, 36, 38
Capron, Allyn, 246
Captain Dodge's Colored Troopers to the Rescue, 217
Carbine and Lance: The Story of Old Fort Sill, 233
Cardis, Luis, 215
Carey, Joseph M., 233
Carmichael, Maj., 128
Carpenter, Capt. Louis Henry, 130, 180, 185-186, 190, 210, 211-215
Carr, Gen. Eugene A., 180
Carranza, Venustiano, 201, 202
Carrizal, Charge at, 201-206
Carrizo Canyon, Battle of, 161
Carroll, Henry, 154, 168, 231
Carroll, J. A., 116
Carrollton, Louisiana, 148
Carson, Kit, 35, 36
Carter, ——, 38
Carter, Jacob V., 167
Carter, Joe, 22
Casey, John F., 250-257
Casper, Wyoming, 232
Catron, Thomas B., 227
Cedar Springs, 144
Certificate of Merit, 145, 159, 161
Chapin, Maj., 32
Chapman, Houston, 231
Charbonneau, Touissant, 7-8
Charles, Clay, 236
Charleston, South Carolina, 106
Chatto, 80
Cheatham, Alexander, 197
Checote, Chief Sam, 167, 168, 169
Cherokees, 28, 110-111, 235-236
Cheyenne, 12, 16, 19, 50, 56, 61, 64, 68, 73, 74, 84-85, 94, 168, 178-179, 181
Cheyenne Agency, 182
Cheyenne Dog Soldiers, 180, 209-210
Cheyenne River Reservation, 220

Cheyenne Wells, Colorado, 210, 212
Chicago, Illinois, 4
Chickamauga, Tennessee, 243
Chickasaws, 23, 120
Chimney Mountain, 112
Chippewas, 4, 206
Chiricahua Apaches, 157, 191, 194-195, 254, 255
Chiricahua Mountains, 191
Chisholm Trail, 186
Chisum, John S., 227, 228
Chitto Tustenuggee, 91
Chivington, John, 19
Choctaw, 108, 109
Choctaws, 16, 30, 112, 120
Choteau family, 46, 47
Christy, William, 178
Churchana, Chief, 240
Cibola, New Mexico, 3
Cimarron Horse Shoe bottom, 249
Cimarron River, 82, 235, 236
Clark, Ben, 49
Clark, William, 3, 10
Clarke, Phil, 206
Clarke, Powhatan H., 194, 197
Clarke, William P., 63
Clark's Fork, 75
Clear Creek, 234
Coahuila, Mexico, 89-90
Coballo, John, 88
Cochise, 191
Cochran gang, 236
Cockrell, Col., 106
Cody, William F. "Buffalo Bill," 68, 241, 243
Coffeyville Daily Journal, 26
Cole, Sgt., 256
Collins, Clay, 236
Collins, Lindsey, 236
Collins, Pvt., 58
Colony, Oklahoma, 85
Colorado Second Infantry, 19
Colorado Volunteer Cavalry, 19
Colorow, Chief, 218
Columbus, New Mexico, 199
Comanche Springs, 148
Comancheros, 152

Comanches, 21-24, 28, 89, 90, 94, 95-97, 149, 152, 168, 180, 185-186, 250, 251
Confederacy, 25, 28-29, 31
Conrad, George, 248-250
Cook County, Texas, 234
Cook, Lt. Col. J. B., 31
Cooper, C. L., 255-256
Cooper, Charles, 195
Cooper, Douglas, 112
Cooper's Texas regiment, 116
Copeland, John, 229
Cornwall, Sgt., 58
Coronado, 3
Costillitto, Chief, 94, 100
Cottage Grove, 38
Couch, Capt., 249
Council Bluffs, 12
Coxey's army, 241
Coxey's Commonwealers, 198
Crane, Yellow Bear, 70
Crawford, Emmet, 59-60
Crawford, S. J., 118-119, 121, 122, 123, 124
Crazy Horse, Chief, 49-50, 61, 62-64
Crazy Woman Creek, 66
Crazy Woman River, 61
Cree Indians, 198, 241
Creek Council House, 168
Creek Nation, 165, 167, 168, 169
Creeks, 16, 28, 88, 91, 168-169
Crook, George, 49, 50, 52, 53, 57, 59, 60, 61, 80, 191
Crow Agency, 70, 72, 75-76
Crow Reservation, 66
Crow Springs, Texas, 154
Crows, 6-7, 9, 12, 16, 19, 52, 54, 72-74, 76
Cuba, 138, 146, 170, 175, 198, 199, 215, 243, 245, 246
Cuchillo Negro Creek, 158
Cuchillo Negro Mountains, 163
Cuffy, ——, 90-91
Curly, 73
Cusak, Lt., 154
Custer, Boss, 74
Custer County, Montana, 66

Custer, George Armstrong, 42, 50, 52-53, 59, 60, 61, 72-75, 137, 212
Custer, Tom, 74
Custer Junction, 241
Custer's Last Stand, 41; *also see* Little Bighorn, Battle of
Cut Nose, 6
Dade, Lt., 240
Daiquiri, Cuba, 170
Dale, Thomas, 229
Dallas, Texas, 23
Daly, George, 164
Daniel, Elijah, 90, 91, 94, 102
Davenport, Iowa, 128
Davidson, John "Black Jack," 182, 185-186
Davis, Britton, 79, 80
Davis, Ed, 179
Davis, Martin, 189
Davis, Wirt, 235
Davison, Paul R., 208
Dawson, Byron, 159, 231
Day, Matthias, 159
De Barthe, Joe, 45
De Gress, Jacob, 90
Deer Creek Agency, 72
Delawares, 27, 29, 185
DeMorse, Charles, 115
Dennis, Gen., 108
Denny, John, 159-160
Denver, Colorado, 19
Department of Arizona, 130, 140, 145, 191, 195
Department of Colorado, 241
Department of Dakota, 140, 197, 241
Department of Louisiana, 140
Department of Texas, 94, 140
Department of the Platte, 169, 221
Devil's River, 100
Division of the Gulf, 136, 147
Division of the Missouri, 136, 221
Dobbins, Gen., 127
Dodge, Capt. Francis S., 219, 220
Dodson, Jacob, 3
Dolan, James J., 227-231

Dona Ana County, New Mexico, 232
Donovan, Jack, 211
Dorman, Isaiah, 41-43
Dorsey, Frank, 158
Doubleday, Abner, 139
Dover, Augustus, 236
Drexel Mission, 223
Duchoquette, Francois, 3
Dudley, N.A.M., 159, 229, 230, 231-232
Duke's Brigade, 130
Dull Knife, Chief, 61
Durfee and Peck, 42
Durgan, Lottie, 22
Durgan, Millie, 22, 23
Durgan, Susie, 22
Duvall's Bluff, Arkansas, 130, 131
D'An Camden Road, 119
D'Orman family, 41
E. O. Standard, 71
Eagle Pass, Texas, 101
Eagle Springs, Texas, 189, 253
Eastern Montana College of Education, 247
8th U.S. Cavalry, 95, 156, 221
18th Iowa Infantry, 119
18th Kansas Cavalry, 178
83rd United States Colored Troops, 125, 128
El Dorado, Kansas, 213
El Moral, Mexico, 89
El Paso County, 38
El Paso, Texas, 148, 149, 205, 215, 217, 253
11th Louisiana, 107, 108
11th U.S. Cavalry, 200, 205
11th U.S. Colored, 124
Elk Creek, 112, 115
Elkins, Stephen B., 233
Ellis, Charles, 216
Ellis, Isaac, 229
Emancipation Proclamation, 106
Espinozas, 36-40
Estevanico, 3
Evans, George, 187
Factor, Dembo, 89, 90
Factor, Hardy, 89
Factor, Pompey, 96-97, 102
Factor, Thomas, 90
Fairplay, 38-39

Feather River, 18
Fechet, Maj., 233
5th Infantry, 213
5th Kansas Cavalry, 106
5th Texas Partisan Rangers, 113
5th U.S. Cavalry, 52, 142, 200, 214, 218, 219, 220
5th United States Colored Cavalry, 130, 148, 214
15th Illinois Cavalry Regiment, 128
15th Indiana, 123
15th U.S. Infantry, 216, 227
54th U.S. Colored Infantry, 124
56th Infantry, U.S.C.T., 127, 128
57th Infantry, U.S.C.T., 128, 131
59th Infantry, U.S.C.T., 128
Finley, Leighton, 189
Finnerty, John F., 53, 54, 56
Fire Bear, 75
Firesides, Gen., 250
1st Cherokee Regiment, 113
1st Choctaw and Chickasaw Regiment, 113
1st Creek Regiment, 113
1st Indian Home Guard, 28, 107, 112, 113
1st Iowa Regiment of African Descent, 126-128
1st Kansas Colored Volunteer Infantry Regiment, 105-117, 118, 119, 120, 122, 123, 124
1st Mississippi Cavalry, 31, 32, 107
1st New Mexico Infantry, National Guard, 200
1st Regiment Missouri Volunteer Infantry— Colored, 129
1st Regiment of Louisiana Native Guards, 107
1st U.S. Artillery, 221
1st U.S. Infantry, 140, 254
1st U.S. Volunteer Cavalry Regiment, 243, 244
First Aero Squadron, 200
First Federal Indian Expedition, 29

First National Bank of Santa Fe, 227
Fisher, King, 101
Fitch, A. T., 235, 236
Fitzpatrick, Mrs., 22
Fitzpatrick ranch, 22
Five Civilized Tribes, 28, 180
Five Scalps, 7
Flat Top Mountain, 23
Fletcher, Nathan, 162
Flipper, Henry O., 182, 183
Flipper's Ditch, 182
Florida Mountains, 157
Ford, John, 21
Foreman, Maj. John, 110, 111
Forsyth, George A., 68, 148, 169, 210-211, 213, 214
Forsyth, James, 223
Fort Apache, Arizona Territory, 80, 143, 191, 192, 193, 196, 240, 255
Fort Apache Reservation, 191
Fort Arbuckle, Indian Territory, 178, 179-180, 181, 182, 234
Fort Assiniboine, Montana, 75, 145, 197, 198, 241, 243
Fort Atkinson, 10, 12
Fort Bascom, New Mexico Territory, 131
Fort Bayard, New Mexico Territory, 140, 156, 157, 207
Fort Belknap, 21, 22
Fort Benton, 71
Fort Bliss, Texas, 216
Fort Bowie, Arizona, 254
Fort Buford, North Dakota, 197
Fort Clark, Texas, 91, 94, 95, 98, 100, 101, 102, 140
Fort Cobb, Indian Territory, 181, 237
Fort Concho, Texas, 97, 186, 187, 190
Fort Craig, New Mexico Territory, 156
Fort Cummings, New Mexico Territory, 156, 164, 232
Fort Custer, Montana, 72, 75, 141, 197, 241, 246

Fort D. A. Russell, 233
Fort Davis, Texas, iv, 140,
    141, 148-149, 152,
    186, 190, 236, 252
Fort Dodge, Kansas, 182
Fort Du Chesne, Utah,
    169, 172
Fort Duncan, Texas, 91,
    94, 101, 140
Fort Elliot, Texas, 139
Fort Ellis, 72
Fort Ethan Allen,
    Vermont, 199
Fort Fetterman, Wyoming
    Territory, 58, 61, 64
Fort Frederick Steele,
    218
Fort Garland, 35, 39, 40
Fort Gibson, Indian
    Territory, 29, 88, 109,
    112, 116, 119, 124,
    136, 167, 168, 178,
    180, 181, 182
Fort Grant, Arizona
    Territory, 140, 143,
    144, 191, 195, 240,
    254, 255
Fort Griffin, Texas, 186
Fort Hale, South Dakota,
    141
Fort Hall, Idaho, 48
Fort Harker, Kansas, 178,
    180, 210
Fort Hays, Kansas, 178,
    179, 210
Fort Huachuca, Arizona,
    140, 199, 200, 208
Fort Jackson, Louisiana,
    140
Fort Keogh, Montana, 75,
    141, 197, 241
Fort Lancaster, Battle of,
    149, 152-154
Fort Laramie, Wyoming,
    20, 64
Fort Larned, Kansas, 178
Fort Leavenworth, Kansas,
    28, 136, 178, 197, 208,
    229
Fort Lisa, 6
Fort Lyon, 19, 181
Fort Manuel, 6
Fort Marion, Florida, 80,
    195
Fort McKavett, Texas, 92,
    140, 154, 156, 186

Fort McKinney, Wyoming,
    65, 66, 221, 232, 250
Fort McRae, New Mexico
    Territory, 156
Fort Meade, South
    Dakota, 141
Fort Michilimackinac, 4
Fort Missoula, Montana,
    141, 245
Fort Myer, Virginia, 170,
    208
Fort Niobrara, Nebraska,
    169
Fort Phil Kearney, 212
Fort Pierre, 46, 47
Fort Pike, Louisiana, 140
Fort Pillow, Tennessee, 34,
    120, 128
Fort Quitman, 140, 189
Fort Randall, South
    Dakota, 140
Fort Reno, Indian
    Territory, 64, 80, 82,
    139, 142, 165, 249
Fort Rice, Dakota
    Territory, 42
Fort Richardson, Texas,
    235
Fort Riley, Kansas, 131,
    165, 178, 181, 248
Fort Robinson, Nebraska,
    47, 49, 62, 63, 64, 160,
    162, 169, 170, 199,
    200, 221, 250
Fort Sam Houston, Texas,
    245
Fort Scott, Kansas, 106,
    109, 118, 121
Fort Selden, New Mexico
    Territory, 156
Fort Shaw, 141
Fort Sheridan, 64
Fort Sill, Indian Territory,
    82, 139, 142, 165, 169,
    181, 182, 234, 235,
    236, 248-249, 250,
    252
Fort Sisseton, South
    Dakota, 141
Fort Smith, Arkansas, 112,
    116, 117, 118, 122,
    124, 236, 238
Fort Snelling, Minnesota,
    141, 184
Fort St. Philip, Louisiana,
    140

Fort Stanton, New Mexico
    Territory, 100, 156,
    158, 226, 227, 229,
    230, 231
Fort Stanton Reservation,
    188
Fort Stevenson, 47
Fort Stockton, Texas, 140,
    148, 149, 186
Fort Supply, Indian
    Territory, 101, 139,
    142, 165
Fort Thomas, Arizona
    Territory, 140, 143,
    144, 145, 191
Fort Tularosa, New Mexico
    Territory, 156, 160
Fort Union, New Mexico
    Territory, 47, 131, 156,
    231
Fort Vasquez, 17
Fort Verde, Arizona
    Territory, 80, 191
Fort Wadsworth, 42
Fort Wallace, Kansas, 180,
    210, 211, 213
Fort Washakie, Wyoming,
    68
Fort Whipple, Arizona
    Territory, 80
Fort Wingate, New Mexico
    Territory, 151, 155,
    156, 166
Fort Worth, Texas, 248
Foster, Cpl., 256
Foster, John R., 158
Four-Mile Creek Canyon,
    39
14th Kansas Regiment,
    119
40th Infantry Regiment,
    136, 158
41st Infantry (colored),
    92, 136, 141
4th Cavalry, 61, 94, 139,
    188, 194, 197, 235,
    240
4th Field Artillery, 200
4th Illinois Cavalry, 31, 32
4th Indian Home Guards,
    118, 121
4th Infantry, 218
Fowler, Jacob, 3
Frederick County,
    Virginia, 15
Free, Mickey, 79, 80

Freeland, A., 159
Freeman, Frank, 226-227
Fremont, John Charles, 3
Fremont County,
    Wyoming, 68
Frohock, William, 152, 153
fur trade, 6, 7-8, 9, 10-12,
    16-17, 46, 47
Gainesville, Texas, 233
Gallino,——, 47
Garland, Colorado, 40
Garland, Samuel, 210
Garnett, Billy, 47, 63
Garnier, Bat, 49
Gatewood, Charles B., 78,
    79, 194
Gavilan Canyon, New Mex-
    ico Territory, 164-165
General Grant National
    Park, 173
General Order No. 2, 105-
    106
George, Sugar T., 113
Gerard, Frederic F., 42
Geronimo, 80, 156, 191,
    194-195, 254, 256
Geronimo Campaign of
    1885-1886, 191
Gettysburg, Battle of, 92
Ghost Dance, 68, 170, 220
Gibbon, John, 52
Gila River, 240
Gilpatrick, James H., 118,
    119, 121, 125
Glass, Dick, 167
Glass, Hugh, 13, 16
Glass, John T., 2, 193
Globe, Arizona Territory,
    240
Goes-Ahead, 73, 76
Goings, Frank, 46
Goings, Nettie Elizabeth,
    46
Golding, Thomas, 165
Gomez, Felix U., 202, 204,
    205
Good Lance, 55
Goodwin, Millard F., 229
Goodwin Trail, 164
Gopher John, 88
Gordon, John, 219
Grabber, 46
Graham, G. W., 180, 209,
    213
Graham Mountains, 144
Grand River, 110, 111

Grant, Gen. Ulysses S., 31,
    107, 128
Grayson, Renty, 94
Great Sioux War, 50
Greaves, Clinton, 157
Greeley, Colorado, 218
Greeley, Horace, 218
Green Peach War, 169
Green River, 65
Greenville, Louisiana,
    136, 148
Grey Eyes, 11
Grierson, Benjamin H., 136,
    181, 182, 187, 188-
    190, 195-196, 197, 250
Grierson, Robert, 189
Griffith, David, 116
Grizzly Creek, 18
Grouard, Benjamin F., 47-
    48
Grouard, Frank, 44, 45-69
Grouard, Lallee, 69
Guadalupe Mountains, 149
Gulf of Mexico, 10
Gunnison River, 36
Gwaltney, Bill, 35
Hamilton, J. M., 148
Hampton Normal and
    Agricultural Institute,
    239, 243
Hanson, Margaret Brock,
    69
Hardscrabble Creek, 36, 38
Hardy, ——, 90-91
Harkins, ——, 38
Harmon, William R., 233-
    235
Hatch, Edward, 136, 148,
    149, 152-153, 217,
    228, 229, 231, 249
Hayes, Rutherford B., 182
Haywood, Charles, 223
Helena, Arkansas, 127,
    130, 131
Henry, Andrew, 10
Henry, Guy V., 198, 221,
    222, 223
Henryetta, Texas, 248
Hickock, "Wild Bill," 181
Hindman, George, 228
Hinks, Lt. Col., 140
Hitchiti, 88
Holbrook, Arizona
    Territory, 195
Hole In The Wall, 65
Holladay, Ben, 48

Hollis, Pvt., 194
Honey Springs, 112
Honey Springs, Battle of,
    113-117, 120
Honor Guard, 173
Hood, Charles C., 237-238
Hooker, Ambrose E., 159
Hopkin's Kansas Battery,
    112
Horn, Tom, 79
Horse, Chief John, 88, 89,
    90, 91-92, 101
Hotchkiss Gun Detach-
    ment (10th), 243-244
Howard, Charles, 215-217
Howell, Bud, 71-72
Hubbard, Gov., 216, 217
Hudson, John G., 126, 128
Hudson's Crossing, 124
Hughes, James B., 243
Hugo, William H., 159
Hunnewell, Kansas, 237
Hunt, George C., 196
Hunt, Wilson Price, 9
Ilsley, Charles S., 233
Indian Affairs, 221
Indian Brigade, 112
Indian Home Guard
    Regiments, 110; also
    see 1st, 2nd, 3rd, 4th
    Indian Home Guard
Indian sign language, see
    sign language
Indian Wars, 53, 130, 135,
    141, 163, 178, 196, 224
Indianola, Texas, 140
Inkpudta, 42
Interior Department, 102
Irvine, Thomas H., 66
Irving, Washington, 5
Island, Harry, 113
Island Mound, Missouri,
    106
Isparhecher (Spi-e-che),
    167, 168-169
Jackson Barracks,
    Louisiana, 140
Jackson County, Missouri,
    25
James, Frank, 66
James, Jesse, 66
Janis, Nick, 47
Jayhawking, 29
Jefferson Barracks, 239
Jenkins' Ferry, Battle of,
    122, 123

Jenness, George, 178-179
Johnson, ——, 237
Johnson, Britton, 21-24
Johnson, C. T., 23
Johnson, Henry, 219-220
Johnson, Jimmy, 22
Johnson, John, 22, 23
Johnson, Jube, 22
Johnson, Lottie, 22
Johnson, Mary, 22, 23
Johnson, Moses, 21
Johnson, Sallie, 22
Johnson County Range
    War, 68, 232-233
Jones, John B., 216, 217
Jones, T. W., 235
Jordon, George, 160, 161
Judson, Col., 113
Juh, 156
July, Sampson, 89, 90
Kansas, 105-106
Kansas City, 19
Kansas Pacific Railroad,
    136, 178
Kansas River, 9
KC Ranch, 232
Keller Station, Virginia, 239
Keokuk, Iowa, 126
Kettle Hill, 243
Kibbetts, John, 89, 90-91,
    102
Kickapoo Springs, Texas,
    154
Kickapoos, 28, 89, 94, 99,
    149, 152, 154, 156,
    187, 188
Kicking Bear, 55
Kimball, George, 231
Kiowas, 21-24, 94, 96,
    149, 168, 180, 185,
    217, 250, 251
Knowles, Horatio, 118,
    119, 121
L. G. Murphy & Com-
    pany, 227
La Veta Mountains, 36
Laguna de Parras, 90
Laguna Sabrinas, Mexico,
    99
Lake Providence,
    Louisiana, 163
Lakota Sioux, 11, 42-43,
    48-50, 52-64, 74, 170,
    220-224
Lame Deer, Chief, 62, 65
Lane, Jim, 105-106

Langston University, 236
Las Animas, Battle of, 159
Las Animas Creek, 159
Lawrence, Kansas, 26
Lawson, Gaines, 140, 182,
    185
Lawton, Oklahoma, 181
Leavenworth, Henry, 10-11
Leavenworth, Kansas, 105,
    255
Lebo, Thomas C., 187-
    188, 194, 196
Lee, Fitz, 198
Lee, Gen., 128, 131
Lee Plantation, 119
Leeper, Mathew, 28
Lee's Battery, 113
Lehmen, ——, 38
Letts, John, 18
Lewis and Clark, 3, 7, 8-9
Lewis, Hamilton, 144
Lewis, Tally, 113
Lexington, 108
Limpia Canyon, 149
Lincoln, Abraham, 38,
    106
Lincoln County, New
    Mexico, 226-232
Lincoln County War, 226-
    232
Lincoln, New Mexico,
    226-232
Lipans, 89, 90, 94, 95, 99-
    101, 149, 187
Lisa, Manuel, 6, 9
Little Bighorn, Battle of
    the, 41-43, 50, 52-53,
    58, 60, 61, 62, 72-75
Little Bighorn River, 42-
    43, 75, 246
Little Bighorn Valley, 52-53
Little Buffalo, 21
Little, Capt., 185
Little Fountain Creek, 38
Little Goose Creek, 52,
    54-58
Little Missouri River, 119
Little Powder River, 65
Little Rock, Arkansas, 117,
    124-125, 128, 131
Little Wolf, Chief, 61
Littlebrant, Lt., 240
Livingston, Montana, 72
Llewelyn, ——, 66
Lochial, Arizona, 206
Loco, 80

Locust Grove, 29
Logan, Rayford, 199
Lone Wolf, Chief, 185,
    213, 251
Los Angeles, 17
Los Mascogos, 89
Loud, Capt., 223
Louisiana Native Guards,
    107
Louisville, Kentucky, 5,
    131
Lowe, Lt., 168
Lower Brule Agency, 46
Lukens, Milton H., 236
Lukum, Milt, 236
Lupton, Lancaster, 36
Machine Gun Platoon
    (10th), 200, 201
Mackenzie, Col. Ranald S.,
    47, 61, 94, 136, 139
Mandan, 8
Mangin, ——, 233-234
Mangus, Chief, 195, 256-
    257
Marcy, Randolph, 27-28
Marfa, Texas, 190
Marmaduke, John S., 119
maroons, 87, 88, 89, 91
Marquis, Thomas B., 76
Mascogan Negroes, 89
Masterson, Bat, 94
Matamoros, Mexico, 90
Mathews, Jacob B., 228
Maxey, Samuel B., 119
Maximillian, 135
Mayes County, Oklahoma,
    110
Mays, Isaiah, 143, 144,
    145
Maysville, Battle of, 113
McBryar, William, 196-197
McCabe, W. P., 202
McCannon, John, 39
McClellan, C. B., 191
McClinton, W. V., 60
McCulloch, Henry, 108
McGlosky, ——, 66, 68
McKenzie, Edward, 162
McKinney, John A., 61
McLaughlin, Agent, 221
McLauren, Mrs., 100
McLauren Ranch, 100
McRae, Jr., Bennie V., 137
McSween, Alexander A.,
    227-232
McSween, Mrs., 231

Medal of Honor, 92, 95, 97, 145, 156, 157, 159-160, 161, 164, 165, 180, 194, 196, 197, 213, 220, 221, 224

Medicine Tail, 75

Meeker, Nathan C., 218-219

Merritt, Col., 220

Merritt, Wesley, 148, 219

Mershon, James H., 236

Mescalero Apache Indian Agency, 227

Mescalero Apache Reservation, 229

Mescalero Apaches, 89, 100, 149, 157, 161, 253

Mexican Central Railroad, 201

Mexican Expedition of 1916; see Punitive Expedition

Mexican-American War, 17, 50

Miles, Gen. Nelson A., 65, 194-195, 221, 257

Military Road, 109

Milk Creek, 218-220

Milk River, 13

Miller, C. E., 256

Miller, Capt., 108-109

Miller, Fred, 75-76

Miller, William, 99

Milliken's Bend, Battle at, 107-109

Mills, Anson, 59, 191

Mimbres Mountains, 158

Mimbres River, 164

Minnatarees, 7

Mississippi River, 5, 31, 105, 107

Missoula, Montana, 246

Missouri Fur Company, 9

Missouri Legion, 11

Missouri River, 6, 7, 8-9, 10, 11, 13

Mizner, Col. J. K., 196, 197, 198

Mogollons, 191

Montague County, Texas, 234

Montano, Jose, 229

Montgomery, Col., 33

Mooers, J. H., 210, 213

Moore, Francis, 147

Moore, George H., 158

Moore, William, 228

Morey, Lewis S., 201-202, 205

Morgan, John Hunt, 130

Morgan, T. J., 220

Mormon Church, 146

Morrow, Albert P., 148, 154

Mower, Col., 140

Moxon, Harry, 73

Murphy, Lawrence G., 227-231

Muscatine, Iowa, 126

Muskogean, 88

Muskogee, Creek Nation, 167, 169

Myers, Joel, 22

Nachez (Naiche), 191

Nacimiento de los Negros, Coahuila, 89-90, 102

Nahina, ——, 47

Nana, Chief, 156, 161-165

Narvaez, Panfilo de, 3

National Guard, 200

National Park Service, 173

Navajos, 81, 157

Nebraska State Historical Society, 46

Ned, Jim, 27-29

Neosho River, 124

New Orleans, Louisiana, 5, 10, 140, 147, 148

Nez Perce, 62

Nicodemus, Kansas, 210

"Nigger Bill," 19

9th Kansas Cavalry, 111

9th Louisiana, 107, 108-109

9th U.S. Cavalry, 82-84, 92, 136, 137, 138, 147-176, 198, 215-217, 219, 221-224, 226, 227-232, 233, 237, 248-250

9th U.S. Cavalry band, 150, 171, 181-182

Noconi Comanche, 182, 185-186

Nolan, Capt., 189

Nolan, Nicholas, 217

Noland, John, 26

North Canadian River, 88

Northern Pacific Railroad, 42, 197-198, 241

Norton, Barney, 144, 145

Nye, W. S., 233

Oakley, Annie, 241

Oglala Lakota, 12, 50, 62

Okeechobee, Battle of, 16

Okmulgee, Creek Nation, 167

Old Ute Pass, 38

Omahas, 10

125th Infantry, U.S.C.T., 131

126th New York Volunteer Infantry, 92

Opothleyahola, Chief, 28

Ord, E.O.C., 187

Oregon Country, 9

Oro Blanco, Arizona, 206

Osages, 28

Osband, Capt. E. D., 31

Osceola, Chief, 16, 88

Ouray, Chief, 218

Overstreet, Monroe, 165

O'Brien, Frank, 233-234

O'Fallon, Benjamin, 12

O'Malley, Ed, 66

O'Neal, Bill, 21

Palmetto Ranch, 129

Palo Duro Canyon, Battle of, 95-97

Papineau, ——, 46

Pappoon, Lt., 213

Parker, Charles, 161

Parker, Isaac C., 236, 238

Parker, Quanah, 94

Parker, Kansas, 250

Patch, A. M., 235-236

Patterson Mercantile Company, 168

Patton, George, 245

Paul (slave), 3

Pauls Valley, 23

Paumoto Sandwich Islands, 45

Pawnee Indian Agency, 236

Pawnees, 61, 181

Payne, Adam (Paine), 95, 102

Payne, David, 82-84

Payne, Isaac, 96-97

Payne, J. Scott, 219

Payne, Titus, 101

Pease River, 95, 217

Peck, Arthur, 194

Peck, Mrs. Petra, 194

Peck Ranch, 194

Pecos River, 96, 149, 152, 154

Penateka Comanches, 23, 185-186

Penn, Delaware, 158

Peppin, George, 228, 229-232
Perry, Charles, 161
Perryman, Jacob, 113
Perryman, James, 94, 100
Pershing, Gen. John J. "Black Jack," 173, 177, 198, 199-206, 245
Philadelphia, Pennsylvania, 247
Philippine Insurrection, 146, 170
Philippine Islands, 138, 170, 173, 198, 199, 200, 244-245, 246, 247
Phillips, Albert E., 200, 201
Phillips, Col., 109, 113
Picottes, 46
Piedras Negras, Mexico, 89
Piegan Indians, 75
Pike, Alfred, 28, 29
Pikes Peak, 19
Pima County Jail, 208
Pine Bluff, 117
Pine Fire, 76
Pine Ridge Agency, 46, 68, 222-224, 225
Pine Ridge Campaign, 146
Pine Ridge Reservation, 170, 220, 221
Pinto Mountains, 194
pirates, 5, 10
Placido, Chief, 29
Plains Indians, 186, 220
Platte River, 16, 65
Plenty Coups, 74, 75
Poison Springs, Battle of, 117, 118-120, 122
Pollack, Edmond, 65
Pollack's Sagebrush Expedition, 65
Pollock, Inspector, 167
Pond Creek, 213
Pony Express, 48
Port Hudson, Louisiana, 106-107
Porter, Kenneth W., 87
Porter, Pleasant, 167
Post Cantonment, 139
Potawatomi, 4
Poteau River, 121
Potter, Joseph H., 139

Pourier, Baptiste "Big Bat," 49, 53-54, 57, 58
Powder River, 47, 65, 233
Powder River, Battle of, 50
Powell, Anthony, 142
Prairie de Anne, Arkansas, 122
Prairie Grove, Battle of, 113
Pratt, ——, 46
Pratt, Addison, 48
Pratt, Choteau, 46
"Prazost," 47
Presidio, The, 173, 176
Pretty Eagle, 74
Proctor, Redfield, 145
Pryor, ——, 75
Pryor, Montana, 70
Pueblo, Colorado, 3, 17, 36, 38
Punitive Expedition of 1916, 138, 173-174, 199-206
Purington, George A., 228-229
Quantrill, William C., 25-26
Rainy Mountain, 21
Randall, John, 179
Rankin, Joseph P., 68
Ransey, Capt., 127
Rattlesnake Canyon, 190
Rattlesnake Springs, 190
Rawlins, Wyoming, 218
Read, Robert D., 244
Real County, 100
Red Cloud, 49
Red Cloud Agency, 47, 62, 63, 64
Red Food, Chief, 185-186
Red Fork, Battle of the, 61
Red Hills, 38
Red Legs, 25
Red River, 22, 119, 122
Red River War, 94-97, 186
Reed, Tom, 49
Reiss, Allen, 100
Remington, Frederic, 179, 217
Remolino, Mexico, 94
Reno, Marcus A., 42-43, 52, 73, 76
Rentie, Pickett, 113
Republic River, 210
Rey, Octive, 107
Reynolds, James J., 50, 128, 140

Rice, Gen., 122-123
Richard, Louis, 49
Ricker Interviews, 46-47
Rider, James, 236
Riley, James, 236
Rio Frio, 100
Rio Grande, 135, 148, 187, 188, 190, 237
Roberts, Andrew "Buckshot," 229
Robinson, Berry, 230
Robinson, George T., 185
Robinson, Governor, 26
Robinson, Lt., 72
Robinson, Wash, 81-85
Rocky Mountain Fur Company, 10
Rocky Mountains, 8, 16, 19
Roman Nose, 210-211, 212
Roosevelt, Theodore, 170, 173, 198, 244
Rose, Edward, 5-13, 16
Rosebud Creek, Battle of, 52
Rosebud Reservation, 220, 221
Ross, Eck, 236
Ross, Saddler, 236
Rough Riders, 170, 198, 244
Royer, D. F., 170, 220
Ruby, Arizona, 206
Ruger, Gen., 75
Ruidoso River, 227
Ryder, Blondy, 206-207
Sable, Jean Baptiste Point du, 3-4
Sabrinas, 97
Sac and Fox Indian Nation, 167
Sacajawea, 7
Sacramento, 18
Saline River, 122, 123, 125, 178
Salt Creek, 23
Salt Lake Valley, 253
Salt Lake City, 48
Salt War, 215-217
Saltville, West Virginia, 130
Samar, 244
San Antonio, Texas, 140, 148, 149
San Antonio River, 99

San Bernardino,
    California, 48
San Carlos Apache Indian
    Reservation, 143, 188,
    191, 197, 240
San Carlos, Arizona
    Territory, 80, 140, 156
San Elizario, Mexico, 215-
    217
San Francisco, California,
    170, 176
San Francisco National
    Cemetery, 173
San Juan Creek, 243
San Juan Hill, 146, 170,
    198, 199, 243-244, 246
San Luis Valley, Colorado,
    35, 36, 40
San-Da-Ve, 101
Sand Creek, 19
Sandoval, Luisa, 17
Sandoz, Mari, 47
Sandy Creek, 211
Sangre de Christo Range,
    40
Santa Cruz Valley, 194
Santa Fe, New Mexico
    Territory, 17, 150, 156,
    171, 182, 195
Santa Fe Trail, 16-17, 81
Santa Rosa Mountains,
    188
Santee Dakota, 42
Santiago, Battle of, 146,
    170, 243, 246
Santo Domingo Ranch,
    202
Sawtelle, William H., 208
Schofield, John M., 165,
    252
Schriemscher, Newton,
    236
Schultz & Brothers Store,
    215
Schwatka, Frederick, 59-60
Scott, Cpl., 194
Scott, Hugh L., 74
Scott, John, 158
Scott, Sam, 167
Scott, William, 206-207
Scott, Winfield, 236
Seaman, H. C., 106
Searchers, The, 21
2nd Cavalry, 50, 53, 243
2nd Cherokee Regiment,
    113

2nd Colorado Infantry,
    111, 112
2nd Colored Light
    Artillery, 158
2nd Creek Regiment, 113
2nd Indian Home Guard,
    28, 29, 112, 115
2nd Indiana Battery, 119
2nd Kansas Battery, 112
2nd Kansas Colored
    Volunteer Infantry
    Regiment, 117, 118-
    125
2nd Massachusetts
    Infantry, National
    Guard, 200
Seminole Nation, 88
Seminole Negro Indian
    Scouts, 86, 87-102, 187
Seminole Wars, 16, 88
Seminoles, 16, 28, 87-102
Seneca, 28
Sequoia National Park,
    173
Sergeant Jim, 2
Seven Cities of Cibola, 3
7th Army Corps, 124
7th Cavalry, 41-43, 52-53,
    58, 60, 137, 174, 198,
    200, 220-224
7th Infantry, 141
17th Infantry, 200
79th U.S. Colored Troops,
    117
Seyga, ——, 38
Shafter, William R., 97,
    99, 139, 187
Shangreu, Lewis, 49
Shaw, Thomas, 161, 162
Shawnees, 16, 28
Shehake, see Chief Big
    White
Sheridan County,
    Wyoming, 233
Sheridan Inn, 68
Sheridan, Philip H., 135,
    136, 147, 169, 180,
    181, 188, 210, 214,
    249
Sheridan, Wyoming, 54,
    68
Sherman, William T., 136
Shields, ——, 89
Ship Island, Mississippi,
    140
Shirley, ——, 185

Shoshones, 52, 61
Shoup, George L., 19, 38
Sibley, Frederick W., 53-58
Sibley Scout, 53-54
Sieber, Al, 79-80
Sierra del Burro
    Mountains, 101
Sierra Nevada Mountains,
    18
sign language, 6, 18, 23
Silent Drill Team, 142
Silver City, New Mexico,
    254
Silver Star, 244, 245
Simon, Capt. Ben, 28
Siones, 12
Sioux Wars, 61
Sioux, 73; also see Lakota
Sitting Bull, Chief, 48, 53,
    62, 64, 221
6th Field Artillery, 200
6th Infantry, 200
6th Kansas Cavalry, 110,
    112, 119
6th U.S. Colored Cavalry,
    130, 148, 194, 200,
    214
16th Infantry, 200
16th Texas, 109
60th Regiment of United
    States Colored Troops,
    126-128
62nd U.S. Colored
    Infantry, 129
65th U.S. Colored
    Infantry, 147
Skipworth's landing, 32
Slaughter, William, 246
slaves, 31
Sleeping Rabbit, 167
Slim Buttes, Battle of, 59
Smith, George W., 164-
    165, 227
Smith, Jedediah, 11-12,
    16
Smith, Kirby, 122
Smith, Lt., 228-229
Smokey Hill River, 178
Snake Warrior, 91
Snakes, 7, 8, 16, 59
Socorro, Mexico, 215-217
Soldier Creek, 57
Solomon River, 178
Sonora, Mexico, 194
South Canadian River, 84
South Park, 36, 38

Southern Cheyenne, 96
Southern Pacific Railroad, 143, 191, 194
Spanish-American War, 138, 146, 170, 198, 215, 246
Sparks, ——, 256
Spilsbury, Lemuel, 202, 204
Spivey, Towana, 182
Spotted Tail Agency, 64
St. Charles, Missouri Territory, 9
St. Joseph, Missouri, 69, 255
St. Louis, Missouri, 6, 15, 16, 19, 126
Staked Plains, 95
Stance, Emanuel, 154, 156
Standing Bear, 49
Standing Rock Agency, 221
Standing Rock Reservation, 220
Stanger, Speed, 49
Stanton, E. M., 106, 130
Steele, Fred, 119, 122
Steele, James M., 124
Stillwater Agency, 72
Stillwater, Oklahoma, 249
Stillwater River, 72
Stilwell, Jack, 211, 212
Stinking Creek, 234
Stockgrowers Association, 232-233
Stoneman, Gen., 80
Stoneman's Raid, 130
Story, Nelson, 72
Stover, George, 46
Sublette, Andrew, 16-17
Sugar Tree Creek, 28
Suggs, Wyoming, 233
Sword Bearer, 75
Sykes, Zekiel, 162
TA Ranch, 232
Tafoya, Jose, 100
Tahlequah, Cherokee Nation, 29
Taos, New Mexico, 36
Tappen, Col., 39
Taylor, Lt., 169
Taylor, Stephen, 162
Tays, John B., 216
Temple, Guy, 161
10th U.S. Cavalry band, 181-182, 191

10th U.S. Cavalry, 75, 81, 82, 97, 99, 136, 138, 144, 160, 177-208, 209, 211-213, 214,
Teresita, 100-101
Terrazas, Col., 257
Terry, Alfred H., 52, 73
Texas Rangers, 128, 215-217
Texas Road, 112, 113
Thayer, Gen., 119, 122
3rd Indian Home Guards, 28, 110
3rd Louisiana Native Guards, 107
3rd Regiment, U.S. Colored Heavy Artillery, 127
3rd U.S. Cavalry (white), 142
3rd U.S. Colored Cavalry, 31, 33-34, 50, 59, 60, 64, 129, 130
3rd Wisconsin Cavalry Battalion, 112
13th Cavalry, 200
13th Louisiana Cavalry, 32
38th Infantry Regiment, 92, 136, 141, 213
39th Infantry Regiment, 136
Thomas, James H., 181
Thomas, L., 131
Thompkins, William H., 198
Thompson, W. A. "Hurricane Bill," 95, 96
Thornburgh, Thomas T., 218-219
Thrapp, Dan L., 257
Tinaja de las Palmas, 189
Titus, Joseph, 187
Tobin, Tom, 35-40
Tongue River, 54, 57
Tonkawas, 29, 90, 95, 96, 97
Touch the Clouds, 63
"Trailer Jack," 53
Trans-Mississippi Army, 125
Trans-Mississippi region, 105, 106
Trevino, Jacinto B., 202, 204

Triplet, Mrs. I. N., 126-127
Triplet, Sgt., 127
Trudeau, Pierre, 211
Tufts, Indian Agent, 167
Tuillo, Mexico, 89
Tularosa, Battle of, 161
Tule Canyon, 95
Tunstall, John H., 227-228, 231
Turkey Creek, 80
20th Infantry, 167, 168, 169, 200
20th Texas Cavalry, 113, 115, 117, 217, 234, 235, 236, 240, 241, 243, 244-245, 246, 250-257
25th Corps, 131
25th Infantry band, 181-182
25th Infantry, 90, 97, 99, 136, 136, 140-141, 142, 146, 158, 184, 187
24th Infantry (Colored), 92, 97, 99, 136, 138, 139-140, 142, 143, 145, 187, 200, 237, 240
24th Infantry band, 181-182
29th Texas Cavalry, 113, 115
23rd Iowa Cavalry, 107
Twin Creek, 54
Two Strike, 55, 223
U.S. Army Cavalry Training Center, 208
U.S. Marine Corps, 142
U.S. Soldiers Home, 145, 159, 160
U.S. State Department, 205
Under Fire with the Tenth U.S. Cavalry, 247
Underground Railroad, 35
Union Colony, 218
Union forces, 31, 32-34
Union Indian Brigade, 28, 29
Union Navy, 108
Ute Pass, 36
Utes, 59, 199, 218-220
Uvalde County, Texas, 90
Valdez, Pedro Avincular, 102

Valois, Gustavus, 161, 163-164
Van Buren, Arkansas, 235
Van Horn, Lt. Col. ——, 141
Vasquez, Louis, 16-17, 19
Verden, Oklahoma, 23
Vicksburg, Mississippi, 31, 33, 107
Victorio, Chief, 142, 156, 158-159, 160, 188-190, 253, 254, 257
Victorio and the Mimbres Apaches, 257
Viele, Capt. Charles, 185, 186, 189, 194
Villa Ahumada, 201-202
Villa, Pancho, 138, 173, 199-206
Vliet, Van, 191
Von Luettwitz, Adolphus H., 59, 60
Wade, James F., 148, 191, 195
Walker, Brigadier General, 109
Wallace, Lew, 231
Waller, Ruben, 211-213
Walley, Augustus, 163-164
Walsh, V. W., 136
Wanderer's Creek, Texas, 236
Wanton, George H., 198
War College, 208
War Department, 31, 106, 141, 199, 208, 243, 245
War of the Rebellion, 105
Ward, John, 96-97
Ward, Maj., 124
Warm Springs, 157, 188
Warrior, ——, 89
Washington, D.C., 80, 81, 88, 145, 160, 170, 207
Washington, George, 27, 81, 101, 232
Washita County, Oklahoma, 85

Washita River, 29, 85, 185
Watie, Stand, 110-111
Watson, James, 197, 240
Wayland Seminary, 239
Wayne, John, 21
Weatherford, Texas, 235
Webb, Wilfred, 146
West Africa, 245
West Point, 173, 182, 183, 201
Wewoka, 88
Wewoka Creek, 88
Wham, Joseph Washington, 143-146
Wham Payroll Robbery, 143-146
Whelock, William, 235
Whipple Barracks, Arizona Territory, 191
White Antelope, 56
White Hat, 63
White, Jonathan, 60-61
White Mountains, 195
White Oak Creek, 119
White River, 127, 128
White River Agency, 218
White Tail Canyon, 194
White-Man-Runs-Them, 73
Whitside, S. M., 221
Wichita Agency, 28, 140, 168, 182, 185-186
Wichita Expedition, 29
Wichita Mountains, 21, 81, 82, 181
Widenmann, Robert, 227
Wild Cat, Chief, 89, 90
Willcox, Arizona Territory, 143
Williams, James M., 106, 110, 114-115, 119, 124, 136
Williams, Moses, 163-164
Williston, North Dakota, 47
Wilson, James, 162
Wilson, Charles "Smokey," 70-77
Wilson, Gen., 71

Wilson, Henry, 25-26
Wilson, John, 25
Wilson, John B., 228
Wilson, John Edward, 77
Wilson, John W., 236
Wilson, William, 223, 224, 225
Wilsons, 89
Windus, Claron, 95
"Winker, Colonel," 102
Wofford, Andrew W., 236
Wolcott, Frank, 232
Wood, Alfred, 30-34
Wood, Doctor, 30
Wood, Margaret, 31
Woods, Brent, 165
Woods, Pearly, 165
World War I, 206
Wounded Knee, Battle of, 68, 141, 170, 221-224
Wounded Knee Creek, 221-222
Wovoka, 220
Wraps-Up-His-Tail, 75
Wray, Colorado, 210
Wright, Henry H., 157, 158-159
Wright, John, 235
Wyman, Maj., 75
Yankton, 11
Yaquis, 206-207
Yard, Maj., 234
Yazoo River, 33
Yellow Hand, 68
Yellowstone, 8, 12
Yellowstone Expedition, 59
Yellowstone River, 6, 13, 66
York (slave), 3
Yosemite National Park, 173
Young, Charles, 173, 201
Young County, Texas, 21
Ysleta, Mexico, 215-217
Zaragoza, Mexico, 89, 99, 187
Zuni, 3